MUSIC IN AMERICAN LIFE

A list of volumes in the series Music in American Life appears at the end of this book.

MORMONISM AND MUSIC

MORMONISM AND MUSIC

A HISTORY

Michael Hicks

University of Illinois Press
Urbana and Chicago

Library of Congress Cataloging-in-Publication Data

Hicks, Michael, 1956–
    Mormonism and music : a history / Michael Hicks.
        p.   cm. — (Music in American life)
    Includes bibliographies and index.
    ISBN 0–252–01618–1 (alk. paper)
    1. Mormons—United States—Music—History and criticism.
    2. Mormon Church—United States—Hymns—History and criticism.
    3. Hymns, English—United States—History and criticism. 4. Music—
United States—History and criticism. I. Title. II. Series.
ML3174.H5   1989
783'.02'693—dc19   88–37886
                                                                   CIP
                                                                   MN

Contents

Preface

One of the biblical passages frequently set to music is the psalm that begins:

> By the rivers of Babylon there we sat down, yea, we wept, when we remembered Zion. We hanged our harps in the willows in the midst thereof. For there they that carried us away captive required of us a song; and they that wasted us required of us mirth, saying, Sing us one of the songs of Zion. How shall we sing the Lord's song in a strange land?[1]

What makes this text such a curiosity is that, while it expresses a reluctance to sing, it is of itself a psalm, a song.

Such are the ironies of music and religion. The asceticism at the heart of many religions implicitly calls their adherents to forswear music's pleasures. But music is so much a part of man's profoundest utterances that religion must rely on music's effects. Augustine struggled with this irony, confessing that in loving music he wavered between the dangers of aural gratification and the benefits of sacred song. Generations of Christians since have vacillated between their evident need for music and their wish to transcend it.

Of all Christian groups, Mormons may have been the most literal in likening themselves to a new Israel, enduring the captivity of a modern Babylon. They have yearned to establish Zion in the New World while considering themselves, like the psalmist, divinely estranged. Yet, unlike the psalmist, they have tried to preserve their singularity as a people by singing, playing, and dancing before an onlooking world. The Mormon quest for identity has shaped Mormon musical life for over 150 years.

Mormonism has grown from what seemed to many observers a disreputable adjunct of revivalism to a small, self-contained nation in the Rocky Mountains and thence to a transcultural brotherhood of faith, authority, zeal, and communion.[2] In the process, Mormons have taken pains to cultivate the ''divine art'' while at the same time cultivating their ''Mormon-ness.'' Consequently, the body of musical work emerging from Mormon culture, be it hymns, folk songs, dance music, or symphonies, has come to have a flesh and bone of its own, an anatomy that is in the image of the religion itself.

All thorough histories of the Church of Jesus Christ of Latter-day Saints[3] have dealt with Mormonism and music. In his *Comprehensive History* of the church, Mormon historian B. H. Roberts wrote that "since it is natural for man to express his highest emotion, perhaps, in music . . . it would be expected that the highly religious emotions attendant upon the religious events of the church of the New Dispensation, would be to give birth to an hymnology and to music of a somewhat special kind. This it has doubtless done." But in the almost sixty years since Roberts wrote this no one has produced a scholarly narrative tracing the evolution of this "music of a somewhat special kind."[4]

Toward that end I present this study. In the chapters that follow I have attempted to braid topical and chronological approaches to the subject, which I hope will allow the general reader to browse and the expert to find subjects handily. In the first seven chapters I take the reader through the nineteenth century, Mormonism's formative period, which was effectually abridged by pressures (from within and without) to end polygamy and Mormon political autonomy. In those times sacred and secular affairs mingled freely in Mormonism, and that mingling is reflected in the treatment of Mormon musical history. In chapters 8 through 12 I treat musical affairs in twentieth-century Mormonism, primarily the "official" musical practices and policies during a period in which the church has attempted to consolidate its identity as a mainstream religion. In these chapters I give special attention to administrative postures toward music and to the personalities and ideas that shaped those postures.

Any history of a religion and an art will be a history of both aesthetic triumphs and petty disputes. For while the joining of religion and art has often led mankind to the summit of his potential in each, both religion and art as institutions have maintained a fundamental enmity. This is doubtless because they make similar claims and demands. Both clamor for people's affection and allegiance. Both promise bliss (one in the next world, the other in this). Both claim to lead their adherents to a better state of existence. And both create disciples who commit themselves to peculiar notions of truth and orthodoxy.[5]

Bearing in mind the conflicts that plague religious music, I have organized my narrative around three points of tension in the history of Mormonism and music: the will to progress versus the will to conserve, the need to borrow from outsiders versus the need for self-reliance, and the love of the aesthetic versus the love of utility. The Book of Mormon itself remarks that there "must needs be an opposition in all things" and the musical life of Mormonism bears that out. But as the Book of Mormon also suggests, these conflicts are signs of life. Without them

Mormonism would be static, dead. This book has been quickened by my wish to illuminate, sometimes by the fires of controversy, how the Mormon people have managed to keep their harps out of the willows and keep the songs of Zion alive.

In so doing I hope to give the growing league of Mormon historians a broader backdrop for their references to music in Mormonism and to shed light on several issues in the church's past. For students of American religion this book may provide a case study of how theology, church government, and music interact in the pressure cooker of religious intolerance and misgiving into which Mormonism has often been cast. Students of religious music in general may find here a story which often reenacts the struggles over music in other churches. And I hope all readers may see herein some ways in which music enables a people to maintain, prosper, and defend their community against all odds.

Several archives, including those of the Library of Congress, the University of Illinois at Urbana–Champaign, and the University of Utah, have been open to me and their staff members have eagerly and competently assisted me. The staff of the Manuscript Archives and Special Collections of the Harold B. Lee Library of Brigham Young University has been especially gracious; BYU archivist David Whittaker has spent many hours of his own time critiquing my work and helping me track down relevant materials. The staff of the Historical Department of the Church of Jesus Christ of Latter-day Saints, notably Glenn Rowe, Steven Sorenson, and William Slaughter, helped me at every turn of my research and supplied some necessary good humor. I hasten to add that, although all quotations from manuscript materials located in the church's archives are used herein by permission, no official church sanction or endorsement of this work should be inferred.

Among the many friends and acquaintances who have blessed my research, I mention here only the most painstaking. Douglas Donaldson and Lynn Carson have both been longtime intellectual patrons of this book, always generous with their minds and time when it came to discussing Mormon musical life. David Kern spent several months as a part-time research assistant. Michael Moody, director of the Music Division of the church, encouraged me along the way and provided both advice and information concerning modern Mormon musical life.

Many of my colleagues in the Brigham Young University College of Fine Arts and Communications and in the Department of Music, notably Merrill Bradshaw, K. Newell Dayley, Thomas Durham, and Steven Johnson, have graciously supported me, loaned me materials from their files, and shared their ideas with me. The college granted me funds for travel and research materials, the department gave me the use of a (by now indispensable) computer, and the University Honors Program allowed me to teach a course in the subject at a crucial time in the formation of my ideas.

Many of the scholars mentioned above have read portions of this manuscript and suggested useful revisions, as have Ian Barber, Davis Bitton, Armand Mauss, and Barre Toelken. Others who have aided me in various substantial ways include: Murray Boren, Bryan Espinscheide, Scott Kenney, John Maestas, Richard Oman, and Marshall Smith. Judith McCulloh and Carol Betts of the University of Illinois Press have patiently counselled and exhorted me, guiding this book to its publication, as have Linda H. Adams and Terry Jeffress. I take the blame for whatever deficiency remains.

Most loving and patient have been my wife, Pam, daughters Rachel and Julia, and son Caleb, who have vicariously fashioned this book along with me. Their understanding of such obsessions has allowed this work to come to pass with more dispatch than one rightly could have expected.

NOTES

1. Psalms 137:1–4.

2. See Thomas F. O'Dea, "Mormonism and the Avoidance of Sectarian Stagnation: A Study of Church, Sect, and Incipient Nationality," *American Journal of Sociology* 60 (November 1954): 285–93.

3. Since Joseph Smith and a handful of disciples legally organized the church nicknamed "Mormon" in 1830, many groups have left the main body of the church and formed separate churches, each laying claim to its own primacy. Since then the nickname "Mormon" has been used commonly to denote the apostolically derived church centered in Salt Lake City, the Church of Jesus Christ of Latter-day Saints.

While other churches that have descended from Joseph Smith possess interesting musical histories of their own, to treat them here would unprofitably burden an already complicated narrative. And to devote only a chapter or two to the musical activities of other groups related to Mormonism would compromise those groups' history, relegating their history to footnotes—a situation which would satisfy neither me nor their members.

4. B. H. Roberts, *A Comprehensive History of the Church of Jesus Christ of Latter-day Saints, Century I*, 6 vols. (Salt Lake City: Published by the church, 1930), 6:244. Perhaps the best published historical treatments of Mormon music so far have been William J. McNiff, *Heaven on Earth: A Planned Mormon Society* (Oxford, Ohio: Mississippi Valley Press, 1940), pp. 156–94, and Howard Swan, *Music in the Southwest, 1825–1950* (San Marino: Huntington Library, 1952), pp. 3–58. Both of these sources treat only the nineteenth century and neither of their authors had access to the massive amount of manuscript material that has come to light in recent years.

5. Art's challenges to religion since the eighteenth century are ably discussed in Jacques Barzun, *The Use and Abuse of Art* (Princeton University Press, 1974), pp. 24–46.

Abbreviations

BYU	Brigham Young University
CMC	Church Music Committee (or Church of Jesus Christ of Latter-day Saints, General Music Committee)
CMD	Church Music Department (or Music Department, Church of Jesus Christ of Latter-day Saints)
CR	*Conference Report*. Salt Lake City: Published by the Church, 1880– .
DN	*Deseret News*
HBLL	Harold B. Lee Library, Brigham Young University
HC	Smith, Joseph, Jr. *History of the Church of Jesus Christ of Latter-day Saints*. B. H. Roberts, ed. 7 vols., 2nd ed. rev. Salt Lake City: Deseret Book, 1964.
HDC	Library-Archives, Historical Department of the Church of Jesus Christ of Latter-day Saints
IE	*Improvement Era*
JD	*Journal of Discourses, Reports of Addresses by Brigham Young and Others*. 26 vols. Liverpool and London: F. D. and S. W. Richards, 1853–86.
JI	*Juvenile Instructor*
MA	*Latter Day Saints' Messenger and Advocate*
OPH	Kate B. Carter, comp. *Our Pioneer Heritage*. 20 vols. Salt Lake City: Daughters of the Utah Pioneers, 1958–1977.
TC	Tabernacle Choir
TS	*Times and Seasons*
UH	Library, Utah State Historical Society
UU	Marriott Library, University of Utah
WE	*Woman's Exponent*
WWJ	Scott G. Kenney, ed. *Wilford Woodruff's Journal: 1833–1898*. 9 vols. Midvale, Utah: Signature Press, 1983.

1

The Genesis
of Mormon Hymnody

Four days after Christmas 1824 Egbert Grandin, editor of the *Wayne Sentinel* in Palmyra, New York, printed this column filler on the newspaper's back page: "Next to theology, I give a place to music: for thereby all anger is forgotten, the devil is driven away, and melancholy, and many tribulations, and evil thoughts are expelled. It is the best solace for a desponding mind." This filler, a passage from Martin Luther's writings, suited the times. With the ground frozen and the partly built Erie Canal unnavigable, commerce tended to slow among the villages along Lake Ontario's southern shores. Farmers, merchants, and tradesmen fell prone to winter melancholy and "cabin fever." One of Grandin's readers, Joseph Smith, Sr., found the winter particularly bitter. To quell rumors that local medical students were grave robbing, Smith had lately been forced to disinter the body of his firstborn son, Alvin, and advertise in the *Sentinel* that the corpse was intact. Moreover, in this first harvest season since Alvin had died, Smith barely got enough crops in to pay the annual farm debt. Work on the new farmhouse all but ceased. And the massive revivals in town that year again drove a religious wedge into his family. While his wife, Lucy, and three children intensified their faith in Presbyterianism, Smith and his namesake, Joseph Jr., refused to go to any church.

Both the elder and the younger Joseph were what was known in the lore of the times as "visionary men." In 1811, while living in Royalton, Vermont, Joseph Sr. had grown anxious about his soul's salvation. But like many citizens of the young republic he retreated from established systems of faith into his own private religion, which was partially defined for him in a series of seven symbolic dreams. In all of them he found himself walking alone, seeking salvation, and being ministered to by heavenly beings who promised him the glory and honor he had not known as a failed New England farmer.[1] His son, Joseph, in turn, reported a vision in 1820 more spectacular and bold than any of his father's dreams. Conscience-stricken by the sermons of a recent revival near Palmyra, young Joseph prayed in the woods for forgiveness and was answered by "a pillar of light above the brightness of the Sun at noon day." In the light, Joseph said, the Lord appeared and proclaimed the young man's sins pardoned.[2]

Revivals like the one that sent young Joseph to his knees occurred so often in upstate New York that the region took on the nickname "the burnt district."[3] At the center of these revivals was the spectacle known as the camp meeting. As many as ten thousand believers and seekers at a time, according to one report, would gather in the wooded hills of Ontario County.[4] There, for several days and nights, as many as seven preachers at once would shout sermons to the multitudes or lead them in favorite sacred songs. When "moved upon by the Spirit," some members of the crowd went into frenzies. Some rolled lengthwise, like logs, often in shallow mud, while others would dance or jerk uncontrollably, "whether with a violent dash on the ground, and bounce from place to place like a football; or hop round, with head, limbs, and trunk, twitching and jolting in every direction, as if they must inevitably fly asunder."[5]

Presbyterians, Methodists, and occasionally Baptists united in the camp-meeting exercises across the state. But the denominations were also constantly at odds, desperately vying for enough converts to fill local meetinghouses. The younger Joseph Smith recalled: "The Presbyterians were most decided against the Baptists and Methodists, and used all the powers of both reason and sophistry to prove their errors. . . . On the other hand, the Baptists and Methodists in their turn were equally zealous in endeavoring to establish their own tenets and disprove all others."[6] Thus, the Ontario County revivals of the early 1820s succeeded at once in lengthening church rolls and yet keeping the sects strictly separate. By the end of the 1823 revivals at least thirteen congregations lay within as many miles of the Smith farm, seven of them with their own meetinghouses.[7]

Two of those buildings belonged to the Quakers. The Society of Friends held no revivals, but their religion had permeated the district since a congregation of them settled en masse in Farmington (adjacent to Palmyra) around 1790. The Friends were well known in this period for rejecting the unqualified praise of music that Luther had expressed. Their mentor George Fox had determined at a young age that the prevalence of psalm singing in Protestant congregations was a sacrilege. The only true singing, Fox felt, was "the melody the true Christians made, in their hearts to the Lord." Later Quaker leaders called music "unfavorable to the health of the soul" and warned specifically against sacred music, which produced "an excitement mistaken for devotion."[8] The Society of Friends encouraged abstinence from singing and music-making of any kind, both in and out of their meetings.

Aside from Quakers, there were more Baptists in Palmyra in 1823 than any other members of religious societies. Most seventeenth-century Baptists had considered singing in public "with conjoined voices" a false tradition, akin to saying form prayers and sprinkling infants. If the believer wished to praise God in song, they felt, he should go to his prayer closet. The opposition to public singing began to give way during the Great Awakening, and in 1742 the Philadelphia Confession added a chapter on "the singing of psalms, etc.," which said that "the whole church in their public assemblies (as well as private Christians) ought to sing God's praises according to the best light they have received." Moreover, the Confession added, public singing was instituted by Christ himself at the Last Supper, "as a commemorative token of redeeming love."⁹ Nevertheless, many conservative Baptists refused to sing, maintaining their prejudice against the practice well into the nineteenth century. Rhode Island Baptist pastor David Benedict, in his 1813 history of the denomination, observed that, although he knew of no Baptist ministers who opposed singing, "their posterity remain in different parts of the State, by whom I have been asked if I was a *Singing Baptist*."¹⁰

Joseph Smith, Jr., reported that he was most drawn to Methodism. Some Palmyrans even recalled that for a brief spell Joseph was "a very passable [Methodist] exhorter" himself.¹¹ Of all the denominations in upstate New York the Methodists were the most active in proselyting and the most avid in cultivating congregational music. Methodism's founders, John and Charles Wesley, had purportedly authored several thousand hymn texts, believing that hymns were perhaps the best means of instilling doctrine in the minds of believers. Hence, as Peter Cartwright wrote in 1856, the early American Methodist circuit riders carried only three volumes in their wagons: the Bible, the Methodist Discipline, and the hymnbook.¹² Moreover, three and a half pages of the Discipline instructed exhorters how to use "the Spirit and Truth of Singing." The book scorned "formality" in music: too-slow singing, the use of new or difficult tunes (at least until the old were mastered by everyone), and singing too many verses at a time—five or six was the limit. It also called for the preacher to interrupt hymns often and cry out to the people: "Now! Do you know what you said last? Did you speak no more than you felt?" And it urged that no voices in the congregation, no matter how discordant, should refrain from singing. Everyone should "throw off all reserve, for we are all infinitely indebted to our good God."¹³

These prohibitions against musical formality implied a certain contempt for church choirs, which nevertheless were allowed into certain gatherings by the Discipline. Many Methodist evangelists discouraged the forming of choirs because choirs tended to cleave the congregations and because, as Cartwright insisted, they would make Methodists "like other heathen churches.''[14] But the Palmyra Methodist Church had a choir in the 1820s. The local Methodist chapel had been built with a singers' gallery, which was presided over by a singing master who fascinated the children by clinking his tuning fork against his teeth to get the pitch.[15]

Presbyterians appear to have favored choirs, and the chapel of the Western Palmyra Presbyterian Church, which most of the Smith family attended, boasted the preeminent choir among the local congregations. As the *Sentinel* reported in 1824, this choir "performed in a manner which we presume has never been equalled in this place. It is indeed a subject of felicitation that our singers, although their number be limited, are manifesting a laudable ambition to excel in this sublime and delightful part of public worship.''[16] The opportunity to sing in such a choir may have held special inducements for some converts, especially for a family as steeped in music as were the Smiths.

Lucy Smith may have been a member of the Palmyra Presbyterian choir, for sacred singing was very much a part of her upbringing. Her husband, Joseph Sr., however, who she recalled could not be persuaded to attend this church more than three times, had taught singing some years earlier. His youngest son, William, recalled that Joseph had been at one time "a teacher of music by note to a conciderable extent. It was from him I learned to sing Old hundred and Grunvik when I was but a child." As was customary among some Protestants, Joseph Sr. led his family in singing a hymn each evening. According to William, who found such nightly kneeling sessions "earksome," the favorite family evening hymn was John Leland's

> The day is past and gone,
> The evening shades appear:
> O may we all remember well
> The night of death draws near.[17]

Although vocal music held a place—however ambiguous—in the public and private worship of many Christian believers in upstate New York, instrumental music did not. Christian leaders, from the religion's early centuries on, had often linked instrumental music to brothels and to the cursed lineage of Adam's wicked son Cain, whose descendant Jubal was said to have been "the father of all such as handle the harp and organ" (Genesis 4:21). Chrysostom, Tertullian, Clement, and other church fathers had condemned instrumental music at the very time they praised vocal music.[18] Their rhetoric continued in the polemics of John Calvin and grew quite fervent among many New England patriots, who associated instruments with the pomp of the old state churches of Europe.

In 1827 Elias Smith of Boston epitomized this view, publishing an editorial in his *Morning Star* which attacked instrumental music in church with the argument that a free nation could not tolerate in its chapels the historic tools of "an unlawful, unrighteous connexion of *politics* and *religion.*" He wrote: "Whenever people come out from this government [that mixes church and state], to submit to Christ only, they 'sing with the spirit and understanding also.' When they go back, become *incorporated,* or are a body *politic,* to sue and be sued—to sell pews for the taxes, take the widow's money to pay the priest, buy *fiddles,* learn young people to sing and play on *instruments,* them [*sic*] you must worship only when you hear the sound of the bass viol, tenor viol, flute, claronet, bazzoon, double bass, &c." Christians in the New World, Smith insisted, must worship "with their hearts and voices, instead of *pipes, catgut, horse hair,* and *rosin.*"[19]

Despite such polemics, instrumental music afforded one of the few pleasures amid the ruggedness of rural life. Many churches, including the Palmyra Methodist Church, allowed bass viols into the choir lofts, even though viols were a species of "fiddle." Reeds, strings, and music books were sold in several Ontario County stores, and instrumental music of various sorts accompanied the itinerant amusements that passed through the village. Throughout the 1820s comic theater troupes performed in local hotel ballrooms, where, on wintry weekday afternoons and evenings, dancing schools were also held. From time to time a carnival, wild animal exhibit, or traveling wax museum would park its wagons in the village. The 1824 tour of the region by the Stowell and Bishop wax museum included "music on an elegant new patent organ." And even the "Grand Caravan of Living Animals" of 1826 enticed the local settlers by advertising "good music."[20]

Of all instruments the fiddle was perhaps the most loathsome and yet the most desired. Brigham Young, who grew up about thirty miles from the Smith farm, recalled that he "never heard the enchanting tones of the violin, until I was eleven years of age; and then I thought I was on the high way to hell, if I suffered myself to linger and listen to it."[21] The reminiscences of regional circuit-riders bespeak the repressive spirit that led to Young's deprivation and guilt. Revivalist James Erwin, for example, recalled with pleasure the conversion of a New York fiddler who, seeing that "he must abandon sin in every form, cross the river of decision and destroy the bridge behind him," not only cancelled the order he had placed for a new violin, but tied a string to his old fiddle in order to carry it away to a neighbor's—he could no longer bear even to touch the instrument. "In him," Erwin wrote, "was fulfilled the promise, 'From all your filthiness and from all your idols will I cleanse you.' "[22] The idea that the fiddle was a species of idol also appeared in Palmyra. When Philander Chase of St. Matthew's Church (a few miles from Joseph Smith's acreage) carved a shingle into a toy fiddle for some local children to play with, members of rival congregations complained that the minister had defiled himself.[23]

Fiddles usually accompanied dancing, and there were few religious folk who doubted the sinfulness of dancing. Those who argued for tolerating dancing called it a needful exercise, a source of vigor, and a refining grace. Those who despised it found its jerking movements undignified, and, in its more novel forms—the waltz, for example—lascivious.

But in rural areas, where newspaper accounts of aristocratic balls and soirées sparked dreams of a more elegant life, dancing schools enticed young people. Consequently, preachers felt they could not relent from condemning dancing, for they almost universally considered it a wicked seduction. Indeed, there was at this time a "universally prevailing idea that balls, dancing and sports of all kinds were a violation of the Christian profession," in which to indulge meant the "forfeiture of . . . Christian character."[24] The *Wayne Sentinel* was known to spoof dancing masters (though, like most papers, it did not hesitate to carry advertisements for dancing schools).[25] The "Advice to Young Ladies" the *Sentinel* printed on 9 February 1825 probably was on the liberal side of many of its readers, but well expressed a characteristic ambivalence toward dancing: "If you dance well, dance but seldom. If you dance ill, never dance at all."

On 21 September 1823, two months before his elder brother Alvin died, Joseph Jr. prayed for God to forgive him his involvement in worldly pastimes. As he related it years later, "left to all kind of temptations, and mingling with all kinds of society, I frequently fell into many foolish errors and displayed the weakness of youth and the corruption of human nature, which I am sorry to say led me into divers temptations, to the gratification of many appetites offensive in the sight of God."[26] These sins, he explained in 1834, amounted to "a light, and too often, vain mind, exhibiting a foolish and trifling conversation." This description, given the climate of the times, undoubtedly referred to the sins of "amusements."[27]

Although still unwilling to go with his mother and siblings to the Western Palmyra Presbyterian Church, Joseph felt remorse for his sins, perhaps due to the sermons preached at a recent revival. Vowing to clear up his standing with God, confess that his mind had been darkened by amusements, and swear off the bad company he had been keeping, he awaited another vision, "for I had full confidence in obtaining a divine manifestation, as I previously had done." In fulfillment of this expectation, Joseph reported, he was visited in the middle of the night by a resurrected ancient American warrior–prophet named Moroni.[28] The messenger quoted Bible passages to the seventeen-year-old and commanded him to uncover a sheaf of golden plates that was buried in the sloping hill ("Cumorah") along which the Manchester road passed. On these plates he would find inscriptions from a lost race, a nation of migrant Hebrews.

To speculate on the racial origins of the Indian was a kind of amusement in early America, especially among frontiersmen, whose surroundings continually manifested the presence of the "red man's" culture. Virtually since Columbus, books and tracts had postulated that Old World Semites, and particularly the "lost tribes of Israel," had somehow ended up in the Americas. But it was difficult to explain how their descendants could have degenerated into the low breed most Americans considered the Indians to be. The natives' primitive customs, including their fabled drumbeating and dancing, seemed to belie their "noble" heritage. After his 1823 vision, however, Joseph began to expound upon the glories of the Indians' golden age, including, as his mother recalled, "their dress, mode of travelling, and the animals upon which they rode; their cities, their buildings, with every particular; their mode of warfare; and also their religious worship. This he would do with as much ease, seemingly, as if he has spent his whole life with them."[29] In his vision of Moroni, in these parlor tales, and eventually in the Book of Mormon, the romance of the Indian took on new breadth. For Joseph claimed to have recovered by divine revelation an inspired account of the American Indians' rise and fall—their ascendance by God's grace and their decline at the hands of his displeasure.

Two years after he reported his visitation by Moroni, Joseph had not yet recovered the gold plates. This was, he explained, because his heart was not pure; he desired the plates for their monetary value. Indeed, his father's crops had worsened and young Joseph had to hire out for wages to a south central New York treasure hunter. Employed near the Susquehanna River, digging for a "lost mine," Joseph lodged at the house of Isaac Hale in Harmony, Pennsylvania. Hale's daughter Emma, one year Joseph's senior, caught the young man's eye. He quickly began to court her.

Living in a predominantly Quaker settlement, Emma and her family were Methodists. Without a meetinghouse for worship, they met in local homes (perhaps at times the Hales' own) and Joseph may have attended the meetings with Emma. Little is recorded of the musical practices of the village at this time. One event, however, is worthy of note. About the time of Joseph's sojourn at the Hale home, a Baptist singing controversy erupted in Great Bend, a few miles away. Deacon Daniel Lyons, who had built the Baptist meetinghouse, fiercely opposed singing in the new congregation there and apparently persuaded many to subscribe to his beliefs. But, according to an 1873 chronicler, "his success only contributed to the scattering of the flock."[30]

After more than a year of seeking without success her father's blessing on their joining, Joseph married Emma in January 1827. He worked on the lost mine venture a while longer until, exasperated with it, he quit and returned with his bride to his father's farm. That September, he reported, the heavenly messenger at last found him worthy of unearthing the golden plates, and in December Joseph moved back to his father-in-law's, eager to translate the ancient record. Before he returned to Harmony, however, he aroused the fascination of a Palmyra landowner named Martin Harris, who in April 1828 left his plow to move in with Joseph and Emma and be the scribe for the book. After Harris misplaced 116 pages of manuscript, Joseph convinced his younger brother's school-teacher, Oliver Cowdery, to be his new scribe. Under Joseph's dictation, Cowdery wrote out more or less the complete Book of Mormon in about three months, inking in the work's final "Amen" on 1 July 1829. By summer's end Cowdery had copied the manuscript and Egbert Grandin was setting the Book of Mormon in type.[31]

The book was a sprawling piece of prose. It chronicled the political and religious intrigues of, on the one hand, the descendants of Lehi, a Hebrew prophet who sailed with his family to the New World about 600 B.C., and on the other, the nation of the Jaredites, a nomadic people who journeyed to the Western Hemisphere after the confusion of tongues at Babel. The core of the work was a narrative describing the resurrected Jesus' visit to the Americas before his ascension. Before and after that episode the book told of the constant change of fortunes among rival clans, their cyclical passage from righteousness to wickedness and back again. Laden with small and large sermons, its narrative closed with a description of a huge battle, telling of only one righteous survivor—Moroni, who buried the book.

The Book of Mormon was immensely complex and at times detailed in its narrative, though often awkward in its language. It had power sufficient to persuade many readers to confess Joseph Smith's seership and religious authority. Fortuitously, the work seemed to address many of the issues debated by contemporary Protestant churchmen, including those concerning music.

In the Book of Mormon sacred singing was virtuous, and was spoken of in distinctly revivalist terms, such as singing "redeeming love" or chanting "ceaseless praise with the choirs above."[32] Indeed, just three hundred words into the manuscript the book described a vision of "numberless concourses of angels in the attitude of singing."[33] The book also made it clear that the Hebrew migrants to America sang in their worship meetings.[34] Unlike the Bible, in which instruments were often mentioned as implements of worship, the Book of Mormon had nothing to say about them, except in a chapter taken directly from Isaiah. About dancing the book was ambivalent. While at times dancing is mentioned without censure, in several instances it seems to be linked to degeneracy, especially in this passage: "Behold, my brethren and the sons of Ishmael and also their wives began to make themselves merry, insomuch that they began to dance, and to sing, and to speak with much rudeness, yea, even that they did forget by what power they had been brought thither; yea they were lifted up unto exceeding rudeness.''[35]

During the harvest months of 1829 and through the frost of 1830, Joseph held cottage meetings, baptized, and ordained elders, all under the aegis of more visions and visitations. On 29 March 1830, three days after the *Sentinel* offered the bound Book of Mormon to the public, Joseph's mother and his brothers Hyrum and Samuel were abruptly disfellowshipped from the Presbyterian Church.[36] Within eight days Joseph brought his now unchurched brothers to a meeting at Peter Whitmer's log house in Fayette, New York, a gathering to establish the ''Church of Christ'' according to state law.

To the unpersuaded the new congregation was the last thing New York needed, another ''Church of Christ'' to add to the heap of sects that already filled the region. But what set this sect apart was the book, and not precisely what was in the book, but that it was there at all. For if the revelation of the Book of Mormon meant anything at all to Joseph's disciples, it was that more revelation could come, and with it, a heaven-led kingdom on earth. Thus, with the Book of Mormon and its guardian in place to nurture it through a troublesome infancy, the new church was born. To distinguish its members from those of other Churches of Christ, outsiders began to call the new dissenters after their founding volume's name: Mormonites, or Mormons.

At that 6 April 1830 meeting Joseph apparently read a draft of the ''Articles and Covenants of the Church of Christ'' that he and Cowdery had penned. This document treated all the customary church particulars: modes of ordination, baptism, the Lord's Supper, and church record keeping, as well as the various obligations of members. But the document did not touch on musical matters. While Smith's account of this meeting mentions no singing, it does note that the new church ''praised the Lord, and rejoiced exceedingly,'' which may imply singing.[37]

On 9 June 1830, the church convened at the Whitmers' for its first Protestant-style conference, its members now numbering twenty-seven. Although Joseph recalled eight years later that the conference opened with singing, the minutes taken at the meeting describe it as opening rather with the reading of the fourteenth chapter of Ezekiel—no singing is mentioned.[38] This may be because the clerk, Oliver Cowdery, felt it unnecessary to note the musical part of the services in his record. Or perhaps Joseph's memory on this point was faulty, for at the next two conferences for which Cowdery served as scribe, 26 September 1830 and 4 August 1831, Cowdery carefully noted the singing.[39] With all the points of order needing attention, Joseph may have neglected the issue of music in the church's earliest days. It is also possible that the new prophet may have vacillated on whether or not to encourage music. His family traditions drew him toward it, but he had seen how controversial music could be, how it could even "scatter the flock." While music was needed to unify, it could easily divide a church.

By the end of the 9 June conference Joseph's parents and most of his siblings had joined the new Church of Christ by baptism. Emma, however, was not baptized until three weeks later. A revelation Joseph delivered to her in July suggests that she may have had misgivings. The document commanded her to "murmur not because of the things which thou hast not seen, for they are withheld from thee and from the world." Urging her to "beware of pride," it told her not to fear, "for thy husband shall support thee in the church." Her calling in the faith was not surprising: she was to be "a comfort unto my servant," her husband, and to be his scribe in Cowdery's stead, "that I may send my servant Oliver . . . whither-soever I will." But one somewhat convoluted passage in the revelation offered Emma a special calling and made it clear that God would take the church's music and her place in it seriously: "And it shall be given thee, also, to make a selection of sacred hymns, as it shall be given thee, which is pleasing unto me, to be had in my church. For my soul delighteth in the song of the heart; yea, the song of the righteous is a prayer unto me, and it shall be answered with a blessing upon their heads. Wherefore, lift up thy heart and rejoice, and cleave unto the covenants which thou hast made."[40]

Aside from what it may have done for Emma, the revelation did two things for the new church. First, it settled the question of whether or not to sing in church, firmly landing on the side of Joseph and Emma's family training. Second, it said that the church's sacred music could be "selected" from the traditions of other churches. With its emphasis on the "song of the *heart*" it savored of the old anti-singing polemics, yet it equated sacred singing with praying, making vocal music, in effect, requisite to worship. But what the revelation did not do was also crucial. It did not command the new believers to write new hymns, although this was commonplace among sects of the time. It said nothing about the matter of musical instruments in (or out of) church. Although it was later used to promote the printing of a hymnbook, the revelation said nothing about publication. Indeed, as it was first delivered to Emma Smith, the revelation appeared to be principally a command to decide what hymns already known to church members were proper to be sung in the Church of Christ. Since choosing songs to be sung was often the duty of a congregational singing master, the revelation may have been designating Emma to lead the tunes.

Within eighteen months, Emma apparently had chosen at least a few of the hymns for the Church of Christ. The first three sets of conference minutes to name the hymns sung by the church (August–October 1831), for example, all refer to the same hymn, John Newton's very popular "Zion," whose first two verses read:

> Glorious things of thee are spoken
> Zion, city of our God!
> He whose word can ne'er be broken
> Forms thee for his own abode.
>
> On the rock of ages founded,
> Who can shake thy sure repose?
> With salvation's wall surrounded,
> Thou may'st smile at all thy foes.[41]

Newton's hymn had already come to have a special ring for the new church because "Zion" was to them no longer the mere dream of a heavenly city. As early as 1829, in Harmony, Pennsylvania, Joseph dictated a revelation to his scribe that commanded church members to "seek to bring forth and establish the cause of Zion." Other revelations, including the one directed to Emma, had referred obliquely to Zion, promising an inheritance there. Then a prophecy given in September 1830 seemed to tease the church with the statement that "no man knoweth where the city Zion shall be built, but it shall be given hereafter." This notion appeared again and again in the revelations that began to pour with astonishing frequency from Joseph. Church members migrated en masse from New York to Kirtland, Ohio, perhaps hoping that there, where Disciples of Christ members were converting to Mormonism in droves, the city of Zion might be built. But at the Kirtland conference, 7 June 1831, Joseph told the brethren in the name of the Lord to wagon to Missouri, which was already gaining a reputation in the states as a land flowing with milk and honey. Arriving in Jackson County, on Missouri's western border, in July 1831, Joseph triumphantly announced: "this is the land of promise, and the place for the city of Zion." Suddenly, John Newton's hymn belonged to the followers of Joseph Smith.[42]

In the next two conferences where the hymn name is recorded in the minutes, Benjamin Cleaveland's "Go on, ye pilgrims" ("A Crumb for the Pilgrims") was sung.[43] The hymn enjoined steadiness in reaching Zion:

> Go on, ye pilgrims, while below,
> In the sure paths of peace,
> Determined nothing else to know
> But Jesus and his grace.
>
> . . . . . .
>
> Then you shall reach the promis'd land,
> With all the ransom'd race
> And join with all the glorious band,
> To sing redeeming grace.

However stirring such hymns may have been to the first Mormons, there was something faintly distressing about singing the old songs in the new church, especially now that it had discovered Zion's hiding place. Sidney Rigdon, the former Disciples of Christ preacher who was now Joseph Smith's right-hand man, alluded to this in a meeting at Kirtland, 25 October 1831. Rising to speak after the opening hymn, "Zion" ("Glorious things"), Rigdon remarked that God was making his children one, binding their hearts to heaven, and, that "in this thing God has taught his children to sing a new song even about Zion which David Spoke of &c."[44] The allusion was clear: the biblical prophecies called for *new* songs to grace the millennial kingdom. If the Mormons had to learn by heart the hymns of the new church—for there was no mechanical press in the church to print up Emma's selection—they should be the "songs of Zion," emerging from within the Church of Christ itself. Both new songs and a press would be supplied by an Ontario County newspaperman named William Wines Phelps.

The eccentric editor of a series of virulent anti-Masonic political sheets, the thirty-eight-year-old Phelps had bought a Book of Mormon in Palmyra two weeks after it came off the press. Believing it divinely inspired, he determined to meet Joseph Smith and question him further about religion. When he arrived in Kirtland in June 1831, just as the wagons were leaving for Missouri, Phelps humbled himself before the prophet, who quickly delivered a revelation calling Phelps to print for the church and write primers "that little children also may receive instruction before me as is pleasing unto me."[45] That September the church elders sent Phelps to Cincinnati to buy type and a press to print a church newspaper in Zion. By the end of April 1832, just as the newspaper was ready to be issued, the brethren ordered that "the Hymns selected by sister Emma be corrected by br. William W. Phelps," then printed in the new paper, *The Evening and the Morning Star.*[46] In June the paper came forth with the first of several installments of "Hymns, selected and prepared for the Church of Christ, in these last days."

In these back-page columns of hymn texts, one discovers what "correcting" meant to Phelps. In Newton's "Zion," for example, the "rock of ages" became the "rock of Enoch"—alluding to Joseph's revelations on the ancient city of Zion founded by that antediluvian patriarch. From Watts's "He dies, the friend of sinners dies," Phelps removed the present tense, substituted "great Redeemer" for "friend of sinners," and deleted the title of "God" for Jesus, putting "Lord" in its place. In other cases, he so thoroughly rewrote Protestant hymns as to make them utterly new in their essence. For example, compare portions of his revamping of Joseph Swain's "O Thou in whose presence my soul takes delight":

Joseph Swain	W. W. Phelps
O thou in whose presence	Redeemer of Israel,
my soul takes delight,	our only delight,
On whom in affliction I call,	On whom for a blessing we call,
My comfort by day and my	Our shadow by day and our
song in the night,	pillar by night,
My hope, my salvation, my all.	Our king, our companion, our all.
. . . . . .	. . . . . .
Or why should I wander	How long we have wandered
an alien from thee,	as strangers in sin,
Or cry in the desert for bread?	And cried in the desert for thee.
Thy foes will rejoice when my	Our foes have rejoiced when our
sorrows they'll see,	sorrows they've seen,
And smile at the tears I have shed.	But Israel will shortly be free.

In Phelps's version Christ becomes the deliverer of his nation rather than the intimate savior. (As in most of his revisions, the first person singular becomes plural.) "Thy foes" become "our foes," who not only will rejoice at the church's sufferings, but already have. Above all, the lyric emphasizes and expands the earlier hymn's allusions to the Israelite epic in the wilderness. In this as in other works by Phelps, the new church is the literal new Israel.[47]

The millennialism endemic to American religion at this time also surfaced in Phelps's "corrections." Compare Watts's popular "Not Ashamed of the Gospel" with Phelps's rechristened version, "New Jerusalem":

Isaac Watts	W. W. Phelps
I'm not ashamed to own my	We're not ashamed to own our
Lord	Lord,
Or to defend his cause,	And worship him on earth.
Maintain the honor of his word,	We love to learn his holy word,
The glory of his cross.	And know what souls are worth.
. . . . . .	. . . . . .
Then will he own my worthless	Then will he give us a new
name	name
Before his Father's face,	With robes of righteousness,
And in the New Jerusalem	And in the New Jerusalem
Appoint my soul a place	Eternal happiness.

In the same way, Phelps changed Watts's familiar nativity hymn, "Joy to the World," into a millennialist chant for Christ's return. His new version, titled "The Second Coming of the Savior," begins: "Joy to the world, the Lord will come, and earth receive her king."

It is difficult to say where Emma's selection ended and Phelps's editorial prerogative began. Even in his first installment of the "selected" hymns, he placed at the top of the page some of his own verses. The first song published in the newspaper, a hymn fittingly called "The Church of Christ," was apparently intended by Phelps as a kind of inaugural hymn for the new keepers of Zion. It was filled with his biting rhetorical style, including these lines:

> Old formal professors are crying "delusion,"
> And high-minded hypocrites say "'tis confusion,"
> While grace is pour'd out in a blessed effusion
> And saints are rejoicing to see priest-craft fall.[48]

Such salty lyrics appeared in the Mormon newspaper side by side with texts such as Michael Bruce's sedate "Zion exalted above the hills":

> On mountain tops the mount of God
> In latter days shall rise
> Above the summit of the hills
> And draw the wondering eyes.

By February 1833 Phelps apparently had exhausted Emma's hymn selection; in that month he proudly printed two "New Hymns." The first of these, "An angel came down from the mansions of glory," sang of the Book of Mormon, calling it

> A heavenly treasure; a book full of merit;
> It speaks from the dust, by the power of the Spirit;
> A voice from the Savior that saints can rely on,
> To prepare for the day when he brings again Zion.[49]

And in June 1833 Phelps began printing a new series of lyrics, entitling them, at last, "Songs of Zion." Virtually all of these looked toward Christ's reappearing, and several spoke plainly of the Mormons' belief that they were living in

> The day when saints again should hear
> The voice of Jesus in their ear,
> And angels who above do reign,
> Come down to converse hold with men.[50]

As copies of *The Evening and the Morning Star* went hand to hand across Jackson County, or were pulled from saddlebags in Kirtland, where many church members continued to gather, the devout of the Church of Christ saw in Phelps's hymns their old traditions being transfigured. The new and "corrected" songs of Zion were passed from mouth to ear and copied into diaries throughout the Mormon communities. What remained was for the newspaper hymns to be bound in books and slipped into the brethren's waistcoat pockets.

NOTES

1. For accounts of some of these visions see Lucy Mack Smith, *Biographical Sketches of Joseph the Prophet and His Progenitors for Many Generations* (Liverpool, England: Orson Pratt, 1853), pp. 57, 70–72, 74.

2. See the earliest extant (1832) account of this vision in Milton V. Backman, *Joseph Smith's First Vision* (Salt Lake City: Bookcraft, 1971), pp. 155–57.

3. On the name "burnt district" see Charles G. Finney, *Autobiography* (Old Tappan, N.J.: n.d.), p. 78.

4. "Genessee Conference," *Methodist Magazine* 9 (August 1826): 313.

5. David Benedict, *A General History of the Baptist Denomination in America, and Other Parts of the World*, 2 vols. (Boston: Lincoln and Edmands, 1813), 2:254.

6. *HC* 1:4

7. On the congregations in the Palmyra area, see the map and statistics compiled by Backman, *Joseph Smith's First Vision*, p. 68.
In about 1818 the Smiths moved onto a 100-acre lot just south of the village of Palmyra. While their address then changed to Manchester, the Smiths would have continued to be more or less residents of Palmyra, since it was the center of commerce for the region, and the location of the nearest post office. In 1823 both Ontario County and Palmyra were divided, creating the new county of Wayne, and the town of Macedon. See Backman, pp. 10–12.

8. See Fox's broadside "Some Queries" in *Gospel Truth Demonstrated in a Collection of Doctrinal Books*, 3 vols. (Philadelphia: M. T. C. Gould, 1831); also the Quaker documents quoted in Frederick John Gilman, *The Evolution of the English Hymn* (London: George Allen and Unwin, 1927), pp. 176–96.

9. See the appendix in Sewall S. Cutting, *Historical Vindications: A Discourse on the Province and Uses of Baptist History* (Boston: Gould and Lincoln, 1859), p. 189.

10. Benedict, *A General History*, 1:218.

11. Orasmus Turner, *History of the Pioneer Settlement of Phelps and Gorham's Purchase and Morris' Reserve* (Rochester, N.Y.: William Alling, 1851), p. 214.

12. Peter Cartwright, *Autobiography of Peter Cartwright, The Backwoods Preacher*, ed. W. P. Strickland (New York: Carleton and Porter, 1857), p. 6.

13. *The Doctrines and Disciplines of the Methodist Episcopal Church in America* (Philadelphia: Henry Tuckniss for John Dickins, 1798), pp. 122–25.

14. Cartwright, *Autobiography*, p. 117.

15. See G. A. Tuttle, "A Historical Sketch of Palmyra Methodist Episcopal Church. Compiled for the one hundredth anniversary celebration held December 10th to 17th, 1911," microfilm of typescript in HBLL, pp. 1–2.

16. 25 February 1824.

17. "Notes written on 'Chambers' Life of Joseph Smith,' " microfilm of holograph and typescript in HDC, pp. 18, 20 of the typescript.

Lucy Smith's father, Solomon Mack, was enamored of Isaac Watts's enormously popular *Hymns and Psalms* and tried, rather feebly, to emulate Watts in a set of verses published in his 1811 *Narrative*. Lucy's sisters Lovina and Lovisa, both of whom died young, composed several of their own hymn texts and sang duets on Watts's lyrics. Lucy recalled Lovina chanting Watts with her dying breath. And Lovisa, whose voice was "high and clear," sang Watts's 116th Psalm ("My God hath saved my soul from death") late in life with "angelic harmony." See Richard Lloyd Anderson, *Joseph Smith's New England Heritage: Influences of Grandfathers Solomon Mack and Asael Smith* (Salt Lake City: Deseret Book, 1971), pp. 33–61, 74–87.

18. See James McKinnon, "The Meaning of the Patristic Polemic against Musical Instruments," *Current Musicology* 1 (Spring 1965): 69–82.

19. "Instrumental Music Religion," *The Morning Star and City Watchman* 5 (October 1827): 107–11. For a survey of instruments in nineteenth-century American church music, see Nathaniel D. Gould, *Church Music in America* (Boston: A. N. Johnson, 1853), pp. 168–83.

20. See ads in *Palmyra Register*, 12 May 1818, 15 September 1818, 13 January 1819; *Wayne Sentinel*, 22 December 1824, 28 July 1826. By 1829 amusements became so plentiful in the region that the village elders of Palmyra passed an act enabling them to execute laws "for the more effectual suppression of vice and immorality" by closing down "shows exhibited by common showmen." See "Palmyra Village Incorporation Act of Mch 29. 1827—And Proceedings to February 2. 1852," microfilm of manuscript record book in HBLL.

21. Sermon of 6 February 1853, *JD* 2:94.

22. James Erwin, *Reminiscences of Early Circuit Life* (Toledo: Spear, Johnson, and Co., 1884), pp. 189–90.

23. Turner, *History of the Pioneer Settlement*, p. 185. On the distinction between "the Lord's fiddles" (bass viols) and "the devil's fiddles" (violins) in this period, see Leonard Ellinwood, *The History of American Church Music* (New York: Morehouse-Gorham, 1953), p. 24; also Henry Wilder Foote, *Three Centuries of American Hymnody* (Hamden, Conn.: Shoe String Press, 1961), pp. 112–13.

24. R. S. Duncan, *A History of the Baptists in Missouri* (St. Louis: Scammell, 1882), p. 221.

25. See the issues for 24 March 1824, 15 September 1824, 27 December 1825, and 17 November 1826.

26. "History of Joseph Smith," *TS* 3 (1 April 1842): 749.

27. Joseph Smith to Oliver Cowdery, *MA* 1 (December 1834): 40.

28. See *HC* 1:9–15.

29. Lucy Smith, *Biographical Sketches*, p. 85. For a study of Indian lore and the Book of Mormon, see Dan Vogel, *Indian Origins and the Book of Mormon: Religious Solutions from Columbus to Joseph Smith* (Salt Lake City: Signature Books, 1986).

30. Emily C. Blackman, *History of Susquehanna County, Pennsylvania* (Philadelphia: Claxton, Remsen, and Haffelfinger, 1873), p. 82.

31. For the history of the book's production, see *HC* 1:18–71.

32. See Alma 5:9, 26; 26:13; Mosiah 2:28; Mormon 7:7. Singing with "heavenly choirs" was a prevalent idea in Protestant hymnody. See also Henry Alline's hymn "Hard Heart of Mine," from his 1786 *Choice Hymns and Spiritual Songs,* whose third verse begins, "The Christians sing redeeming love / And talk of joys divine." Most Book of Mormon references to music appear in quotations from Isaiah.

33. 1 Nephi 1:8.

34. Moroni 6:9.

35. 1 Nephi 18:9.

36. For the Presbyterian records of this affair see Backman, *Joseph Smith's First Vision,* pp. 182–83.

37. *HC* 1:78. The "Articles and Covenants," as they were first known in the church, are now found as Doctrine and Covenants 20.

38. Compare *HC* 1:84 with *Far West Record: Minutes of the Church of Jesus Christ of Latter-day Saints, 1830-1844,* ed. Donald Q. Cannon and Lyndon W. Cook (Salt Lake City: Deseret Book, 1983), p. 1.

39. *Far West Record,* pp. 3, 9.

40. Doctrine and Covenants 25.

41. *Far West Record,* pp. 9, 14, 20. Here and throughout the book, I have usually normalized the spelling and punctuation of song texts, especially where variants exist.

42. See Doctrine and Covenants 6–57, passim—especially 6:6; 28:9; 52:1-3; 57:2.

43. *Far West Record,* pp. 25, 37. The text given above is from Cleaveland's *Hymns on Different Spiritual Subjects,* 4th ed. (Norwich, Conn.: John Trumbull, 1792), pp. 25-26. Compare W. W. Phelps's "corrected" version, as it appeared in *The Evening and the Morning Star* (July 1832).

44. *Far West Record,* p. 20.

45. Doctrine and Covenants 55:4.

46. Compare *HC* 1:270 with *Far West Record,* p. 46.

47. The "corrected" hymns mentioned here all appear in the first seven issues of *The Evening and the Morning Star* (June–December 1832). See Michael Hicks, "Poetic Borrowing in Early Mormonism," *Dialogue: A Journal of Mormon Thought* 18 (Spring 1985): 132–34.

48. Although no title is given in the first issue of *The Evening and the Morning Star,* a notebook of hymn texts apparently kept by Wilford Woodruff (now in HDC) has "What fair one is this in the wilderness travelling" under the title "The Church of Christ."

49. See *The Evening and the Morning Star,* February 1833. Phelps used the same rhyme ("rely on" / "Zion") in his altered version of the Disciples of Christ hymn "From the regions of love, lo, an angel descended." There he changed the words "who has bled for our pardon" to "whom our souls may rely on."

50. From "The happy day has rolled on," *The Evening and the Morning Star,* June 1833.

2

The Early Hymnbooks

In 1640 the first book published in North America, the Bay Psalm Book, came off the press. From that date onward the continent brought forth hundreds of volumes of sacred verse for public worship. Although beset by quarrels over the propriety of enlisting "man-made" poetry in the praise of God, by the eighteenth century virtually all religious orders of the New World tolerated or even encouraged the use of books containing psalm paraphrases and hymns, or "spiritual songs."[1] The literary virtues of these texts ranged from the jarring imagery of Benjamin Keach—

> Repentance like a bucket is
> To pump the water out;
> For leaky is our ship, alas,
> Which makes us look about[2]

—to the solemn lyricism of writers such as Isaac Watts, whose fluid diction came to permeate the consciousness of the whole republic.

More than a few congregations, however, appear to have been split over the use of hymnbooks. Some believers argued for retaining the traditional method of "lining out" the psalms or hymns to be sung: the minister or deacon would read each line, after which he would lead the congregation in singing it. Those who favored congregational songbooks argued that lining out destroyed the flow of the music, breaking each song or hymn into a series of disjunct phrases. And this became more objectionable as poets increasingly continued thoughts from one line into the next, a practice of which Watts was the undisputed master. The opponents of congregational songbooks argued that using them would destroy the unity of the congregation by diverting their attention away from the leader to the printed page. Allowing each person to look at his own book, they insisted, would inject even more confusion into what was already a chaotic situation.

But psalmbooks and hymnbooks prevailed, if for no other cause than the Americans' irresistible urge to put things into print. This trait was especially prevalent among Christian believers, for whom a book, the

Bible, was the final arbiter of salvation. Putting musical texts into books seemed to give them a legitimacy and durability that could not be matched by oral tradition.[3] Hence, dozens of editions of Watts, the Wesleys' hymns, and nondenominational camp-meeting collections appeared on the bookstore shelves of early nineteenth-century America.

In the early 1830s Mormon leaders began to consider producing their own hymnbook, a collection based on Emma Smith's selection, W. W. Phelps's adaptation, and the collective versification of the new church members. But as the church's doctrines and authority structure evolved, hymnbooks seemed to be at the center of struggles over orthodoxy. In the ebb and flow of early Mormonism the unity that hymnody could provide was crucial to the church's survival. But consecrating texts to the printed page was bound to raise questions of *imprimatur* that would finally be settled only when the church itself divided.[4]

On 20 July 1833, angered by the *Evening and Morning Star*'s apparent welcoming of free blacks into the church in Missouri, a mob of several hundred Jackson County citizens tore down Phelps's house, dismantled the church press, and scattered the type in the street. The newspaper was scuttled and the church's first book, titled *A Book of Commandments for the Government of the Church of Christ,* a collection of Joseph Smith's revelations then at the press, was forestalled. The destruction of the press allowed Smith to move church publishing back to Ohio, under his close inspection and out of Phelps's control.

In January of that year Smith had complained that Phelps was trying to hide a "bad spirit" by "mak[ing] great pretensions when the heart is not right," and requested him to make the *Star* more interesting, "for if you do not render it more interesting than at present, it will fall, and the Church suffer a great loss thereby."[5] The Kirtland high priests—at that time the highest church officers under Joseph—similarly complained that a December 1832 letter they had received from Phelps "betrays a lightness of spirit that ill becomes a man placed in the important and responsible station that he is placed in."[6] Because of church leaders' worries about Phelps's competence and the threat of renewed terrorism in Zion, Oliver Cowdery in December 1833 hauled a new press into Kirtland and took over Phelps's old job as editor of the *Star.*

Despite his concerns about Phelps, Smith invited him to come live with him in Kirtland in spring 1835, explicitly to help him revise his manuscript revelations for publication, and implicitly to continue collaboration with Emma on the hymnbook, which Smith apparently wanted ready before the Kirtland Temple (a sacred structure for performing priesthood ordinances) was finished. Smith's reservations notwithstanding, Phelps was useful to Joseph because he had carefully sifted through Joseph's documents while publishing many of them in the *Star* and typesetting them for the *Book of Commandments*. By August 1835 the collection of revelations, just under half the size of the Book of Mormon, was bound and ready for sale at one dollar per copy.[7] On 14 September the Kirtland high priests formally appointed Phelps to the work of revising and adapting hymns, a work in which he had already long engaged himself. Within a few months, probably by January 1836, the Kirtland print shop issued a 127-page hymnal in an edition of around 1,000 copies.[8]

Naming Emma Smith as the sole compiler, the title page declared the work *A Collection of Sacred Hymns for the Church of the Latter Day Saints*, reflecting the 1834 change of the church's name from "Church of Christ."[9] Its preface claimed that the church needed such a collection of texts (not tunes) adapted to their increasingly communitarian beliefs and expectations for an imminent millennium. Citing the pertinent phrases in the July 1830 revelation to Emma Smith, the preface defined "the song of the righteous" as "a prayer unto God," and expressed the hope that the hymns would "answer every purpose till more are composed or we are blessed with a copious variety of the songs of Zion." With ninety hymns, the collection was relatively spare, containing more hymn texts than many camp-meeting pocketbooks, but fewer than most denominational hymnbooks.[10] Of the ninety, only thirty-eight had appeared in the *Star* or its successor, the *Latter Day Saints' Messenger and Advocate;* and the hymnbook omitted ten others that had appeared in those papers (including one of the first of Emma's selection, "Go on, ye pilgrims").[11]

At least fifty hymns in the new collection were overtly borrowed and rewritten Protestant hymns, seventeen of them by Watts and the rest by John Wesley, Steele, Heber, Ken, Medley, Newton, Leland, Elizabeth Scott, and Thomas Taylor, to name only a few of the recoverable authors. Among the forty hymns probably written by Mormon authors, most have been attributed to Phelps, who had a penchant for rolling, dactylic verses: his first lines include "Awake, O ye people! the Savior is coming," "An angel came down from the mansions of glory," "Now let us rejoice in the day of salvation," "There's a feast of fat things for the righteous preparing," "The Spirit of God like a fire is burning," and "What fair one is this in the wilderness traveling."

Alexander Campbell, from whose Disciples of Christ church many Kirtland Mormons had been converted, wrote in his 1828 *Psalms, Hymns and Spiritual Songs* that a hymnbook was "as good an index to the brains and to the hearts of a people as the creed book."[12] The new Mormon hymnbook provided an eloquent example, surveying in its texts the breadth of Mormon experience and dogma. A large number of hymns dealt with the Second Coming, while many others dealt with the building up of Zion as a decidedly earthly kingdom: Watts's "There is a land of pure delight," for example, was changed to "There is a land the Lord will bless." Five of the hymns dwelt on the glories of the natural world, in conjunction with the Mormon idea of making heaven on earth.[13] The collection also contained six each of morning and evening hymns for family worship, i.e., one for each day of the week except the Sabbath. Four "farewell hymns" appeared, drawn primarily from songs sung by parting circuit riders at the close of their revivals. These were now adapted for use by Mormon missionaries, who were circulating throughout the frontier in search of their own proselytes. The book also contained two of Watts's temple psalm paraphrases (for use at the Kirtland temple dedication), several communion (or "sacrament") hymns, and three popular meditations on death.[14]

The whole book opened not with Phelps's "The Church of Christ" or even "Glorious things of thee are spoken," but rather with the anonymous text "The Freedom of the Will." This hymn, which had first appeared in Elias Smith and Abner Jones's 1805 camp-meeting collection, *Hymns Original and Selected for the Use of Christians,* constituted a powerful assertion of the Saints' right to believe and worship as they pleased in the face of persecution:

> Know then that ev'ry soul is free,
> To choose his life and what he'll be;
> For this eternal truth is given,
> That God will force no man to heaven.
>
> He'll call, persuade direct him right,
> Bless him with wisdom, love, and light;
> In nameless ways be good and kind,
> But never force the human mind.
>
> It's my free will for to believe:
> 'Tis God's free will me to receive:
> To stubborn willers this I'll tell,
> It's all free grace, and all free will.

The collection featured some of Phelps's best writing, including his "Hosanna to God and the Lamb" (better known by its first line, "The Spirit of God like a fire is burning"):

> How blessed the day when the lamb and the lion
> Shall lie down together without any ire;
> And Ephraim be crowned with his blessings in Zion
> As Jesus descends with his chariots of fire—

and likewise some of his worst, as in "Now we'll sing with one accord":

The commandments to the church,
Which the saints will always search,
(Where the joys of heaven perch)
Came through him [Joseph Smith] from Jesus Christ.

Most of Phelps's work lay somewhere between these extremes. Many of his verses consisted of eccentric yet robust lyrics, such as those for "The Red Man," which dealt with the Hebrew birthright that Mormons believed the Indians possessed. It adapted its opening from the anonymous camp-meeting song "Come tell me, wandering sinner," which had appeared in Campbell's hymnal.

"Wandering Sinner"	"Red Man"
Come tell me, wandering sinner,	O stop and tell me, red man,
Say whither do you roam?	Who are ye, why you roam?
O'er this wide world a stranger,	And how you get your living?
Have you no Savior known?	Have you no God, no home?

Another of Phelps's creations reflected his interest in the sanctity of marriage. The sole hymn in the "On Marriage" section of the hymnbook, Phelps's nuptial song began:

> When earth was dress'd in beauty,
> And join'd with heaven above,
> The Lord took Eve to Adam,
> And taught them how to love.
>   . . . . . .
> And bless'd them as an altar,
> For chaste and pure desire,
> That no unhallowed being
> Might offer there "strange fire."[15]

The hymnbook did not suggest tunes for its texts, as Campbell's hymnbook did, but undoubtedly some of the texts were sung to five- or six-note folk tunes, often in minor modes, if contemporary tunebooks give a good representation of the style. Certain hymn tunes were more or less fixed. Phelps's "Redeemer of Israel," for example, was adapted from Swain's "O thou in whose presence," which was universally sung to the tune "Davis." The newspapers in which many Mormon hymns first appeared designated their tunes. ("The Spirit of God," for example, was meant to be sung to "American Star.") In some of these cases any of a number of known or as yet unknown melodies bearing the same title may have been intended. Hence, deducing the tunes to which early Mormon hymns were sung has proved, in most cases, impossible. The only explicit tune names for Mormon hymns in this period appear in the minutes of the Kirtland Temple dedication services.

Virtually the whole musical content of that occasion can be reconstructed. Six hymns were sung, two of them to the same tune, probably that to which "The Spirit of God" continues to be sung today. "Adam-ondi-Ahman" was meant for the tune "Prospect of Heaven."[16] The other tunes mentioned in the minutes ("Dalston," "Weymouth," and "Sterling") appear in many tunebooks of the period. All of the five tunes used at this dedication service employ major scales.[17] The most interesting and durable of the five, the "Spirit of God" tune, seems to derive from an instrumental source, probably a band tune. Mormons undoubtedly felt in its martial strains the pomp of a new nation being born.

Perhaps the most gifted of the poets of the church's first decade was apostle Parley Pratt. Some months prior to the appearance of Emma Smith's hymnbook, Pratt had published at Boston a pocketbook of verse containing a long, pseudo-epic poem called "The Millennium" and eleven moderate-length hymns. In these and in other writings Pratt displayed a passion for converting gentiles and defending the faith. These converged in his 1837 book, *A Voice of Warning and Instruction to All People,* which became the cornerstone of Mormon missionary work in the eastern United States, Great Britain, and eventually the world. Fortuitously, its publication and Pratt's own charisma combined immediately to set in motion the events that would reshape the church's scarcely born hymnody.

In 1837 Pratt converted a well-to-do New Yorker named David Rogers, a visionary of both the mystical and mercantile realms. Rogers quickly discerned that Mormonism was beginning to flourish in many areas outside of Missouri and Ohio, that he and other converts wanted new hymns to bolster their new beliefs, and that Emma Smith's hymnbook was unavailable outside of the church's principal gathering places. He discovered a market for reprinting the Mormon hymnbook in New York and thereby furnishing it to the growing Mormon congregations in the East, not to mention the missionaries departing to Europe from eastern ports. Rogers later claimed that the necessity of such a venture was confirmed to him in a dream in which Christ appeared and commanded him to produce a new hymnbook.[18]

Rogers's volume imitated Emma Smith's in many details. The title and title-page layout, the quantity of hymns, the actual numbering of many hymns, and even the preface were taken directly from Emma's. Yet Rogers omitted forty of the hymns found in the earlier collection, even some of those by Mormon authors. He also mistakenly repeated one text ("Awake, O ye people!" appears both as no. 7 and no. 51) and added five from Pratt's book of verse and at least twenty-four others by Mormons, including a dedicatory hymn for the book by Rogers himself (a hymn which, of course, no one would sing). The new hymns continued in the style of those in Emma Smith's book. Many adapted existing Protestant hymns, and most continued the bold, millennialistic rhetoric of the Saints. Several were quasi-revivalist invitations to outsiders to repent, believe the new gospel, and gather to Zion. Hymns nos. 70 and 71 are typical of these:

> No. 70 (''Praise ye the Lord in latter days'')
>
> His kingdom he has set up now,
> That's ne'r to be destroy'd;
> Go ye into the kingdom, go
> And worship there your Lord.
>
> No. 71 (by ''D. W.'' [David Whitmer?])
>
> The Lord in glory will appear
> When Zion he doth build;
> And all behold from far and near,
> The world with glory filled.
>   . . . . . .
>
> To Zion now we will repair,
> Far in the pleasant west;
> And with the Saints the blessings share
> Of thousand years of rest.

For the time being, however, the Saints found no rest. They openly declared that they would consecrate Missouri's rich farmland to the cause of Zion. Their aggressive rhetoric, some of it in their hymns, frightened and enraged their neighbors. After numerous skirmishes, the governor of Missouri issued an order on 27 October 1838, demanding that Mormons flee the state or be massacred. Three days later a Mormon village was attacked by vigilantes, leaving seventeen dead. The next day, church leaders were imprisoned on charges that they were leading a secret vigilante group of their own. Hearing of the troubles in Missouri, David Rogers donated money for the relief of poor Saints and became a land agent for the church, looking for a suitable region in which the Mormons could settle.

Discerning a milder, if still not wholly tolerant, religious climate in Illinois, the Saints in Missouri (and some in Ohio) began migrating to the west central part of Illinois in May 1839, converging on a tract of marshy land situated at a sharp bend in the Mississippi. The prophet soon dubbed this land ''Nauvoo'' (his transliteration of the Hebrew for ''beautiful and restful dwellingplace'').

By 1 July 1839 the prophet and apostles met to compile a new hymn-book. They apparently considered reprinting or adapting Rogers's work, since he had brought copies of it with him to Nauvoo. At the next general conference of the church one of the apostles, Lyman Wight, publicly lashed out at Rogers, charging that he had no authority to sell such a work, especially one that appeared to be masquerading as Emma's. He insisted that the Rogers hymnal be "utterly discarded" by the church, presumably in favor of a new collection, which Brigham Young, the senior apostle, intended to have compiled and published.[19]

Three weeks later the Nauvoo high priests met and voted that Emma Smith, having a divine right to do so because of the revelation of July 1830, should compile the new hymnbook. They also voted to forbid Young to publish the apostles' work.[20] Whether or not they ever notified Young of this remains in question, for he had left for the East Coast in September. But it is doubtful he would have recognized the high priests' authority over him in any case, since he was convinced that the apostolic office, instituted in 1835, was superior to that of the high priest, a point which many high priests were as yet unwilling to concede.

Young's companion, Parley Pratt, wrote to Nauvoo in November that no hymnals could be found in New York and that he could guarantee sales of one thousand copies "in these parts" the moment a new collection could be printed. Recognizing that debt had nearly paralyzed the church in Illinois, Pratt offered to have the hymnals printed himself, feeling confident that any investment he made would immediately be repaid. Hyrum Smith, Joseph's older brother, wrote back to Pratt, informing him that the hymnbook (along with other church works) must be printed in Nauvoo, under Joseph's scrutiny, in order that it might be "a standard to all nations." Hyrum added that he longed to see the hymnbooks and other church works "flowing through the land like a stream imparting knowledge, intelligence and joy, to all who shall drink at the stream." Within two weeks after Hyrum wrote this letter the Nauvoo high priests voted to print ten thousand hymnbooks, as soon as the means could be obtained. Hyrum told Joseph the work must be produced "under your immediate inspection. I am afraid some have been induced to tarry and assist Parley in these undertakings."[21]

But the citizens of Nauvoo simply could not sustain the printing and binding of ten thousand new books at this time. Most of its residents were poor; many of them had been driven from their homes in Missouri, and their Illinois acreage would take some time to be productive. Furthermore, while the high priests were trying to raise money for printing, they were also exhorting Saints of means to give money to the poor and to help pay off the town plots' outstanding debts. Since most of the old hymnbooks were owned by citizens of Nauvoo, the city had no market for a new edition. And if the books were sent abroad, the shipping costs and duties would have exceeded the cost of the books themselves.

Sometime during 1839 a Mormon missionary in New York named Benjamin Ellsworth published his own solution to the hymnbook problem.

His volume reprinted the 1835 preface, then proceeded to reprint Rogers's collection through hymn no. 89, adding fifteen more hymns (all but two of them by Mormons). Nearly all of these additional hymns were texts that originally appeared in Emma Smith's hymnal but were omitted from Rogers's, or originally appeared in Mormon newspapers but were omitted from Emma Smith's. The publishing history of this book, as well as its reception, is unclear. But the unnamed offense for which Ellsworth was disciplined at a subsequent church conference may well have been his issuing of yet another unofficial hymnbook, not to mention a hymnbook that was based on Rogers's problematic work.

On 6 April 1840, the tenth anniversary of the church's founding, the Nauvoo high priests formally brought charges against David Rogers for selling his hymnbook "as the one compiled and published by Sister Emma Smith." (He was found guilty, but was immediately forgiven and restored to full fellowship.) On the same day Young, Pratt, and four other missionaries landed in Liverpool. Within ten days of the landing they and other missionaries met and agreed that Young, Pratt, and John Taylor (another of Pratt's 1837 converts) should compile, revise, and publish a hymnbook in Manchester, on the premise that British converts were discarding their old Protestant hymnals—"for the Bible, religion, and all is new to them."[22]

Although the Manchester missionaries did not seek Joseph's formal blessing on their project, two other apostles did ask about publishing such a work on the European continent. Joseph declined that request on the grounds that "a new edition, containing a greater variety of Hymns, will be shortly published or printed in this place [Nauvoo]; which I think will be a standard work." However, Joseph added, if the necessity arose they had the liberty of reprinting the 1835 Kirtland hymnbook.[23]

By late May, Young was shopping for print shops and binderies in Manchester. Pratt, meanwhile, had completed dozens of new hymns at the rate of two or three a day; almost fifty of these would be added to the collection.[24] All of Pratt's hymns that survive were uniquely Mormon, emphasizing Joseph Smith's restoration of the ancient gospel and the building of Zion. At least one of them was a rewriting of one of the hymns in Rogers's collection, "An angel from on high" (by "R. B."). A comparison clearly shows Pratt's flair for turning abstractions to concrete images.

"R. B."	Pratt
An angel from on high	An angel from on high
Descended to the earth	The long, long silence broke—
Behold him drawing nigh	Descending from the sky
Proclaiming loud the truth	These gracious words he spoke:
To witnesses who chosen were	Lo! in Cumorah's lonely hill
The heavenly message to declare.	A sacred record lies concealed.

During the final compilation of hymns Taylor fell too sick to work on the project and two local brethren were called in to help.[25] In early June the compilation was done and Young complained in a letter to his wife that "I have had perty much of it to due myself."[26] Pratt, however, felt equally oppressed by the amount of writing, editing, and proofreading he had to do. He complained in a letter to his wife that he had not been able to leave his house more than twenty-four hours in the preceding three months, nor did he expect to "for months or years to come."[27]

By late July, 3,000 copies were in print. But it quickly became evident that misspellings and typographical errors abounded in the work. Now recovered, John Taylor pointed out to Young that a hasty revision was in order and suggested a local Mormon man of letters to do the work.[28] Sick, exhausted by the project, and disappointed at the huge number of errors that were being reported in the hymnbook, Young apparently began to doubt that he and his peers had acted properly in printing the volume, especially since the express permission of the prophet had not been obtained. Although Young's wife wrote to Brigham that Joseph had approved of the hymnbook plans in her presence, the apostle's conscience was not eased. On 5 September, Young wrote to Joseph, directly asking about the hymnbook for the first time: "Have we done right in Printing a hymn book?"[29]

In October another apostle arrived with a letter written by Joseph, dated 19 July, which approved the publication of a hymnbook in England. Because much of the ink was "bloted out," Young construed the letter to be a rebuke for having undertaken the book. He wrote bitterly to his wife that he had not had the opportunity to ask Joseph's permission before making the hymnbook, that he had done "the verry best that I knew how," and that he would face Joseph directly on the matter if necessary.[30] But Smith's actual assessment of the new hymnbook became clear in a subsequent letter to the apostles dated 15 December 1840: "as far as I have examined it I highly approve of it and think it to be a very valuable collection."[31]

Joseph's approval was surely based in part on the continued delay of the Nauvoo hymnal. Nauvoo church printer Ebenezer Robinson, who had worked on the 1835 hymnal, had fallen desperately sick. After a long respite in Cincinnati, he returned to Nauvoo in late fall of 1840, determined to upgrade his print shop and get out the new hymnal.[32] But by the time the work was ready in spring 1841, the apostles in Britain had voted to produce a second edition of their own work.

The titles of the Manchester hymnal's various sections bespoke the special concerns of Mormonism ten years after its birth. Beyond the old morning, evening, baptismal, sacrament, and farewell hymn sections,

sections of hymns on several subjects were added, including "Priesthood," "Second Coming of Christ," and "Gathering of Israel." The idea of priesthood—the divine authority of Christ to administer the gospel and its ordinances—had emerged as a prime concern of Mormons and had become a point of debate between Mormon missionaries and the Christians to whom they preached. The quest for the restoration of the order and power of the primitive church energized many contemporary denominations. However, for the Latter Day Saints, the visits of ancient apostles to Joseph Smith and Oliver Cowdery to confer divine authority had wholly settled the question: this was the authentic Church of Christ.

Partly because the Saints saw the return of the ancient priesthood as a preparation for the Millennium, their expectations of the imminent return of Christ intensified with each year. The fervor for the Savior's return provoked hymn adaptations such as "Behold the great redeemer comes," the Manchester hymnbook's adaptation of Samuel Medley's "I know that my redeemer lives."

I know that my redeemer lives;	Behold the great redeemer comes
What comfort this sweet sentence gives;	To bring his ransomed people home;
He lives, he lives who once was dead	He comes to save his scatter'd sheep,
He lives, my ever living head.	He comes to comfort them who weep.
He lives to bless me with his love,	He comes all blessings to impart,
He lives to plead for me above,	Unto the meek and contrite heart,
He lives my hungry soul to feed,	He comes, he comes to be admired,
He lives to bless in time of need.	He comes to burn the proud with fire.

The British missionaries also saw their work as the consummation of ancient prophecies that the chosen bloodline, Israel, would be gathered to Zion. Many of the songs in the collection bid those pure in heart and blood to flee spiritual Babylon and gather to the United States. These songs had traditional revivalist titles such as "Come, sinners, to the gospel feast," "Sinners, believe the gospel word," and "Repent, ye Gentiles all."

Numbering thirty-three hymns more than even the Manchester collection, the 1841 Nauvoo hymnal substantially retreated from the Zionism of all the earlier hymnbooks. It omitted Phelps's "Redeemer of Israel" in favor of Joseph Swain's original "O thou in whose presence." It also removed Phelps's "corrections" of Watts's "He dies, the friend of sinners dies" and "There is a land of pure delight." Both of these changes were symptomatic of the book's strong tendency to return to revivalist, grace-oriented phraseology, an intimacy with Jesus and the cross, a personal rather than communal tone, and a confessional rather than rejoicing spirit. In the new book Emma Smith included Watts's and Newton's widely known but heretofore shunned titles: "Amazing Grace! how sweet the sound," "Am I a soldier of the cross?," "Begone unbelief, my Savior is near," "I love the Lord, he heard my cry," "Plung'd in a gulf of dark despair," "Salvation! O the joyful sound," "With joy we meditate the grace," and "When I survey the wondrous cross." The collection also contained similarly toned hymns, such as Robinson's "Come, thou fount of every blessing," Evans's "Hark the voice of love and mercy," Steele's "Stretched on the cross the Savior dies," Cowper's "There is a fountain filled with blood," and the anonymous "Lord, what a thoughtless wretch." What motivated this shift in emphasis is difficult to say, but it undoubtedly reflects in part the absence of Phelps's influence in the compilation of the hymns: he was excommunicated in 1839, and when restored to fellowship early in 1841 he was promptly sent on a mission.

The Nauvoo general conference minutes of October 1841 give some sense of what texts might actually have been used by the Saints.[33] Over three days, ten hymns were recorded as being sung, two of them twice ("Come let us anew" and "My soul is full of peace and love"). Of those ten, six were more or less unaltered Protestant hymns (two by Wesley, two Watts, and one each by Williams and Taylor). Three others appear to be indigenous Mormon texts, and one other ("We're not ashamed to own our Lord") was a hybrid. The last hymn sung at the conference, "Hail the day so long expected," had a chorus that showed the millennial glee of the Nauvoo Saints, as well as their hostility to the outside world: "Babylon is fallen, is fallen, is fallen / Babylon is fallen, to rise no more."

The retrenchment implicit in Emma's 1841 selection came at an unpropitious moment in the evolution of Mormon doctrine. In the years 1842–44 Joseph Smith forcefully expanded his theology, partly due to his continual confrontation with the death of friends and relatives, including his father and his younger brother. As he pondered the huge death toll in the city, Joseph began to teach the use of vicarious ordinances for the salvation of the dead, to emphasize the literalness of the resurrection and the constant presence of departed spirits and to institute special "higher" ordinances, especially for use in the temple. These last included the endowment ceremony, which initiated its participants in the symbols and rites of the afterlife, and "celestial marriage"—a "sealing" of man to wife (or wives) for this life and the one to come.

As these and other doctrines came to prominence, Emma's work seemed more and more obsolete, and many new hymns and poems appeared in the pages of the new church newspaper, *Times and Seasons,* as well as in William Smith's paper, the *Wasp* (later the *Nauvoo Neighbor*).

With her 1841 edition probably already out of print, Emma Smith began in February 1843 to call for newly adapted hymns, apparently for yet another fresh compilation.[34] This new hymnal was never produced, perhaps because the quorum of apostles had taken over the Nauvoo print shop. Meanwhile, the British press had issued a second edition of the Manchester hymnal, 1,500 copies.

In 1844 an obscure but important hymnal was printed in the county adjacent to Joseph's birthplace in Vermont. Jesse Little and G. B. Gardner's *A Collection of Sacred Hymns for the Use of Latter Day Saints* was in fact a kind of modest singing school tunebook. Containing forty-eight texts, the work gave tunes and bass lines to thirty-one of them, and included two pages of scales, solmization syllables, key signatures, and note values. The work clearly was modelled upon the 1841 Nauvoo hymnbook: all of the thirty-one texts that were set to tunes in Little and Gardner's book had appeared in the 1841 book (seven of those had been unique to it). Among the unset texts in the new book were four by Pratt (only one of which had Emma included in her work), one new text by Phelps, and at least three texts by a Mary Page. Page's texts resembled Phelps's in their homespun qualities, with verses such as:

> Behold a wonder in the west!
> The church of Christ and yet oppress'd;
> Though first, in size, appears but small,
> It soon will fill our earthly ball.

The seventeen texts without tunes were all Mormon. But of the thirty-one texts with tunes, twenty-one were Protestant hymns, which roughly duplicated the ratio of non-Mormon to Mormon hymns mentioned in the 1841 conference minutes.

The character of the tunes differed somewhat from those that prevailed in contemporary tunebooks. Whereas a large number of American hymn tunes were in minor modes, all of Little and Gardner's tunes were in major. Nineteen of them (61%) used seven-note scales, as opposed to the much smaller percentage (23%) in the tunebooks surveyed by George Pullen Jackson.[35] Conversely, only four (13%) were pentatonic, as opposed to Jackson's survey (23%). The tunes, which are probably all borrowed—though not all of their sources have yet been identified—ranged from the folk-hymn oriented "Adam-ondi-Ahman" to the last hymn, "Awake and sing the song," whose tune was a Lowell Mason–like adaptation of Handel's "He shall feed his flock." The question remains whether all the tunes notated in this volume were those that were employed generally by the Saints, those corresponding only to the compilers' tastes, or some combination of the two.

In June 1844 Mormons were stunned when Joseph Smith and his brother Hyrum were shot to death in a surprise attack on the jail in which the brothers were being held.[36] The double assassination sent the faithful reeling and left several factions in the church vying to succeed Joseph. The principal claims to oversee the church came from the competing hymnbook compilers: from Joseph's family (led by Emma Smith) on one hand, and from the apostles (led by Brigham Young) on the other. Although the masses of the church were divided in their loyalties, the majority eventually offered their allegiance to the apostles, who in late winter 1846 led the famous "exodus" from Illinois to the Rocky Mountains. This large and cohesive group, filled with the apostles' British converts who had immigrated to Nauvoo, discarded Emma Smith's hymnal and kept the Manchester collection. For not only was the latter better known to the immigrants, it was the work better-suited to the expanding theology of Joseph's last years. And it is with the pioneer group that followed the apostles and retained their hymnbook that the name "Mormon" eventually descended into history.

When the first wagons pulled out of Nauvoo on 4 February 1846, the church was not yet sixteen years old, but the body of distinctive hymn texts that would dominate its worship services for a century and a half was almost fully formed. In two weeks Phelps would celebrate his fifty-fourth birthday, and, although he would remain prolific for another twenty-six years, nearly all of his contributions to Mormon hymnbooks had already been published. Parley Pratt's principal hymns all had been composed. While Mormonism would continue to produce new hymns, they would seldom achieve the vigor and intensity of the early hymns. In the Utah period the making of "official" hymnbooks would become increasingly routine and systematic, while the making of hymns would become a deed more of service to the church than of revelatory passion. In a similar manner the act of singing itself would become the object of musical reformers seeking to codify its principles and turn the song of the righteous into a science.

NOTES

1. Paul enjoined the early Christians to speak to one another in "psalms, hymns, and spiritual songs" (Ephesians 5:19; see also Colossians 3:16). For a representative eighteenth-century discussion of the meaning of these terms, see John Gill, *A Discussion on Singing of Psalms as a Part of Divine Worship* (London: n.p., 1734), pp. 18–23.

2. From Keach's 1691 *Spiritual Melody,* excerpted in H. Wheeler Robinson, *The Life and Faith of the Baptists* (London: Kingsgate Press, 1946), pp. 48–49.

3. For discussions of psalmbooks and hymnbooks in colonial America, see Foote, *Three Centuries of American Hymnody,* pp. 143–86 (and on the

controversy over "lining out," pp. 373–82); also, George M. Stephenson, *The Puritan Heritage* (New York: Macmillan, 1952), p. 102. On the printed word in Protestantism, see W. Lloyd Warner, *The Family of God: A Symbolic Study of Christian Life in America* (New Haven: Yale University Press, 1961), pp. 62–63.

4. Several treatments of Mormon hymnody have appeared over the years. The best are Helen Hanks Macaré, "The Singing Saints: A Study of the Mormon Hymnal, 1835–1950" (Ph.D. diss., University of California at Los Angeles, 1961); Newell Bryan Weight, "An Historical Study of the Origin and Character of Indigenous Hymn Tunes of the Latter-day Saints" (Ph.D. diss., University of Southern California, 1961); David Sterling Wheelwright, "The Role of Hymnody in the Development of the Latter-day Saint Movement" (Ph.D. diss., University of Maryland, 1943); and William Leroy Wilkes, Jr., "Borrowed Music in Mormon Hymnals" (Ph.D. diss., University of Southern California, 1957). Also very useful is the unpublished study by Bruce David Maxwell, "Source Book for *Hymns*" (privately distributed, 1982), copy in HDC.

5. *HC* 1:317.

6. *HC* 1:319.

7. This was priced somewhat high for a 281-page work because Joseph hoped to recoup the Missouri printing losses. See W. W. Phelps to Sally Phelps, 16 September 1835, photocopy of holograph in HDC.

8. On Phelps's appointment see *HC* 2:273; cf. W. W. Phelps to Sally Phelps, 11 September 1835 and 14 November 1835, HDC. See also Peter Crawley, "A Bibliography of the Church of Jesus Christ of Latter-day Saints in New York, Ohio and Missouri," *Brigham Young University Studies* 12 (Spring 1972): 503–5. It is not known how many copies of the hymnbook Frederick Williams's print shop issued, but on 2 April W. W. Phelps took 500 copies with him to the Saints in Clay County, Missouri (*HC* 2:434). At least that many copies probably remained in Kirtland, although only about 250 families, many of them not Mormon, then lived in Kirtland. How much growth in church membership Joseph Smith may have anticipated, or how much capital could be invested in hymnbooks, is not known. For a study of the economic system under which these early publications were undertaken, see Lyndon W. Cook, *Joseph Smith and the Law of Consecration* (Provo: Grandin Book, 1985).

9. In 1838 the church's name became "Church of Jesus Christ of Latter Day Saints." Subsequently, the form "Latter-day Saints" was adopted by the Utah-based church.

10. The 1836 edition of the Methodist hymnal, for example, contained 697 texts, and even the fourth edition of Alexander Campbell et al., *Psalms, Hymns, and Spiritual Songs* (Bethany, Va.: Alexander Campbell, 1835) contained 242.

11. I am counting the hymns in both the original and reprint editions of the *Evening and Morning Star*. In 1835 Oliver Cowdery and Frederick G. Williams reprinted the *Star* in a quarto format, adding three hymns not in the original.

12. This statement, from the preface to his hymnbook, was first published in *The Christian Baptist* 5 (3 December 1827): 395.

13. "There's a power in the sun," "See all creation join," "The sun that declines in the far western sky," "Through all the world below," and "Earth with her ten thousand flowers."

14. "Hark, from the tombs a doleful sound," "Why do we mourn for dying friends," and "Why should we start and fear to die?"

15. On Phelps's intense concerns over marriage, see especially his letter to "Beloved of the Lord" (his wife, Sally?), 9 September 1835, HDC. Compare the song written by the early convert John Carter, which begins "Thus saith the Lord: 'I hate divorce,' " John S. Carter, Diary 1831–33, holograph in HDC. No reference to the singing of "When earth was dress'd in beauty" has been found in the minutes of church conferences. "The Red Man," however, was quite frequently sung throughout the nineteenth century.

16. The source of the tune to "The Spirit of God" has not been found, although the present tune was published to those words as early as 1844—eight years after the Kirtland temple dedication—in J. C. Little and G. B. Gardner, *A Collection of Sacred Hymns for the Use of Latter Day Saints* (Bellows Falls, Vt.: Blake and Bailey, 1844). The present "Adam-ondi-Ahman" tune also appears in that work, and its apparent source, "Prospect of Heaven," appears in Walker's 1835 *Southern Harmony*.

17. "Spirit of God" and "Weymouth" use seven-note scales; "Dalston" uses a six-note scale (with a raised fourth scale degree); "Prospect of Heaven" is a conventional pentatonic (major scale degrees 1–2–3–5–6), while "Sterling" uses only major scale degrees 1–2–3–4–5.

18. See the dedicatory hymn (no. 90) in Rogers's *A Collection of Sacred Hymns for the Church of the Latter Day Saints* (New York: C. Vinten, 1838).

19. See *TS* 1 (December 1839): 31 (cf. Minutes for 7 October 1839, Joseph Smith Papers, HDC), and *HC* 4:14.

20. *HC* 4:17–18.

21. *HC* 4:22, 47–49, 51.

22. See *TS* 1 (June 1840): 120–22. In this letter to Smith, Brigham Young, without asking permission to print new books in Manchester, reminded Joseph that it would be utterly impractical to send hymnbooks from the States to England. Brigham was keenly aware that, all expediency aside, Joseph's wife, Emma, was the official hymn-compiler for the church. His indirect discussion of the hymnbook left the matter open to Joseph to forbid the project, without forcing the Prophet to explicitly sanction a hymnal produced without Emma.

23. Orson Hyde and John E. Page to Joseph Smith, 1 May 1840, Joseph Smith Letterbook, HDC; *HC* 4:123–24.

24. Parley Pratt to Brigham Young, 4 May 1840, Brigham Young Papers, HDC; Parley P. Pratt, *Autobiography,* ed. Parley P. Pratt [Jr.] (Salt Lake City: Deseret Book, 1938), p. 304.

25. Heber C. Kimball to Vilate Kimball, 27 May 1840, HDC.

26. Brigham Young to Mary Ann Angell Young, 12 June 1840, Philip Blair Papers, UU. Within a month Young presented a copy of the hymnbook to a conference assembled in Carpenter's Hall, who voted to receive the book and endorse the labors of those who had produced it. Extant receipts show that some

of the printing was done at the firm of W. R. Thomas on 19–27 June. The entire cost of printing 3,000 copies, paper and all, was £258. Nearly all of the binding, however, was done after the book had been accepted by the congregation—why go to the huge expense if the congregation did not approve the collection? Receipts saved by Young account for 2,459 hymnbooks being bound during the period 23 July through 4 September, usually fifty copies a day.

27. Parley Pratt to Mary Pratt, 6 July 1840, HDC. Pratt was also occupied publishing the British Mormon newspaper, *Latter Day Saints' Millennial Star.*

28. John Taylor to Brigham Young, 23 July 1840, typescript in John Taylor Papers, UU.

29. Ronald W. Walker, "The Willard Richards and Brigham Young 5 September 1840 Letter from England to Nauvoo," *Brigham Young University Studies* 18 (Spring 1978): 474. On Young's wife's report of Smith's approval see Willard Richards to Brigham Young, 24 October 1840, Young Papers.

30. See the note under the letter of Brigham Young to Joseph Smith, 7 May 1840, Joseph Smith Letterbook; Brigham Young to Mary Ann Angell Young, 12 November 1840, Blair Papers.

31. Dean C. Jessee, comp. and ed., *The Personal Writings of Joseph Smith* (Salt Lake City: Deseret Book, 1984), p. 482.

32. See the letters of Angeline Robinson (25 December 1840) and Ebenezer Robinson (27 December 1840) to Brigham Young, Young Papers.

33. *TS* 2 (15 October 1841): 576–77.

34. See her notice in *TS* 4 (1 February 1843): 95.

35. See George Pullen Jackson, *Spiritual Folk Songs of Early America* (New York: Dover, 1964), pp. 16–17.

36. For a survey of the conditions surrounding the Smiths' imprisonment and killing, see Dallin H. Oaks and Marvin S. Hill, *Carthage Conspiracy: The Trial of the Accused Assassins of Joseph Smith* (Urbana: University of Illinois Press, 1975), pp. 6–29.

3

Schooling the Tongue

"I will sing with the spirit," the apostle Paul wrote, "and I will sing with the understanding also." Paul's phrasing entered the prose of many spokesmen for sacred music in nineteenth-century America and even into the preface of the first Mormon hymnal. For the Mormons, Paul's dichotomy came to mean, on the one hand, singing in tongues and, on the other, singing the prescribed hymns. But in time the doctrine of singing "with the understanding" led the Mormons, along with many American religious societies, well beyond the making of hymnbooks to the founding of singing schools, the training of choirs, and the setting forth of "vocal science."

Speaking in tongues had sprung up from time to time in the old camp meetings. In the heat of evangelical fever, tongues—ecstatic, unintelligible syllables—accompanied the well-known shouts, barks, and whimpers. A more sedate form of tongues had appeared among the early Quakers, and by the early 1830s the Irvingites of Great Britain claimed the gift in abundance. In all cases the gift was said to attest to God's sanction of a new faith by linking believers to the primitive church. Its very oddity made it a unique symptom of divine indwelling, and a sign to be sought.[1]

The earliest account of tongues in Mormonism describes the ecstatic singing of Lyman Wight, a former Campbellite Disciple. Wight had taken charge of the new Kirtland Church of Christ while the first missionaries to that area returned to New York. Burning with charisma, Wight held up his hands before an 1831 congregation, and as his palms appeared to glow, he sang "a song which no one ever heard before, and which they said was the most melodious that they ever listened to. It was sung in another tongue."[2]

Joseph Smith first sanctioned speaking in tongues in a meeting in the fall of 1832 in Kirtland. The new convert Brigham Young had arrived in town, and when he met to pray with the elders, he began to speak in strange syllables. The elders were instantly divided over the manifestation, the majority ascribing it to the devil. Joseph, however, proclaimed it divine and then joined in himself. Soon the house was ringing to the ecstatic chants of a dozen mouths or more. Within a few weeks Joseph had begun singing in tongues as well, and sometime the following year singing in tongues appeared in the church at Missouri. By December at least one missionary of the church was tallying his labors thus: "five . . . have spoken in tongues, and three have sung in tongues."[3]

What strikes the reader of early Mormon accounts of singing in tongues is the mellifluousness and grace with which the songs seem to have been executed. The setting to music of strange syllables became a small art form unto itself. Lyman Wight's early tongues-singing was thought supremely melodious. A tongues duet in the Kirtland Temple was reportedly sung "simultaneously . . . beginning and ending each verse in perfect unison, without varying a word . . . as though we had sung it together a thousand times." Elizabeth Ann Whitney of Kirtland sang in tongues with a voice remembered as both "birdlike and full of symphony." And so far was the Mormon practice from the strenuous exercises of revivalism that at least one Mormon woman sang in tongues for two hours while sleeping.[4]

The principle of divine translation fascinated Mormons; it was the power by which their founding book had been brought forth. Consequently, Mormons widely sought and expected the gift of "interpretation of tongues." Indeed, interpretation became a necessity at times, because some Mormon elders freely spoke in tongues during their Sabbath sermons, leaving many of their listeners bewildered.[5] Some of the early interpretations of singing in tongues were copied down by clerks and occasionally revised into formal hymns. Several early "Songs of Zion," as published in early Mormon newspapers, derive from tongues-singing. One interpretation of tongues written into the Kirtland Revelation Book was adapted by Phelps into a hymn for his newspaper.[6]

Kirtland Revelation Book	Phelps
Age after age has rolled away,	Age after age has roll'd away
according to the sad fate of man	Since man first dwelt in mortal clay
countless millions forever gone.	And countless millions slept in death
	That once supplied a place on earth.

Many interpretations came in couplets, rather than in simple prose, often with jangling rhymes like those found in Lucy Smith's "Moroni's Lamentation."[7]

> I have no home, where shall I go?
> While here I'm left to weep below
> My heart is pained, my friends are gone,
> And here I'm left on earth to mourn.

I see my people lying around,
All lifeless here upon the ground;
Young men and maidens in their gore,
Which does increase my sorrows more.

My father looked upon this scene
And in his writings has made plain
How every Nephite's heart did fear,
When he beheld his foes draw near.

With ax and bow they fell upon
Our men and women, sparing none;
And left them prostrate on the ground—
Lo here they now are bleeding round.
   . . . . . .
Thus sung the son of Mormon, when
He gazed upon his Nephite men;
And women, too, which had been slain,
And left to moulder on the plain.

Many songs in tongues had similarly distinct Mormon themes, such as "the travelling of the Nephites," "the fame of Joseph," and even the sufferings of the Missouri Mormons—this last of which came in language akin to "Moroni's Lamentation" ("our brethren lay bleeding on the ground / with their wives and children weeping around").[8]

For ten years from the first "official" introduction of singing in tongues, the Mormons' passion for it waxed and waned. From time to time the music broke out in massed assemblies or in lamplight parlor gatherings. But Joseph distrusted the messages interpreted from tongues, some of which contradicted his own revelations. In 1833 he cautioned the Missouri Mormons that "Satan will no doubt trouble you about the gift of tongues, unless you are careful; you cannot watch him too closely." Six years later he warned his apostles, who were about to head eastward and set sail for Europe, "every . . . singing is not of God," adding that the devil knew tongues as well as the best of Saints. And in 1842, speaking to the churchwomen of Nauvoo (who often spoke and sang in tongues), Joseph announced: "If you have a matter to reveal, let it be in your own tongue; do not indulge too much in the exercise of the gift of tongues, or the devil will take advantage of the innocent and unwary. You may speak in tongues for your own comfort, but I lay this down for a rule, that if anything is taught by the gift of tongues, it is not to be received for doctrine."[9]

On the other hand, Joseph Smith rejoiced in sweet tunes, whether sung with the spirit or the understanding. Although his wife, Emma, was a capable singer, Smith is known to have called upon the Young brothers

(Brigham and Joseph), the Hancock brothers (Levi and Solomon), and the father and daughter duo Titus and Eunice Billings to come and sing for him when he was depressed.[10] He found himself particularly drawn to the soprano voice of his bishop Newel Whitney's wife, Elizabeth Ann. When she sang for Joseph, Elizabeth's eulogizer recalled, "he would sit as it were spell bound . . . for the time so absorbed, as to forget his sorrows."[11] Just after Christmas 1835 Joseph promised Elizabeth that if she would open her mouth in faith God would give her the power to sing in the "pure language" of Adam and Eve, a gift he said would stay with her as long as she used it to bless others. Believing his words, she arose in a meeting in Kirtland and began to sing in tongues to the tune of Phelps's "Adam-ondi-Ahman." Parley Pratt then interpreted her song into a rhyming ballad of something over ten stanzas, a kind of chronicle of the divine priesthood beginning with Adam, whose garden, the Mormons then believed, had been located in western Missouri.

> In ancient days there lived a man,
> Amidst a pleasant garden,
> Where lovely flowers immortal bloom'd,
> And shed around a rich perfume;
> Behold his name was Adam.

Later stanzas spoke of the Old Testament patriarchs and even of the Book of Mormon peoples.

> By that same faith they built a ship,
> And crossed the mighty ocean,
> Obtained the choicest land of Earth,
> Foretold the great Messiah's birth,
> And all the great commotion.[12]

Vocal training began to thrive in America during the eighteenth-century debates in New England over "regular" versus "old-way" (or "usual-way") singing. The semi-improvisatory oral tradition of old-way singing freely ornamented melodies with scoops, slurs, and emotion-laden hiccoughs, and it executed tunes in ponderously slow tempi. When an entire congregation indulged in it, the effect was raucous and discordant to those versed in regular singing, that more reverent form of singing that followed the printed notes. In order to foster regular singing the Puritan fathers had instituted weekly classes in proper vocal production, diction, solmization, and note reading. From 1762 on, the colonies were flooded with tunebooks for the use of singing schools and by 1800 over 130 different tune collections had been published. Among the most influential of these was Smith and Little's 1798 *The Easy Instructor,* which varied the shape of the noteheads according to each pitch's position in the scale.[13]

As the frontier expanded to the west and south, Smith and Little's system spread to dozens of other tunebooks, many of which became the textbooks of itinerant singing masters who set up schools from village to village. With the proliferation of shape-note singing by vagabond musicians (often barely trained themselves), "usual-way" singing continued in frontier churches. And because the dereliction of many singing masters provoked opposition to their trade, many people viewed any purveyors of singing lessons as the offscouring of decent society.[14]

Joseph Smith took obvious pleasure in hearing others sing. His own father had taught singing "by note" (i.e., regular singing). But the undercurrents of denominationalism in early Mormonism left some resistance to musical formality in the church; the residue of Campbellism in particular argued against musical training. Campbell refused to allow choirs among his congregations and rebuked any rehearsing of sacred songs. "Although I commend . . . zeal in the cause of good music in the assemblies of the saints," Campbell later explained, "I cannot . . . approve of the plan of teaching any one to practise for improvement upon the sacred songs which are only to be sung in the worship of God. I have always remonstrated against this custom as a species of profanity. It is . . . a most unholy thing to learn to sing by a constant repetition of our most devotional songs amidst the levity and blunders of a singing school."[15]

Nevertheless, two weeks after Joseph promised Elizabeth Ann Whitney what she called "the gift of singing inspirationally" (singing in tongues) he organized the church's first singing school. He had planned for the church to have a formal choir at least since summer 1833, when he drew up plans for the Kirtland Temple: its main floor boasted four large singers' galleries, one for each corner of the hall, each holding five twelve-and-a-half-foot benches.[16] In January 1836, with only finish carpentry yet to be done in the temple, it became imperative that a choir be formed and trained. Joseph's two counselors in the highest governing body of the church—the "first presidency"—had both come out of Campbellism, as had many eminent Mormons in Kirtland. Accordingly, Joseph reported that he was able to organize a "singing department" in the church (on Monday, 4 January 1836) only "after some altercation."[17] Searching for a singing master for the new school, Joseph overlooked the church's then best-known musician, Levi Hancock, and chose Marvel Chapin Davis, a thirty-four year old whom Joseph baptized the day before the singing school was organized.[18]

Meeting two evenings a week, the temple singing school consisted of any Saints who had interest; its members were neither called nor hired. Adolescent and adult Saints "from the young adult to the old gray heads"[19] began rehearsing six texts from Emma's collection. Ten days before the temple dedication Joseph visited the group's Wednesday night rehearsal and cryptically recorded in his diary that "they performed admirably, concidering the advantages they have had."[20]

When dedication day arrived the choir must have been astonishingly large—numbering perhaps two hundred—since it appears to have filled the temple's singers' galleries. (There were probably fewer than 250 families living in Kirtland at the time.[21]) According to Joseph Smith's description of the event, the choir needed at least three music leaders to direct it, no doubt to cope with the spatial arrangement of the group.[22] Its singing profoundly stirred the congregation and, according to some accounts, brought down angels. So accustomed was the church to singing "with the spirit" that some of the congregation believed that Phelps's new hymn "The Spirit of God" was given by God on the spot, when it was sung to the tune of the well-known "Now let us rejoice." It seemed a kind of interpretation without tongues.[23]

Jonathan Crosby and his wife, Caroline, new converts from Massachusetts, moved into Kirtland three days after the singing school was organized under Davis. Having been a bass viol player in the Congregational Church for several years—"until the fulness of the gospel took me away," he wrote—Crosby had been trained in a singing school in 1833. The following year he attended other schools with his new bride, where, as she wrote, "[we] enjoyed ourselves quite well."[24] Along with fellow Kirtland resident Luman Carter, Jonathan Crosby took over the school a year after Davis began it. Here, formal Mormon-sponsored musical training appears to have begun: according to the local Mormon newspaper "instructions in the principles of vocal music" were given every Sunday night.[25]

It is difficult to say whether Crosby and Carter's choir advanced beyond the singing of Emma's hymns. Every dollar of Ohio church money went to support the ailing Kirtland Bank, and to pay off temple debts. The depression of the local economy discouraged the importation of tunebooks. This no doubt left the church singing school to learn tunes and to harmonize by ear. Moreover, the Campbellite tradition was to shun tunebooks because they fixed the worshipping eye on a man-made page.[26]

Meanwhile, the troubles in Missouri so unsettled the Saints there that musical training had little appeal. In 1835 Joseph Smith seems to have excused the Missouri churchmen from singing altogether by reminding them of the psalm about Israel's ancient trials. "When the children of Zion are stranger[s] in a strange land," he wrote, "their harps must be hung upon the willows: and they cannot sing the songs of Zion."[27]

When the church relocated to the banks of the Mississippi, M. C. Davis stayed in Ohio, where he worked as a physician and apparently had no more contact with the church. Benjamin Wilber, an elder from New York, began leading the choir in Nauvoo. Whether Wilber had any formal training is unknown, but a Protestant minister who visited Nauvoo in 1842 described him as appearing to be a professional singing master.[28] The principal function of the choir in Nauvoo's first years was to sing for church conferences and funerals, most of which were held in a sloping natural amphitheater nine blocks north of Joseph's riverside homestead. (Funerals, even mass funerals, were especially frequent in early Nauvoo because the marshy platte bred clouds of malaria-bearing mosquitos in the summers of 1839–41.) At first the choir's repertoire appears to have consisted primarily of hymns.[29] By 1843, with church leaders beginning to espouse Freemasonry, the choir began to learn Masonic songs.[30]

Many of the British converts to Mormonism who filled the steamboats to Nauvoo in the early 1840s were probably accustomed to more elaborate sacred music than were most American Mormons. In addition, the British emigrants practiced singing hymns while on their long sea journeys, and thus arrived in Nauvoo with months of practice in choral singing.[31] The gradual flow of British tastes and expertise into Nauvoo encouraged and empowered trained musicians in the church to elevate Mormon singing habits, to push Mormon music into the realm of music "by note."

As early as November 1841, over five hundred British Saints had arrived at the Nauvoo docks. At that time, the Nauvoo choir sent a petition to the board of regents of the city's school system (the so-called "University of Nauvoo") asking that wardens be appointed "for the regulation of music in this city." Upon calling the four wardens, one for each municipal ward, the mayor, John Bennett, insisted in somewhat ambiguous terms that they "prohibit the *flat* sound of the notes, and adopt the *broad*." Joseph cheerfully seconded this motion, adding, "I was always opposed to anything *flat*."[32]

All the members of this new regulating board lately had come under the influence of the University of Nauvoo's eloquent "Professor of Music," Gustavus Hills. A mapmaker, newspaperman, aspiring poet, and associate justice of the Nauvoo municipal court, Hills had been a Methodist exhorter in Middlesex County, Connecticut, before being converted to Mormonism in December 1840. In less than a week after his baptism, Hills reached Nauvoo and was ordained an elder. Upon the death of *Times and Seasons* co-editor Robert Thompson (August 1841), Hills went to work at the press. Hills quickly began to stock Lowell and Timothy Mason's *Sacred Harp* in the print shop's book section.[33] On Christmas Day, 1841, he founded the Nauvoo Musical Lyceum, a forum for advancing the ideals of Lowell Mason's Boston Academy of Music. Hills led the Lyceum in adopting Mason's *Manual of Instruction* as "a guide for instruction in the art of sacred singing in the schools of this city." The Lyceum also adopted William Porter's *Cyclopedia* (written under Mason's direction) for advanced study. Hills became assistant editor of *Times and Seasons* on 15 January 1842 and began to write up the Lyceum's proceedings for the newspaper. His accounts included this reverent column:

> We are pleased to see the laudable zeal manifested by some of our *musical* friends, to bring about a uniform and tasteful style of sacred singing. Among a people emigrated from different countries, with different prejudices and habits as we are, this is no easy task, and we can but admire the improvements made, and the judicious order established within a few months past. By the by, we peeped in the other evening, during the performance of the Musical Lyceum, and heard what will make us try to peep in again.
>
> A proper and expressive articulation of the words constitutes the life and soul of music; intelligence thus clothed with the robes of melody, and harmonic numbers, moves gently over the spirit, imprints her heavenly footsteps, and awakens all its energies. We should not be so sure that the performances before hinted at were good, were it not that we are sure we have a tolerably *good ear* for music, or an ear for good music and we are delighted, whereas our *devil,* who is known to have a bad ear for good music, and a good ear for bad music, was quite differently affected; he crowded in edgewise, but soon deserted,—said he could not stand the racket.

But for all his noble intentions, Hills and his crusade succumbed to scandal. Both Hills and his friend Mayor John Bennett had persuaded a number of women to embark in an early but disapproved form of Mormon polygamy, a marriage system which Bennett called "spiritual wifery," but which went beyond the spirit in its consummations. (Bennett, a physician, apparently had promised abortions to "spiritual wives" who conceived.) After an open affair with Sarah Pratt, whose husband was proselyting in England, Bennett was cut off from the church. The Saints then disfellowshipped Hills (August 1842) when the young Mary Clift announced she was carrying Hills's baby.[34] Plummeting from grace in the eyes of his public, Hills quickly lost his musical eminence, although, ironically, he retained his municipal judgeship.

As Hills's influence began to wane, the singing school's role in Mormonism expanded. In the seven years after M. C. Davis began the first choir, choral music had begun to take precedence over congregational music in Mormon gatherings. In 1842 the new women's organization of the church, the Relief Society, founded its own choir to sing hymns for its occasional gatherings. By 1843 a number of Mormon settlements outside of Nauvoo had formed their own groups.[35] Meanwhile in Ohio W. W. Phelps endeavored to keep alive the Kirtland choral tradition. Called to be caretaker for the now desolate temple there, Phelps hosted the Mormon emigrants who occasionally passed through on their way to

Nauvoo and played the part of the choirmaster, often standing alone in one of the choir galleries and singing solo.[36]

When Benjamin Wilber left on a mission to the eastern states, Stephen Goddard, a fine bass singer and one of the musical wardens of the city, took over the choir, which by the time of Joseph's death had at least forty-five singers: twenty-seven women and eighteen men.[37] Under Goddard their repertoire ventured beyond hymns and Masonic songs to the contrapuntal anthems of William Billings and others. (The Mormons apparently had overcome the common objections to such works that they were too complex to be understood by the common man, that the polyphony obscured the words, and that they kept the public from joining in.[38]) A review of Goddard's choir reveals his popularity:

> One word for the leader of the Choir. When in the great congregation of an assembled multitude, numbering variously from five to ten and sometimes twenty thousand. [*sic*] The high praises of Jehovah are sung, and every heart beat high in unison to the joyful lay as it echoes from the general throng. We are ready to reflect upon the loftiness, theme, and the grandeur, and harmony with which such scenes are associated—and we are ready to enquire who is the mover of this mighty mass. Notice being given for music, all eyes are eagerly placed upon one individual—the hymn and tune are found—the voices are tuned—at a moment the enwrapt feelings of thousands blend in one common anthem or hymn of holiest song and the reviving countenances of the throng, forces the conviction on the mind that *God* (dard) was there.[39]

In the beginnings of Mormonism Joseph and his followers emphatically declared the need of the common people to band together, economically, culturally, and spiritually. In Nauvoo, a city relatively free from gentile hostility, the Mormons determinedly advanced their own culture, attempting to make a heaven on earth patterned after the glories of the world's great cities. Arguments for the advancement of music in Mormondom included one writer's hyperbole that "rising generations in coming time will look upon you [the patrons of music in Nauvoo] as the founders of the greatest city in the west, and the greatest benefactors of the age in which you lived."[40] To unify the Saints in spirit, congregational singing sufficed. But the boisterous chanting of the masses could not suit the building of God's kingdom in Zion. Mormon leaders began to side with the American spirit of musical reform, epitomized by Lowell Mason, who wrote that to indulge in congregational singing, "everything that belongs to taste in music must be given up."[41] In Mormondom, choirs ascended above congregations and musical formality overtook spontaneous expression.

One of the last acts of the Nauvoo citizenry was to build a public music hall near the temple, primarily to give the choir a resonant hall in which to perform. Joseph had often complained of the burden that constant open-air preaching laid upon him.[42] Before the hall was built, virtually all of the choir's performances had been outdoors, in the grove where Joseph preached. As one appreciator of the choir wrote in 1844, their "zeal can only be made manifest by the difficult circumstances under which they are laboring, by singing in the open air and that too frequently in windy weather; that we have an imperfect idea of the thrilling delight such a body of music placed under different circumstances would produce."[43] The music hall was built in response to such pleas, but served the choir for less than a year. In the thaw of 1846 the Saints loaded wagons to push westward into the Great Basin, and the choirs returned to the open air.

Beginning afresh in the wilderness, the Saints needed some time to recover the cultural richness they had found alongside the Mississippi. The loose rocky soil of the Salt Lake Valley was a far cry from the fine dark earth of the Midwest; for a few years crops festered and the quest for survival outran the need for musical art. But the continual meetings of the Mormons required sacred vocal music. Within a week of entering the Salt Lake Valley the first company of pioneers chose a site for a new temple and erected on it a bowery of heavy timber posts and branches under which the people could hold religious and civil meetings. Before a crowd of perhaps several hundred in August 1847 a small choir led by Goddard sang for the Saints' first conference in the land they called "Deseret," a Book of Mormon-derived name for the honeybee, a symbol of industry and cooperation.

Choirs in early Deseret sang hymns for religious meetings as well as for quasi-religious gatherings such as the convocations of the Deseret Theological Institute. They also sang patriotic and devotional songs for the two principal public holidays, the fourth of July and the twenty-fourth of July (the anniversary of the Saints' entry into the valley). Given the evident need for singing groups, choirs of one sort or another sprang up in virtually every settlement. These choirs were often formed at Brigham Young's request, and he made certain that musically gifted church members were part of each new colonizing group in the region.

Mormonism had made great strides in Wales and in 1849 hundreds of Welsh converts immigrated to the Great Basin. Because the Welsh had strong choral traditions, a large group of these immigrants inevitably banded together. They performed new devotional works such as "Wend ye with the Saints today," and hero songs like "Joseph and Hyrum," usually in dialect set to familiar Welsh tunes. A visitor to a church conference in 1852 wrote of the Welsh choir's power to "exhilirate all present by singing one of their hymns, to one of their charming, wild, romantic airs."[44] For that conference an oblong, arched adobe structure capable of holding 2,500 Saints had been set up at the site of the bowery, in order to relieve the Welsh group and the transplanted Nauvoo choir of having to sing in the open air. Taking its name from the new building, the Nauvoo choir, which had attracted some of the Welsh singers into its ranks, began to call itself the "Tabernacle Choir."

Choirs were formed in the smaller settlements of what would become Utah and Idaho as well as in many foreign branches of the church.[45] One such was the Bradford (England) Mormon choir. Apostle Wilford Woodruff, not one given to doting on musicians, wrote in his 1845 diary that the Bradford choir was "splendid."[46] The director of the choir for the years 1853–54, Joseph Beecroft, recorded in his own journal some of the workings of the choir, at times revealing some of the conflicts that inevitably accrued to the blending of religious authority and musical art. Upon being appointed to lead the group Beecroft discovered that the local church elder, Joseph Bentley, had inexplicably forbidden two of the best female singers to continue performing with the group, and had also warned another Mormon against "Blowing his Sax Horn" with the choir. Beecroft immediately threatened to resign the choir unless the singers were restored to its ranks—principally because without them the ratio of men to women in the choir would have been six to two. Beecroft had his way, and on Monday nights the choir began to rehearse hymns such as the Watts-Phelps "We're not ashamed to own our Lord." The choir had no tunebooks, but Beecroft wrote out parts for the singers himself.[47] Instrumental players occasionally dropped in on the practices and by July 1854 Beecroft could report that "We had a ful choir consisting of 3 Claranetts five violins two violincellos one ophaclyde one octive one cornopian two male and four females . . . two males and two female singers for tenner and 2 male alto, and a great number of Bass singers." The quality of the singing to which he was accustomed, however, may be guessed at by this diary entry from his first Christmas in the States (1856): "The day was kept as a general Holyday, but there was no music nor singing. Awaking some time in the morning I heard a sound and thought some were singing, but on listening attentively I found it was Pigs that was squealing, and I felt disappointed."[48]

In 1852 Willard Richards, former secretary to Joseph Smith and now counselor to Brigham Young, began to urge that music be taught in Utah schools, "and from them reach our domestic circle." As part of his campaign for music education he republished an article by a Reverend Todd in the church newspaper, the *Deseret News,* an article which argued for "the happy influence of music upon domestic life and social habits." Todd's article emphasized that Americans should not lag behind Europeans in cultivating music: "almost all foreigners are proficients." An ideal example, said Todd, could be found in a small German village group he encountered in his travels, a choir that was able to perform almost all of Haydn's *Creation*.[49]

The prospect of a rural community mounting oratorios impressed Brigham Young perhaps less for how it might sound than for how it might foster a spirit of cooperation. Young had inherited Joseph Smith's desire to make the Mormon people culturally fit for the second coming of Christ. The best means for this, thought Young, was not to enforce asceticism, but rather to gather together the fruits of human culture and have the whole society cultivate them. Taking the golden age of David's Jerusalem as a model, Smith and Young both believed they could transform their diverse followers into a cohesive society whose glory would gradually fill the earth.

As part of his dream to have the Saints bring their treasures to Zion from throughout the world—and especially from Europe—Young directed James Smithies to oversee a new "Deseret Philharmonic Society" in 1855. This association would "promote the love and study of harmony throughout the Territory," especially the harmony of sacred choral music. The society's secretary, Jonathan Grimshaw, sent out a call to converts coming to Deseret that "we are much in want of the Oratorios of Handel, Haydn, Mendelssohn, etc.; the Masses of Mozart, Haydn, Beethoven, etc., and *new* works of merit." All musicians known to be in the territory were automatically enrolled as members of the society. "We shall also be glad," wrote Grimshaw, "if our musical brethren and sisters will report themselves to this society on their arrival here."[50]

At about this time, two French travellers heard a Mormon choir in Utah and recorded that the group "executed a piece of one of our greatest masters; and we feel bound to say that the Mormons have a feeling for sacred music, that their women sing with soul, and that the execution is in no notable degree surpassed by that which is heard either under the roof of Westminster, or the frescoes of the Sistine Chapel."[51] Nevertheless, the Philharmonic Society had only fleeting success, due in part to the setbacks that music schooling suffered in the 1850s in Utah.

The first setback involved the churchwide "reformation" that began in the fall of 1856, during which Brigham Young's counselor Jedediah Grant led a purge of sinful conduct among the Saints. Although he did not explicitly decry the musical habits of the people (except for their obsession with dancing), Grant's rhetoric was laden with puritanism and subtly called into question the propriety of singing schools and music lessons. Church musician William Clayton approached President Young with the prospect of beginning a new musical organization in the city expressly devoted to performing music "adapted to the reformation and the spirit of the times." But Clayton worried about the propriety of even that, telling Young that "if there is a shade of doubt on your mind in regard to it we drop it where it is. If it is all right . . . we will meet and go ahead, but we feel careful not to engage in any thing which would not meet with your hearty approval.''[52] No record of Young's reply has been found.

The second setback involved the march on Utah by General Johnston's army in 1857, which brought on a storm of hysteria among the Saints, who considered the army's mission as a direct attack by the United States. Opening old wounds, the march of Johnston's troops braced the Saints for conflict and for a season dispelled their quest for refinement.

It was not only Brigham Young's zeal for advancing Mormon culture but also his worries over public health that led to Mormon vocal music training on a mass scale. Young suffered throughout his life from bouts with ''lung fever'' and had lost his mother and several wives, including the bride of his youth, to consumption. Like most Americans he thought the best remedies for these (and virtually every other ailment) were fresh air and exercise. Benjamin Rush, the best known of American physicians, popularized the idea that ''the exercise of the organs of the breast, by singing, contributes very much to defend them from those diseases to which our climate, and other causes, have of late exposed them.''[53] Further, Rush claimed that singing could restore victims of consumption to full vigor. Rush's ideas gained currency in lectures such as the one heard by the Mormon apostle Wilford Woodruff in September 1848. The apostle learned that ''it is found not profitable to confine the scholar in one place not [*sic*] more than an hour'' and that students should use ''gymnastics &c filling the lungs with air & exploding it suddenly with sounds like O, Bo, Ba &c loud to exercise the lungs making them stand strait.''[54] During the reformation in Utah, Young began preaching the pursuit of fresh air, explaining that ''when people are obliged to breathe confined air, they do not have that free, full flow of the purification and nourishment that is in the fresh air, and they begin to decay, and go into what we call consumption.''[55] As his passion for education swept the territory in the late 1850s Young worried that the confinement of students to their desks during school hours would restrict their breathing and ruin their health. In Utah as in many parts of the country, the call for physical education to promote health brought vocal training into the schoolhouse.

On 30 June 1858 the *Deseret News* published an article drawn from the *Musical World* entitled ''Vocal Music Corrective to Health,'' based on Rush's principles. The article probably attracted the attention of David Calder, a Scottish-born clerk in Young's employ. Calder had been troubled at the prevalence of lung afflictions in the United States. He had written to his aunt Mary in 1852 that ''in my visits to the cemetery I found that almost all the causes of death were the diseases of consumption, and the lungs. I believe that people are greatly to blame themselves, especially the ladies, for bringing upon themselves those diseases. Were the ladies to lace less, wear stouter shoes to protect their feet from the damp, less afraid of the rays of the sun, and take more outdoor exercise, there would not be so many cases of consumption. I never saw a more sickly or delicate sett of women anywhere as I have seen here.''[56]

Trained in the Hullah system of note reading, Calder had recently been converted to the Curwen Tonic Sol-fa method because it seemed better equipped to promote singing in various keys. In 1859 Calder began ordering music books from New York's Firth and Pond to sell to singers in Salt Lake City.[57] At about the same time he approached Young on the matter of teaching the Curwen system in the schoolhouse Young was then building for his own bountiful offspring. Believing that vocal training such as Calder's could be a boon to health throughout the state of Deseret, Young eagerly accepted. He promised Calder the schoolhouse rent-free for evening use, along with custodians to clean, warm, and light it.[58]

Inaugurating his new singing school, which was free to all comers, Calder wrote a declaration of principles for the *Deseret News,* 19 December 1860, which included this explanation:

> It is an established fact that singing is conducive to health. Nothing is better calculated to produce the power of free and lengthened respiration; and as one of the best preventives of, and surest remedies for, weakness of the chest, vocal music stands pre-eminent. It imparts vigor to the organs connected with the lungs, and thereby conduces to a healthy state of every part of the body.
>
> To introduce vocal music as a branch of education in our schools, in my opinion, would be the best physical exercise at present within our reach. It would also be a most pleasing and interesting relaxation from the dry and tedious studies of the school room, and greatly aid to strengthen the mental powers of the children.

Calder quickly enrolled four hundred students in his classes and within eighteen months had turned the school into a more or less official arm of the church, taking the name ''The Deseret Musical Association.'' Brigham Young was its honorary president.[59]

The association made its first public display in the twenty-fourth of July parade, 1862. The young women in the group wore white gowns with blue sashes at their waists and flower wreaths on their heads. To show the contrast between the Curwen system and traditional notation the singers carried two banners. One depicted the ''old notation''— musical notes—while the second showed the Tonic Sol-Fa notation. To the onlooking Saints the display suggested that the new singing method represented the triumph of simplicity and finesse over the complex abstractions of the past. Calder had brought ''science'' to singing.[60]

The new singing-school choir dwarfed the Tabernacle Choir. In 1863 the Tonic Sol-Fa singers performed with two hundred young women and sixty young men, all dressed in white.[61] But as late as April 1861 the Tabernacle Choir had only "about a dozen persons," according to one report.[62] Richard F. Burton visited a meeting in the bowery next to the Tabernacle in about 1860 and wrote that the church choir consisted of two women and four men who "sang the sweet songs of Zion tolerably well—decidedly well, after a moment's reflection as to latitude and longitude."[63] Measured against these intimate musical rites, the massive gathering of three Utah choirs for conference in the Tabernacle, 30 March 1862—the Tabernacle Choir, Calder's choir, and the Fourteenth Ward Choir—must have dazzled the assembled Saints.

An amateur musician attending this conference found the musical effect only mediocre: the choirs, he wrote, "sang pretty well considering that two of them never sang before so many thousands of people."[64] But Brigham Young was utterly taken with the spectacle, especially with the sight of hundreds of children singing by note. In the months following the 1862 conference he had songbooks printed in Curwen's notation and began proselyting for the Tonic Sol-Fa system on his yearly tours of the territory. His "Instructions to Latter-day Saints in the Southern Settlements" reveal how far the system had become to him—and hence to the church he led—a means of building the City of God and exalting its earthly citizens:

> We are progressing in this branch of mental improvement. Some of our brethren have been indomitable in their perserverance to divert the minds of our youth from an excess of frivolous and light amusements to the more useful and profitable habits of study and learning. I might here mention Elder David O. Calder, who has successfully been teaching, in Great Salt Lake City, the 'Tonic Sol Fa' method of singing. He teaches three distinct classes, altogether numbering five hundred scholars, twice a week. Every accomplishment, every polished grace, every useful attainment in mathematics, music, and in all science and art belong to the Saints, and they should avail themselves as expeditiously as possible of the wealth of knowledge the sciences offer to every diligent and perservering scholar.[65]

For Young and his followers musical training could steer a Saint toward Zion. Vocal music was a "useful art," an endeavor that brought delight and well-being. It improved not only the body but the spirit and the understanding also. Perhaps most important, the concord that resulted from trained choirs symbolized the beauty of cooperative effort, the founding principle of Zion. And these choirs and their sacred anthems had their counterparts in the bands and ballads that began to fill the Mormon nation.

NOTES

1. The most extensive scriptural passage on speaking in tongues is 1 Corinthians 14, which seems to argue both for and against the practice. This passage also contains what many consider the only allusion to singing in tongues—Paul's casual mention of "singing with the spirit."

2. Josiah Jones in Milton V. Backman, Jr., "A Non-Mormon View of the Birth of Mormonism in Ohio," *Brigham Young University Studies* 12 (Spring 1972): 310.

3. On these incidents see Helen Mar Whitney, "Life Incidents" (title changes variously with installments), *WE* 9 (1 August 1880): 39; Zebedee Coltrin, Diary (1832–34), HDC, 14 November 1832; *Far West Record,* pp. 63, 66; "The Book of John Whitmer, Kept by Commandment," typescript published as *John Whitmer's History* (Salt Lake City: Modern Microfilm, n.d.), p. 9; *HC* 1:323; and the letter of Moses Nickerson, 20 December 1833, *HC* 2:40.

4. See Edward W. Tullidge, *The Women of Mormondom* (New York: Tullidge and Crandall, 1877), pp. 208–9; "Elizabeth Ann Whitney," *WE* 10 (15 March 1882): 153–54; and James B. Allen and Thomas G. Alexander, eds., *Manchester Mormons: The Journal of William Clayton (1840–1842)* (Santa Barbara and Salt Lake City: Peregrine Smith, 1974), p. 162.

5. See *The Life and Testimony of Mary Lightner* ([Dugway, Utah]: Pioneer Press, n.d.), pp. 4–5.

6. The first verse of the hymn is given. Compare the entire texts of the Song, "sang by the gift of Tongues and Translated" (27 February 1833) in "Kirtland Revelation Book," manuscript in HDC, and the first of the "Songs of Zion" in *The Evening and the Morning Star,* May 1833.

7. See *The Evening and the Morning Star,* January 1834; also *William Smith on Mormonism* (Lamoni, Iowa: Herald Steam Book and Job Office, 1883), p. 33.

8. *Far West Record,* p. 66; *WWJ* 1:146 (20 April 1837); Benjamin Brown, *Testimonies for the Truth: A Record of Manifestations of the Power of God, Miraculous and Providential* (Liverpool: S. W. Richards, 1853), p. 12.

9. Joseph Smith letter of 2 July 1833, *HC* 1:369; also *HC* 4:607 and Andrew F. Ehat and Lyndon W. Cook, *The Words of Joseph Smith* (Salt Lake City: Bookcraft, 1980), p. 12. Apparently one song in tongues about this time called upon one of the apostles, Heber C. Kimball, not to go to England; see Helen Mar Whitney, "Scenes and Incidents," *WE* 10 (15 May 1882): 185. After the exodus to the Salt Lake Valley, the practice of singing in tongues seems gradually to have diminished. But it did continue into the twentieth century. A patriarchal blessing given to one Mormon woman on 13 June 1904 suggested that the gift of singing in tongues was still to be given, but had practical uses: "Thou hast been blessed with the gift of singing, and thou wilt become perfect in this gift; and will be blessed with the gift of tongues; and thou wilt sing in tongues. A time will come in thy life when thou wilt be required to sing in tongues; thou wilt be among a class of people, and the Lord will bless thee with their language" (holograph in Emma Lucy Gates Papers, HBLL).

10. See *JD* 9:89 on the Young brothers' singing. Levi Hancock was appointed music leader for church conferences and for the Kirtland High Council (Kirtland

High Council Minutes, HDC, 17 August 1835, and *MA* 1 [August 1835]: 161). Hancock was also the interpreter for Lucy Smith's tongues-singing (see *William Smith on Mormonism,* p. 33). On the Billings family duets see "A Sketch of the Life of Eunice Billings Snow," *WE* 39 (August 1910): 14.

11. "Elizabeth Ann Whitney," p. 153. Newel Whitney had been converted to Mormonism after a night of "singing the songs of Zion" at his house with Elizabeth and some prominent Mormons. See "Philo Dibble's Narrative," *Early Scenes in Church History: Eighth Book in the Faith-Promoting Series* (Salt Lake City: Juvenile Instructor Office, 1882), pp. 77–78. On Whitney's singing see also her daughter-in-law, Helen Mar Whitney, "Life Incidents," *WE* 9 (15 August 1880): 42, and 12 (1 September 1883): 50.

12. For a full account of this episode see "A Leaf from an Autobiography," *WE* 7 (1 November 1878): 83.

13. For accounts of early American singing controversies see Charles Hamm, *Music in the New World* (New York: Norton, 1983), pp. 33–41, 261–75; Robert Stevenson, *Protestant Church Music in America: A Short Survey of Men and Movements from 1564 to the Present* (New York: Norton, 1966), pp. 21–31; Foote, *Three Centuries of American Hymnody,* pp. 74–123. On singing style see Nicholas Temperley, "The Old Way of Singing: Its Origin and Development," *Journal of the American Musicological Society* 34 (Fall 1981): 511–44.

14. "Schools," *The Musical Magazine* 2 (October 1836): 94.

15. *Millennial Harbinger* 18 (1847): 179.

16. *HC* 1:360. The quadripartite singers' galleries were designed in part so that the large assembly room could be divided by curtains into four smaller meeting rooms, if necessary, each with its own choir. For a mention of choir singing heard while the curtains were drawn see *WWJ* 1:126 (23 March 1837).

17. Jessee, *Personal Writings,* p. 124.

18. What was odder than Smith's bringing a singing master into the faith one day before forming a church choir was that Davis had joined the church once before. Living with the Mormons in Kirtland at least since October 1833—when the town's non-Mormon "Overseers of the Poor" tried to evict him—Davis worked as a laborer on the temple. In March 1835 he was made an elder in the church and on 17 August he was listed in their minutes as a member of the Kirtland High Council, the most powerful body of church leaders under Joseph himself. A month later, without explanation, Davis's name was dropped from the council roster. Although there is no record of his excommunication, only that act of disfellowship, according to the church doctrine of that time, would have necessitated that he be rebaptized. That Joseph was keenly aware of Davis's reentry into the church is demonstrated by the fact that, when recounting in his diary the twelve people that were baptized on 3 January 1836, Joseph selects only one of the converts for mention by name: M. C. Davis.

19. Caroline Barnes Crosby Journal (1807–82), microfilm of holograph HDC.

20. Jessee, *Personal Writings,* p. 169. Compare also the statement that Joseph was a "constant attendant" at the early singing schools, in Joseph Young, *History of the Organization of the Seventies* (Salt Lake City: Deseret News, 1878), p. 15.

21. Marvin S. Hill, C. Keith Rooker, and Larry T. Wimmer, *The Kirtland Economy Revisited: A Market Critique of Sectarian Economics* (Provo, Utah: Brigham Young University Press, 1977), pp. 14, 18.

22. See Joseph Smith's description of the physical arrangement of the dedication in Jessee, *Personal Writings*, p. 172.

23. Brown, *Testimonies for the Truth*, p. 11.

24. Jonathan Crosby, Autobiography (1807–52), HDC; also Caroline Crosby Journal.

25. *MA* 3 (January 1837): 444. Luman Carter was ordained an elder the same day as M. C. Davis.

26. See *Millennial Harbinger* 18 (1847): 179.

27. Joseph Smith to Hezekiah Peck, 31 August 1835, in Jessee, *Personal Writings*, p. 347.

28. Henry Caswall, *The City of the Mormons; Or, Three Days at Nauvoo, in 1842* (London: J. G. F. and J. Rivington, 1842), p. 9.

29. See the conference reports in *TS* 1 (April 1840): 92–95; 2 (15 April 1841): 386–88; and 2 (15 October 1841): 576–80. See also "The Funeral of Ephraim Marks," *Wasp*, 16 April 1842.

30. The first of these appeared to be "To heaven's high architect all praise" (tune: "Arlington") and "Genius of Masonry descend" (tune: "Sudbury"); see the *Nauvoo Neighbor*, 21 June 1843. Later Masonic songs appear on the broadside "Hymns to be sung at the Dedication of the Masonic Temple, April 5th, 1844," copy in HBLL.

31. See Helen Mar Whitney, "Scenes and Incidents," *WE* 11 (15 November 1882): 90; Charles Dickens, *The Uncommercial Traveller and Reprinted Pieces* (London: Oxford University Press, 1958), pp. 224, 231; and the letter of William Clayton, *Latter-day Saints' Millennial Star* 4 (August 1842): 74–76.

32. "Choir of the Stake of Zion in the City of Nauvoo," *TS* 3 (1 January 1842): 653. The wardens were Titus Billings, Stephen Goddard, Dimick Huntington, and John Pack. For short biographies of each of these men see Andrew Jenson, *Latter-day Saint Biographical Encyclopedia*, 4 vols. (Salt Lake City: Andrew Jenson History Company, 1901, 1914, 1920, 1936), 1:242; 4:704; 4:748; and 4:714, respectively.

33. Gustavus Hills Diary (1804–46), photocopy of manuscript in HDC; *TS* 3 (15 January 1842): 663, 664; and *HC* 4:454. See the ads for Mason's *Sacred Harp* in *TS* 2 (15 October 1841): 582.

34. Hills confessed to the church courts, paid Clift two hundred dollars, and agreed to pay her twenty-five dollars a year for three years if the child thrived. See the paternity settlement in Newel K. Whitney Papers, HBLL; also Danel W. Bachman, "A Study of the Mormon Practice of Plural Marriage before the Death of Joseph Smith" (Master's thesis, Purdue University, 1975), p. 227.

35. Minutes of the Nauvoo Relief Society, HDC, passim. For mention of the Waldo County (Maine) and Lima (Illinois) branch choirs, see *TS* 3 (15 February 1842): 698–99, and 4 (15 August 1843): 303.

36. See Mary Ann Weston Maughan Autobiography, microfilm of holograph in HDC, [p. 42].

37. "The Concert," *Nauvoo Neighbor,* 12 March 1845.

38. See *Doctrines and Discipline of the Methodist Episcopal Church,* pp. 122–24. For references to Billings's anthems "Heavenly Vision" and "Denmark," see the conference minutes in *TS* 6 (15 April 1845): 869–70, and the concert program in *Nauvoo Neighbor,* 26 February 1845.

39. "Nauvoo Music and Concert Hall," *Nauvoo Neighbor,* 30 October 1844. On Goddard see also Helen Mar Whitney, "Scenes and Incidents in Nauvoo," *WE* 10 (15 September 1881): 58; and 11 (15 November 1882): 90. Goddard is listed as a bass in the choir roster inserted in Thomas McIntyre Journal, microfilm of holograph in HDC.

40. "Nauvoo Music and Concert Hall."

41. Lowell Mason, *Musical Letters from Abroad* (New York: Mason Brothers, 1854), p. 88.

42. See, for example, Joseph Smith Diary (kept by Willard Richards), photocopy of typescript in author's possession, 21 May 1843.

43. "Nauvoo Music and Concert Hall." For more on the hall, see chapter 4, below.

44. J. W. Gunnison, *The Mormons or, Latter-day Saints, in the Valley of the Great Salt Lake* (Philadelphia: J. B. Lippincott, 1856), p. 37. See also *DN,* 3 and 10 August 1850.

45. On the Edinburgh Choir see Thomas McIntyre, Journal, 7 February 1858–12 March 1859; on the Christiania (Norway) Choir in the 1860s see Charles L. Olsen, Autobiography, microfilm of holograph in HBLL, pp. 38–56.

46. *WWJ* 2:516–17 (22 February 1845).

47. See also Charles Olsen, Autobiography, p. 38: "Singing by notes (not by ear) was adopted. As no psalmody or other music book was printed by the church, the only way to get individual music was for each member to have his own blank music-book and for someone to transcribe from the 'Partitur' (the leader's score) the part wanted."

48. Joseph Beecroft, Journals, microfilm of holograph in HDC, 6 and 20 November 1853; 21 May, 9 July, 15–16 November 1854, and 25 December 1856.

49. "Music," *DN,* 10 January 1852.

50. "Deseret Philharmonic Society," *DN,* 1 March 1855. Grimshaw, a clerk in the church historian's office, had already attempted to answer in the press the question, "Why is not vocal music, such as choruses, quartets, glees, etc. appreciated in this country as in the old countries and the eastern States?" His somewhat timid reply was that the words were too often hard to understand. Choristers, he suggested, should inform congregations of their texts before singing. Wordbooks should be passed out at all performances so that people could follow along ("Music," *DN,* 2 February 1854).

In August 1856, three days after the citywide festival of the "Literary and Musical Assembly" of Deseret, Grimshaw announced that he "could not stand the hard times" and no longer had faith in Mormonism. He packed and returned to England (*WWJ* 4:433 [4 August 1856]).

51. Jules Remy and Julius Brenchley, *A Journey to Great-Salt-Lake City,* 2 vols. (London: W. Jeffs, 1861), 2:56.

52. William Clayton to Brigham Young, 2 January 1856, quoted in James B. Allen, *Trials of Discipleship: The Life Story of William Clayton, A Mormon* (Urbana: University of Illinois Press, 1987), pp. 266–67.

53. Benjamin Rush, *Thoughts upon Female Education* (Boston: Samuel Hall, 1787), pp. 9–10.

54. *WWJ* 3:367–69 (19 September 1848).

55. *JD* 4:92.

56. Calder to "My Dear Aunt," April 1852, in David O. Calder Papers, HBLL.

57. Calder to Firth, Pond & Co., 30 March 1859, in David O. Calder Letterpress Copybook, HDC.

58. "New School House," *DN*, 12 December 1860; also David O. Calder to Ward & Co., 31 December 1862, Calder Letterpress Copybook. On the Tonic Sol-Fa system itself see the article "Tonic Sol-Fa," Stanley Sadie, ed., *The New Grove Dictionary of Music and Musicians*, 20 vols. (London: Macmillan, 1980), 19:61–65.

Calder's new free singing school put out of business the school advertised by Sarah Cooke three weeks before Calder's school was announced (*DN*, 21 November 1860).

59. "Deseret Musical Association," *DN*, 7 May 1862. See also Edward W. Tullidge, *History of Salt Lake City* (Salt Lake City: Star, 1886), pp. 770–72.

60. See the parade report, *DN*, 30 July 1862, and "The Concerts in the Tabernacle," *DN*, 17 December 1862.

61. *WWJ* 6:141.

62. *Daily Missouri Republican*, 4 May 1861.

63. Richard F. Burton, *The City of the Saints and Across the Rocky Mountains to California*, ed. Fawn M. Brodie (New York: Knopf, 1963), pp. 285–86. Burton noted that the choir sang only hymns when he heard them. Cf. the comment of Samuel Bowles, *Across the Continent* (New York: Hurd and Houghton, 1865), pp. 117–18, likening the Tabernacle choir singing to that of old Methodist camp meetings.

64. A. Karl Larson and Katherine Miles Larson, eds., *Diary of Charles Lowell Walker*, 2 vols. (Logan, Utah: Utah State University Press, 1980), 1:222.

65. *JD* 10:224.

4

Bands and Ballads

It is difficult to say why early Mormons gradually came to blend their Protestant heritage with the secular culture of the gentiles. It may have been their belief that "the weak things of the world shall . . . break down the mighty and strong ones" that enabled them to take lowly elements of popular fashion and transform them into implements of worship. It may also have been Joseph Smith's explanation that spirit was simply a refined form of matter that allowed them so freely to adapt secular forms into sacred.[1] Perhaps, too, the Saints in their growing theological isolation sought to find at least some common cultural ground with the surrounding world. Whatever their underlying rationales, Mormons quite early in their history began to infuse their culture with fife, drum, and brass band music, comic and sentimental parlor songs and ditties.

When intolerance and terrorism began to plague the Missouri Mormons in the 1830s Joseph Smith urged his people to wage their own war of liberation. Forming a militia to quell mob actions against the Saints in Missouri, Smith fused Mormonism with Yankeeism. Perhaps inadvertently, this fusion brought military music into the Mormon Zion. Smith's militia, appropriately called "Zion's Camp," left Kirtland on 1 May 1834 and reached the Mississippi on 4 June, its number having grown to over two hundred. Crossing the river required nearly two days and many trips on the single flatboat available. Levi Hancock, a member of the last company to cross, spent the day whittling a fife from a large elder branch. (Other than the old French horn used for bugle calls, this was the first instrument in the camp.) To impress the rest of the camp members, Hancock's captain, Sylvester Smith, had his company march from the flatboat to the new campsite in Missouri accompanied by Hancock's fife. Unfortunately, the fife music provoked Joseph's watchdog to attack the foot soldiers, angering Sylvester Smith and aggravating a small feud that had been brewing between him and the Prophet for much of the journey.[2]

By summer's end the campaign ran out of steam, many members of the camp contracted cholera, and Joseph announced that the whole affair had been a divine test of the militia's resolve. When Zion's Camp returned to Kirtland, Joseph resumed work on the temple and began to reorganize and expand the church hierarchy "out of the camp boys," an idea he conceived when the Young brothers, Brigham and Joseph, were singing to him.³ The first full-fledged Mormon military band seems not to have appeared until the Fourth of July 1838 dedication of a new temple site in Far West, Missouri. In this ceremony a procession marched around a cellar pit dug for the building "to the notes of a small band of music" led by Dimick Huntington, a thirty-year-old drummer from New York. The band played five more tunes throughout the day, after which Levi's older brother, Solomon Hancock, sang a twelve-stanza song (composed by Levi the day before at Joseph's request) on the southeast cornerstone of the plot:

> Come, lovers of freedom, to gather
> And hear what we now have to say,
> For surely we ought to remember
> The cause that produced this great day.
> Oh, may we remember while singing
> The pains and distresses once born
> By those who have fought for our freedom
> And often for friends called to mourn.⁴

Throughout the following months Missourians and Mormons clashed. In November the citizens of Far West were forced to surrender to a mob-militia. Joseph and others were taken into custody and jailed, and the Saints driven from the state. As the Saints gradually resettled in Illinois they were determined to protect themselves from outsiders. To do so Joseph instituted in February 1841 the Nauvoo Legion, a chartered all-Mormon municipal militia. Joseph overlooked both Levi Hancock and Dimick Huntington for the post of Chief Musician of the Legion and chose Edward Duzette, a recently converted drummer of remarkable skill. With Hancock and Huntington as his assistants, Duzette was ordered to "enlist and organize a Band of Musick, not to exceed twenty men." The unschooled Duzette demurred, but Smith convinced him that this was a call from God.⁵

By March the band had mustered its quota: nine drummers (including Duzette and Huntington), five fifers (including Hancock), two cymbal players, and one man each on bugle, clarinet, tambourine, and triangle.⁶ This band made its first public appearance at the Nauvoo Temple cornerstone laying on the eleventh anniversary of the church's founding (6 April 1841). At the ceremony, according to the church newspaper *Times and Seasons,* "their soul stirring strains met harmoniously the rising emotions that swelled each bosom." The church poetess, Eliza Snow, echoed this sentiment, describing with admiration the

Legion parade horses stepping "to the sound of the soul stirring music that's moving around."[7]

During the first decade of Mormonism relatively inexpensive keyed-brass instruments became popular in the States. Cornets (or "cornopeans"), saxhorns, bugles, and ophicleides combined to produce a stunning effect in the open air. Their piercing tones well suited them to parades, political gatherings, and summer entertainments. Throughout the nation brass bands began to be formed in major cities. In Britain the bands likewise flourished, especially among the growing class of factory workers, for whom, perhaps, the new brass instruments symbolized the finest fruits of industry—machines that made music.[8]

In building a Zion in Illinois, Joseph Smith not only wanted to gather citizens from the British working classes but also to elicit the prestige due a city of Saints. On the frontier in the early 1840s perhaps nothing less than a brass band would confirm Nauvoo's pretensions to greatness. In November 1840 Brigham Young wrote to his wife from the British mission that "we have a grate meny musisions in the church, we shall have musick in the church." His fellow apostle Wilford Woodruff wrote similarly that the Mormon movement was attracting the best musicians from many English parishes, gravely worrying their pastors.[9] By 1842 many trained British instrumentalists had been converted and had immigrated to Nauvoo. Among these was an entire municipal band who, according to a later account, were baptized en masse and crossed the Atlantic to be with the main body of Mormons in Illinois.[10] Many of these members brought brass instruments and the fervor of the new brass band movement with them. And like the British choirs, the bands performed often on the ships' decks.

In April 1843 Duzette was called on a mission to Ohio and Levi Hancock became the new Chief Musician. Although Hancock was a faithful supporter of instrumental music in the church, he seems not to have known how to lead these more sophisticated musicians, who were beginning to group themselves around the British immigrant William Pitt.[11] On 4 November 1843 the musicians of the Legion's second division signed a petition complaining at having to play field music under the command of fifers and drummers, i.e., under Hancock and Huntington. The document proposed that this group, led by Pitt, be separated from the Legion band, be renamed "The Nauvoo Brass Band," and be subject only to Joseph Smith. In January Hancock counterproposed that the group be reunited, its membership expanded, and, by the same token, that membership in any municipal brass band be restricted to fifteen members. Because these factions of musicians could not agree, the Legion officers dissolved both bands. Two weeks after the disbanding, the Legion struck from the charter all passages that referred to a "Chief Musician."

Joseph settled the matter a week later by repealing the organizing of the Brass Band, reinstating the Legion band, but allowing the musicians of the second division to remain a unit under Pitt's direction (though still subject to the Chief Musician).[12]

Members of this division, though, later insisted that the Prophet had instigated their move for independence from Hancock. They claimed that Smith called them to a meeting in 1842, appointed Pitt the director, and asked them to begin playing the music that Pitt had brought in a trunk from England. Gustavus Hills, the disfellowshipped founder of the Nauvoo Musical Lyceum, was to arrange new pieces and copy parts.[13] The Prophet became the group's steady patron, calling on them for instrumental music at meetings, parties, excursions, picnics, civic ceremonies, and parades.

One of the band's functions during the summer months was to salute new immigrants and to escort them through the streets of the city, a practice that persisted well into the Utah period. Eventually, when the Nauvoo Temple's tower was finished, the Band serenaded the Saints in the grove from atop the steeple, giving an "effect . . . as near heavenly as anything we can think of."[14] A resident of Nauvoo recalled that the constant band music during this period made life in Nauvoo seem "one continual holiday for us children, who had very little idea of the meaning of it."[15]

Joseph had named himself to the rank of Lieutenant-General in the Legion and had begun to fancy hearing soldier songs sung to him in parlor gatherings. According to Benjamin Johnson, a confidant of Joseph during this period, the Prophet most often requested to hear folk and popular songs dealing with military life.[16] One of these, Thomas Campbell's "The Soldier's Dream," is a monologue of a soldier who falls asleep on the battlefield and dreams of returning to his family and friends.[17] Another, "The Soldier's Tear," a selection from George Alexander Lee's 1834 opera *Music and Prejudice,* is a narrative of a soldier leaving home for the battlefield, wistfully surveying his village for the last time, and wiping a tear from his cheek. Its last stanza moralizes in typical early American fashion:

> Go, watch the foremost ranks
> In danger's dark career;
> Be sure the hand most daring there
> Has wiped away a tear.[18]

"The Massacre at the River Raisin," a narrative of the notorious episode in the War of 1812, had been sung for Joseph when he was jailed in Missouri, and apparently remained a favorite in Nauvoo.[19] A fourth song mentioned by Johnson, "Wife, Children, and Friends," again treated the theme of the soldier remembering his home:

The soldier whose deeds live immortal in story,
Whom duty to far distant latitudes sends,
With transport would barter whole ages of glory
For one happy day with wife, children, and friends.
Though valor still glows in his life's waning embers,
The death-wounded tar who his colors defends
Drops a tear of regret as he dying remembers
How blest was his home with wife, children, and friends.[20]

In April 1843 Joseph personally selected the building site for the Nauvoo Music Hall.[21] Such a hall would not only provide an enclosure for the Brass Band, the church choir, and local solo singers and players, it could also become a way station for touring recitalists and perhaps even blackface minstrels. The nightly steamboat shows of these minstrels were faintly heard along the shores, delighting the Saints with, as one resident recalled, riverboat love songs such as:

My skiff is by the shore,
She's light and free;
To ply the feathered oar
Is joy to me.
And as she glides along,
My song shall be,
Dearest maid, I love but thee![22]

Nothing came of the plans for this hall until after Joseph's death, when the Nauvoo Music Association, an alliance of musicians in the city, began issuing certificates for capital stock in the venture at $2.50 a share in late 1844.[23] Because that winter turned out to be the mildest in recent memory, construction continued throughout the season and the hall was finished by February 1845. The 30' x 50' x 11' building boasted a platform with seats and desks for musicians, three chandeliers, and "sounding jars" in the rafters to enhance the acoustics.[24] Each night of the opening concert series (3–5 March) consisted of a lecture on the ethical effects of music, delivered by one of the church apostles; ten selections by the choir, including contrapuntal anthems; seven selections by the band, primarily overtures and marches; a solo by John Kay, a local policeman with a celebrated baritone voice; and a string trio.[25] Among the premiered songs was John Taylor's tribute to Joseph Smith, "The Seer," rather transparently modelled after Barry Cornwall's popular song "The Sea":

Cornwall	Taylor
The sea! the sea! the open sea!	The Seer, the Seer, Joseph the Seer.
The blue, the fresh, the ever free!	I'll sing of the prophet ever dear.
Without a mark, without a bound	His equal now cannot be found

It runneth the earth's wide regions round.	By searching the wide world around.

. . . . . .

I'm on the sea! I'm on the sea!	He's free, he's free, the Prophet's free;
I am where I would ever be.	He is where he will ever be.

. . . . . .

I've lived since then in calm and strife	Beyond the reach of mobs and strife
Full fifty summers a sailor's life.	He rests unharmed in endless life.[26]

The band and choir opened each night's concert with a dedicatory hymn by Parley Pratt that expounded on the place music had achieved in Mormonism:

Truth is our theme, our joy, our song,
How sweet its numbers flow;
All music's charms to truth belong,
To truth ourselves we owe.

. . . . . .

'Twas truth first formed our band and choirs,
On Zion's western plains;
'Twas truth that tuned our earliest lyres
In sweet, harmonious strains.

Sacred to truth this Hall shall be,
While earth and time remains;
Where the band and choir in harmony
Shall swell their sweetest strains.[27]

The program of a festival scheduled to coincide with the church's April 1845 conference suggests that Nauvoo tastes were not far from those of most American cities, except perhaps that the Mormons felt at ease in mingling sacred and secular airs, or as one reviewer noted, "the sacred, sentimental, and comic, and done up to the very sense of the heart."[28] On a typical night of this three-night festival the band played two overtures, two grand marches, a "finale," and a number with the choir entitled "God Save the Band"; soloists sang "Isabel," "The Hole in the Stocking," "Lary O Gallagin," "Is there a heart that never loved," "Soldier's Tear," and "O Adam"; a duo sang "The Catholic Priest"; various glee groups sang "Hail Joseph Smith," "Forgive Blest Shade," "Pilgrim Saints," "Hark the Lark," and "Hark the Fisherman"; and William Pitt played one solo each on flute and violin.[29]

The Nauvoo Music Hall hosted only a few visiting gentile musicians. Their concerts, apparently, were sparsely attended.[30] More often than not the hall was used for a schoolroom and a church meetinghouse. Even so, in the summer of 1845 Joseph Smith's only surviving brother, William, noted that, because of the bands and the music hall, the city had become as "famed for its exquisite music, as it already is for its great beauty."[31]

That summer, mobs threatened Mormon homesteads throughout the county. The conflagration of terrorism that was to follow was foretold by a common vision experienced by the Nauvoo Legion drummers. During a break from a parade drill, the players' eyes were drawn to their stacked drums and they began to see drops of blood appearing on the drumheads.[32] When the fulfillment of that omen came, the Saints prepared to abandon Nauvoo and sold the Music Hall to the local Methodist congregation for $310.

In 1846 Brigham Young called upon the Saints to "gather without delay to the place appointed," asking them to go "with sweet instruments of music and melody and songs. . . . for the time has come for the Saints to go up to the mountains of the Lord's house, and help to establish it upon the tops of the mountains."[33] By this time the Nauvoo bandsmen had become a veritable subculture of Mormonism. The musicians formed their own cooperative enterprise on the move west, sharing wagons and food and hiring themselves out to nearby towns on each leg of the journey, playing for kegs of drink, grain, fresh meat, and other commodities.[34] Brigham Young also appears to have kept the best players close to his own wagons to serenade his family, and occasionally called upon them to entertain the Saints. The players visited the wagons of the sick and tried to stimulate and cheer them with marches and anthems. And during their stay at Winter Quarters, Nebraska, the musicians began borrowing a carriage in order to serenade in the streets, thus enabling the brass players in particular to bring the music to the people while at the same time freeing them of the labor of marching as they played.[35]

The Nauvoo Legion Band formally reorganized itself on 9 April 1850 in a curious attempt to reconcile its factions. William Clayton led the fight for reorganization on the grounds that Joseph had originally formed only one band, "The Nauvoo Band." Clayton considered the restoration of the group essential to establishing Joseph's dream of Zion in the Rocky Mountains: "I have as firm a motive in the organizing of this band as I would have in being baptized—the minute I see any division in this Band, that moment I leave it, but still do not consider that I leave the 'Nauvoo Band.' "[36] The meeting lasted well into the night, with band members confessing their sins and, occasionally, their lack of skill.[37] Duzette acknowledged that he had never been competent to lead the band, and two other players owned that they did not play well because they were "too religious"—their upbringing had kept them away from musical training. Others, however, requested that Pitt henceforth "give us all a fair chance'' in playing solos, and another asked that parts always be provided for all players, "for I have not so much natural ability for Music as some." A total of twenty-seven members enlisted that night and John Anderson was chosen to lead the band until Pitt arrived in the valley. He accepted, but refused to arrange parts, "for it takes a scientific man to do that."

Three days after this reorganization, at Brigham Young's behest, the band began to solicit money for the building of a huge team-driven carriage. This carriage would allow the band to ride in parades and to escort visitors and immigrants from the canyon passes into the valley. Young himself gave $7.50 of his own money and channeled $24.00 from church funds into the building of the carriage.[38] At daybreak, 24 July 1850, the third anniversary of the Saints' entry into the valley, the new 9'x 29' carriage was unveiled and pulled through the city by sixteen mules. One of the imbibers of the day toasted the carriage as "a just emblem of the largeness of a true Mormon heart; may it never be dishonored by those who have the honor to enjoy a ride in it."[39]

As for the old fife and drum corps, however, a report on Brigham Young's fall muster of the transplanted militia tersely summed up the situation: "It is to be hoped that the first Cohort will hereafter be better supplied with music."[40]

Early in 1852 a wind band led by the Sicilian-born convert Domenico Ballo entered the city and challenged the supremacy of Pitt's band. A former clarinetist of the Royal Guards of Naples and the West Point Band, Ballo converted to Mormonism in St. Louis in 1847 and immediately organized a military band among the Mormons there. The whole group made its way that fall to the Mormon settlement of Council Bluffs, Iowa, but apparently could not raise the means to move to the Salt Lake region until 1851. Once he arrived, Ballo revamped his group into a rigorously trained band of at least twenty players: seven B-flat clarinets, one E-flat clarinet, two piccolos, four cornets, one ophicleide, three bass horns, one tenor trombone, and drums. Ballo's playing took the community by storm. Young was particularly fond of the group, with one reservation: he disliked the tone of Ballo's E-flat clarinet and on at least one public occasion asked Ballo to stop playing so that he could hear the rest of the band.[41]

About the time of Ballo's arrival in Salt Lake City, Young instituted the "Deseret Dramatic Association," a volunteer community theatrical troupe with an orchestra to be led by William Pitt and a hall to be built for its performances. On the day of the association's founding in 1852, a four-man committee was appointed to meet with Ballo "for the purpose of bringing about a reconciliation" between his band and the Nauvoo Band, i.e., to put Ballo and his band under Pitt's command.

Understandably, Ballo refused this offer. When the two leaders refused to settle, Pitt was sent on a proselyting mission and one Jacob Hutchinson was unanimously appointed orchestra leader.[42]

The Dramatic Association continued maneuvering to get Ballo into its company. In January 1853 they tried to organize a benefit concert for the near-destitute Sicilian, but Young, grieved at Ballo's resistance, discouraged the idea. In May a motion was made to elect Ballo to take over the association's conductorship. Ballo was notified of his appointment but he refused to accept it. The association told him he could not refuse, and to sweeten the offer they collected eighty pounds of flour, the cash equivalent of twenty more pounds, and two dollars' worth of meat for Ballo, who suddenly accepted the post (and the contributions).

Ballo's new "orchestra," with fiddles augmenting the brass and wind players, became the church's more or less official band. It performed for entertainments in the newly built Social Hall, for serenades on Young's mansion balcony, for meetings of the Deseret Theological Institute, and for church meetings. On all occasions, worship meetings not excepted, the band played traditional military and popular music as well as transcriptions of European sacred and operatic pieces, sometimes accompanying the choir or solo singers. A visitor in 1852 described church instrumental music thus: "While the congregation is assembling and departing from the house, it is usual for the large and excellent band of music to perform anthems, marches, and waltzes, which drives away all sombre feelings, and prepares the mind for the exciting and often eloquent discourses."[43] By 1855 Ballo's group had performed for the Saints selections from Mehul, Mozart, Meyerbeer, Bellini, and Rossini in addition to the usual compliment of original and transcribed patriotic airs and marches (especially "Auld Lang Syne," "Yankee Doodle," and "La Marseillaise").[44] Ballo ensured the excellence of his broad and often difficult repertoire by rigorous training and constant review of his musicians. From time to time he dropped members from the band because, as one of them ingenuously wrote in his diary, "they could not play."[45]

Ballo placed himself at Young's disposal with a devotion that some Mormons recalled "amounted almost to idolatry."[46] Young's reciprocal devotion became obvious to all the citizens of the city, including the members of rival bands. In 1855 Young announced plans to build another hall exclusively for Ballo's group and drew up a set of by-laws for the now more or less official municipal and church band.[47] Built partly with church monies, the 60' x 35' x 14' arched hall would revert to church ownership if the band ever dissolved, even though band members did most of the labor.[48]

A few weeks after Young announced plans for the music hall, apostle George A. Smith wrote to the editor of the *St. Louis Luminary* concerning the Nauvoo Brass Band's apparent decline. "Some think there is nothing of the Nauvoo Brass Band left but the name; there are however about a dozen active members still in the band who were in it in Nauvoo when organized by the request of our martyred Prophet; and it is constantly receiving an accession of talent by almost every emigration. Joseph blessed this band, and it is bound to ride over all prejudice."[49] To enhance its reputation eight members of the Brass Band embarked that summer on a tour of seven northern Utah settlements. Relying on local church leaders to promote their performances, the band played brass music as well as orchestral and vocal pieces in schoolhouses and boweries. Settlers, most of them downcast at the continuing devastation of their crops by drouth, grasshoppers, and Indian "gleaners," crowded to hear the band (except in one instance, "owing to a thunderstorm in the evening, and the indifference of the bishop").[50]

Within a year of this tour, brass bands were formed in Ogden and Farmington, two of the larger settlements. The Ogden group was large and used conventional forces: four B-flat cornets, alto saxhorn, three trombones, bass horn, two tubas, and a drummer. The Farmington band, however, had a unique instrumentation: in addition to its single trumpet, three cornopeans, two trombones, and ophicleide, it had an E-flat clarinet and a clavichord, but no bass horns or tubas. Because this band—which called itself "The Deseret Brass Band"—was so close to Salt Lake City, it could be led by a member of the Nauvoo Brass Band itself, who brought the group arrangements and parts from the city.

As the brass band movement spread through Deseret, the Nauvoo Legion maintained outposts in many settlements, most of them with at least a rudimentary fife and drum corps. By 1862 each of the Mormon settlements of Provo, Springville, Spanish Fork, Nephi, Ogden, and Smithfield, to name but a few, had both a brass band and a martial band. Local newspapers reported that the bands played well, although in one instance a visiting gentile mistook the sound of an approaching band procession for a herd of cows. The noise turned out to be the Parowan band serenading the visitor with "John Brown's Body," one of the many secular tunes favored by Utah bands.[51]

The Mormon bands all seem to have considered their work a religious duty: they were to spread music through the nation of Zion, elevate the people's tastes, stir their hearts with hymns and martial airs, and provide a social pastime for Saints. These bands regularly played for Mormon church services, and no evidence suggests that anyone debated this practice. Joseph the Prophet had encouraged the bands and good Saints would not question their presence in the church. Indeed, some of the Mormon bandsmen cheerfully flouted sectarian bans on instrumental music. They took pride in being able to consecrate the "weak things of the earth''—even musical instruments—to the glory of their God.[52] In rejecting sectarian culture, Mormons embraced secular culture, which seemed to them not only richer but far more tractable.

The Mormons' ease with secular culture was reflected even in their ''religious'' music. The *New York Herald* of 6 July 1857 observed that Mormons ''do not confine themselves to sacred music. All the popular songs of the day—English glees, negro melodies, and even sentimental ballads—they bring into their service. Their hymns are for the most part sung to familiar 'profane' airs.''[53] What made the Mormon practice of song adaptation noteworthy to the *Herald* and to other observers was perhaps the Mormons' habit of retaining the essential character of the secular models. John Taylor's ''The Seer'' poses a good example of this. Three other Mormon adaptations of ''The Sea'' suggest both the breadth of the Mormon poetic spirit and the occasional narrowness of its craft. W. W. Phelps's version, ''The Sky,'' was the most awkward of the lot, beginning:

> The sky, the sky, the clear blue sky—
> O how I love to gaze upon it!
> The upper deep of realms on high—
> I wonder when the Lord begun it?[54]

Joseph Cain's song ''The Bee'' was a tribute to the Mormons' beloved symbol of industry and cooperation. It begins, ''The bee, the bee, the honey bee / Which flies and hums from tree to tree.'' Four years later, Eliza Snow produced a tribute to Utah's newspapers: ''The Press, the Press, the Printing Press / Of noble Art the world to bless.''[55]

''The Sea'' was a popular model for new Mormon songs partly because oceanic immigration was so vital in building the Mormon populace. Well into the 1870s more than one half of the adult population of Utah was foreign-born. A great many of them had recently emigrated from Europe, especially from Great Britain and Scandinavia. Many villages in Utah became outposts of old-world culture and many of the best musicians in Mormondom in the mid-nineteenth century were European emigrants. By the same token, scores of American missionaries crossed the Atlantic eastward to proselyte and publish. (The church's main printing enterprise had been seated in England since 1840.) While on their journeys, many of the immigrants and missionaries alike composed sea songs of their own, for music was one of the few comforts and diversions of ocean steamer passage in those times.

In 1853 Daniel Tyler composed a song rather typical of this variety, a composition in which he had ''the prayers of my bretheren and the Spirit of the Lord to help me.'' Its chorus and final verse show the ingenuous nature of these songs, as well as an evident struggle to find a good rhyme:

> Then let us cross the briny deep
> With breezes soft and mild
> O Lord in safety do thou keep
> That we may feel thou hast smiled
>
> Our wives and children then we'll greet
> The seers and prophets too
> Our joy will be full and complete
> As friends say how do you do.[56]

That same year Henry Maiben wrote a rollicking chanty about the company with whom he travelled, a song typical of those that would make Maiben a favorite comic songster in Utah:

> We have a noble President
> You'd scarce find such an one, sir;
> He stands near six-feet-six in height
> And weighs near twenty stone, sir.
> But best of all he's full of love,
> He's frank and open-hearted
> And as sincere as any that
> From Babylon has departed.
>   Chorus:
> Then sing aloud ye Saints of God
> In one united chorus:
> Old Babylon we'll leave behind
> For Zion is before us.[57]

The lustiness with which such songs were sung seems to have appealed to the ship's gentile crews, as this anecdote from the journal of Peter McBride suggests: "Part of the Manchester Choir was on board and there was lots of singing. One song in particular being, 'We, we won't marry none but Mormons,' and when the ship landed, Capt. Reed made a speech to the Saints in which he said, 'The song says, "I won't marry none but Mormons," and I will say, if I ever bring immigrants again, "I'll carry none but Mormons." ' "[58]

Aside from hymns, many of the songs that filled Mormon conferences and gatherings in Nauvoo and early Utah bordered on the comic: "The Merry Mormons," "A right good man is Brigham Young," "A Comical Way," "The Bone of Contention," and "The Mormon Creed," to name only a few.[59] A number of W. W. Phelps's songs in this period provoked unintended mirth. Consider, for example, his three different adaptations of the very popular Irish song "The Last Rose of Summer," which had been another of Joseph Smith's most frequently requested songs. Between March and October of 1856 Phelps wrote "The Last Flake of Snow," "The First Rose of Summer," and "The Last Foolish Mormons," line by line, all of them clearly derived from the Irish song.[60] Some other songs used well-known popular songs to satirize sectarian religion, such as the enduring parody of "The rose that all are praising," called "The God that others worship":[61]

"The Rose"	"The God"
The rose that all are praising	The God that others worship
Is not the rose for me	Is not the God for me
Too many eyes are gazing	He has no parts nor body
Upon that costly tree	And cannot hear nor see
But I've a rose in yonder glen	But I've a God that lives above
That shuns the gaze of other men	A God of mercy and of love
For me its blossoms raising	A God of revelation
Oh, that's the rose for me	Oh, that's the God for me
Oh, that's the rose for me	Oh, that's the God for me
Oh, that's the rose for me.	Oh, that's the God for me.

Another adaptation of "The Rose" appeared in John Taylor's "The Upper California," a song sung by the Saints during their exodus from Nauvoo (its chorus ran, "Oh, that's the land for me"). Apostle Taylor complained to an 1857 audience that his song was not being sung enough: "We have got to do it, yes," he said, adding that the song should be a kind of "Yankee Doodle" to the Saints.[62]

Perhaps the most popular type of Mormon satire song was that in which the Saints lampooned their persecutors, as in their version of the song sung in the War of 1812, "The Hunters of Kentucky," which they called "The Mobbers of Missouri":

"Hunters"	"Mobbers"
You gentlemen and ladies fair	Come gentlemen and ladies too
Who grace this famous city,	Who love your country's glory,
Just listen if you've time to spare	Hark, if you've nothing else to do
While I rehearse a ditty,	While I relate a story,
And for the opportunity	But mark what's done like days of old
Believe yourselves quite lucky,	By mortals in their fury,
For 'tis not often that you see	For 'tis not often you behold
A hunter from Kentucky.	Such mobbers as Missouri.
Oh, Kentucky!	Oh Missouri!
The hunters of Kentucky!	The mobbers of Missouri![63]

Some of the most deeply felt of the Mormon songs composed in the church's second and third decades were laments on the assassination of Joseph the Prophet and his brother Hyrum (known as "The Patriarch"). Solomon Hancock's was characteristic both for its sentiment and its jangling rhymes:

Joseph and Hyrum both are gone,
For them my heart don't cease to mourn;
To think they both were in jail
And a mob should fall on them and kill.

. . . . . .

Soon as they came to the jail door
The bullets from their guns did pour,
Which brought poor Hyrum to the floor,
A laying weltering in his gore.

Hyrum cried out, I'm a dead man,
Joseph said, oh brother Hyrum
And then he to the window flew,
As if determined to go through.[64]

John Taylor's "O give me back my prophet dear" was somewhat more sophisticated, though, as did a number of Mormon songs, it took for a model "The Indian Student's Lament."[65]

"Lament"	"My Prophet Dear"
O give me back my bended bow	O give me back my prophet dear
My cap and feather, give them back	And patriarch, O give them back
To chase o'er hill the mountain roe	The Saints of latter days to cheer
And follow in the otter's track.	And lead them in the gospel track.

One of Phelps's ventures into this genre was "A Voice from the Prophet: Come to Me," patterned after another sentimental song of the American Indian, called "The Indian Hunter":

"Indian Hunter"	"Voice from the Prophet"
Let me go to my home	Come to me, will ye come
In the far distant west,	To the saints that have died,
To the scenes of my childhood	To the next better world, where
That I love the best,	The righteous reside,
Where the tall cedars are and	Where the angels and spirits
The bright waters flow,	In harmony be,
Where my parents will greet me,	In the joys of a vast Par-
White man, let me go.	adise, come to me.[66]

The songs of Stephen Foster captivated the Saints just as they did the whole nation. "Gentle Annie" became a favorite tune with Brigham Young: it was scored into the Nauvoo Brass Band part books and was widely disseminated in Utah through David Calder's importation of the *Gentle Annie Songster.*[67] The sentiment of Foster's "Hard Times Come Again No More" also appealed to the Mormons. Its words were copied into journals, several Mormon adaptations were written, and the song was sung often. In one instance it was used to soften the hearts of the federal troops during their sojourn in Utah. As one pioneer recalled, "it melted the heart of Colonel Johns[t]on to hear the song and note the general appearance of the innocent urchins."[68]

The songs of black (and blackface) Americans seem also to have tantalized the Saints. Diaries reveal that Mormons encountered this music from many sources: from the Mississippi riverboat minstrel shows, from the black crew members of emigrant ships, from some of the white and free black immigrants themselves, and even from the few slaves in the Saints' midst. As early as January 1853 a local minstrel troupe, "The African Band," performed "a series of negro melodies" at the Social Hall.[69] By 1855 apostle Wilford Woodruff was warning Mormon mothers against teaching their children "negro songs" because, he argued, "whatever seed is sown in the minds of our children the same kind of fruit will be produced."[70] Nevertheless, such songs swept through the territory, often by way of the Nauvoo Legion troops. Brigham Young tolerated the songs, but asked that the musicians not blacken their faces. The child of a minstrel performer quoted Young as saying to her father: "What if you should die suddenly with faces like that? What a disgrace it would be and your standards lowered."[71] While some singers took Young's advice, the Mormons' passion for black and blackface music intensified with the coming of one of Young's great enterprises: the Salt Lake Theatre.

In the spring of 1861, having just completed his private schoolhouse, Young began construction of an elaborate theater which was to replace the Social Hall in housing plays and musical entertainments. Although the local dramatists had been working steadily for nearly a decade, their performances were still not thought "first rate" by the *Deseret News*. The paper did, however, praise the music—"the combination of talent in that department is under the direction of Ballo, which is enough to say."[72] Clearly Young had been grooming Ballo for just the kind of post that the new theater would provide. Young seems to have expected that the acoustics of the new hall would enrich the orchestra's already pleasing sound and that, in turn, the superior sound would attract more good musicians into the group. But on Sunday, 8 June 1861, at the close of a typically full day conducting the musicians at the Bowery and the Tabernacle, Ballo walked home, stepped into his yard, and fell over dead.

Salt Lake City grieved profoundly. Some residents feared that Ballo's death would mean the death of good music in Mormondom.[73] For Mormons versed in the band music and ballads of these early years it was difficult to imagine how Ballo's abilities could be replaced, let alone

improved upon. But in late September a young British musician named
Charles John Thomas arrived in town looking for work. Thomas had
already gained some repute among English and East Coast Mormons.
Within a year of his arrival in Utah he had taken over Ballo's band, the
Theatre orchestra, and the Tabernacle Choir, and had built the groundwork
for a succession of musical dynasties that would dominate Mormon culture
well into the twentieth century.

NOTES

1. For the doctrines referred to, see Doctrine and Covenants 1:19 and 131:7–8.
2. George Albert Smith, History of Zion's Camp, photocopy of typescript,
HBLL, 4 June 1834.
3. *HC* 2:180, *JD* 9:89.
4. Mosiah Hancock Reminiscence, holograph in HDC, pp. 6–7, and
Elders Journal 1 (August 1838): 60.
5. *HC* 4:30 and Minutes of Nauvoo Band Meeting, 9 April 1850, pencil copy
from holograph made by Alice M. Rich (6 September 1932), HDC.
6. "A List of Names Belonging to the Band of the Nauvoo Legion,
March 1st 1841," holograph in Newel Whitney Papers.
7. *TS* 2 (15 April and 1 July 1841): 377, 467.
8. See Margaret Hindle Hazen and Robert M. Hazen, *The Music Men:
An Illustrated History of Brass Bands in America, 1800–1920* (Washington, D.C.:
Smithsonian Institution Press, 1987).
9. Young to Mary Ann Angell Young, 12 November 1840, Blair Papers, and
TS 2 (1 March 1841): 331.
10. See Thomas L. Kane, *The Mormons: A Discourse Delivered before the
Historical Society of Pennsylvania: March 26, 1850* (Philadelphia: King and
Baird, 1850), p. 32.
11. For background on Pitt, see the eulogy by Wilford Woodruff, *DN,*
1 March 1873.
12. See Nauvoo Legion Minutes, holograph in HDC, 4 November 1843;
13, 26 January, and 10 February 1844.
13. Horace G. Whitney, "The Nauvoo Brass Band," *Contributor* 1 (1880):
134–37.
14. *Nauvoo Neighbor,* 13 August 1845.
15. Helen Mar Whitney, "Scenes in Nauvoo," *WE* 10 (1 October 1881): 66.
For a time, according to a local anti-Mormon postmaster, "you could not miss
[a military parade] any day of the year (Sundays excepted)" during this period.
See Warren A. Jennings, ed., "Two Iowa Postmasters View Nauvoo: Anti-Mormon
Letters to the Governor of Missouri," *Brigham Young University Studies* 11
(Spring 1971): 279.
16. See Dean R. Zimmermann, *I Knew the Prophets: An Analysis of the
Letter of Benjamin F. Johnson to George F. Gibbs, Reporting Doctrinal Views
of Joseph Smith and Brigham Young* (Bountiful, Utah: Horizon, 1976), p. 19.

17. There are many different musical settings of Campbell's text from this period, the most often published being that of Thomas Attwood (1765–1838).

18. The song appeared in at least nine different imprints before 1836.

19. See Linda King Newell and Valeen Tippetts Avery, *Mormon Enigma: Emma Hale Smith* (Garden City: Doubleday, 1984), p. 78.

20. See Sigmund Spaeth, *Read'em and Weep: The Songs You Forgot to Remember* (Garden City, N.Y.: Doubleday, 1927), pp. 21–23. An original sheet of the song (1830?) is in the British Museum. Apostle Erastus Snow published the text on the back of an 1851 pamphlet, under this heading: "Had the author of the following lines known the calling and mission of the Latter-day Saints, he would have, most unquestionably, represented them in his song; as it is, we offer it to our readers, assuring them that we often appropriate it to our own use" (*One Year in Scandanavia* [Liverpool: F. D. Richards, 1851], p. 24).

21. *HC* 5:368.

22. Helen Mar Whitney, "Scenes in Nauvoo," *WE* 10 (15 September 1881): 58.

23. A share certificate is pasted in the back of Edwin Harley Diary, photocopy of holograph in HBLL, vol. 2.

24. *HC* 7:363–64 and *Nauvoo Neighbor,* 12 March 1845. Unfortunately the building was so poorly ventilated that on the third night of the opening concert series the upper part of the windows had to be removed to give the singers and players enough air. See *Nauvoo Neighbor,* 23 April 1845.

25. The program is in *Nauvoo Neighbor,* 26 February 1845; see also "The Concert," ibid., 12 March 1845.

26. The full text of "The Sea" may be found in Barry Cornwall [Bryan Waller Proctor], *English Songs and Other Small Poems* (London: Edward Moxon, 1832), pp. 1–2.

27. The text appears in William Burton Diary, holograph in HDC; also in an unsigned manuscript from the period, Newel Whitney Papers.

28. *Nauvoo Neighbor,* 16 April 1845.

29. "Grand Concert" (7–9 April 1845), broadside in HDC.

30. See the note on the appearance of the Slater sisters, *Nauvoo Neighbor,* 23 April 1845; compare this with a similar note in the *Chicago Daily Journal,* 23 January 1845.

31. *Nauvoo Neighbor,* 16 July 1845. See also the account of this meeting in William Clayton Diary, typescript excerpts published as *Clayton's Secret Writings Uncovered* (Salt Lake City: Modern Microfilm, 1983), 9 July 1845.

32. Aroet L. Hale Reminiscence, holograph in HDC.

33. Quoted in Leonard J. Arrington, *Brigham Young: American Moses* (New York: Knopf, 1985), p. 156.

34. See Charles Smith Diary, typescript in HBLL, p. 13, and *William Clayton's Journal: A Daily Record of the Original Company of "Mormon" Pioneers from Nauvoo, Illinois, to the Valley of the Great Salt Lake* (Salt Lake City: Deseret News, 1921), passim.

35. *WWJ* 3:125 (5 February 1847).

36. Nauvoo Band Minutes, 9 April 1850. The quotations that follow in this paragraph also derive from this source. For a survey of Mormon bands in this

period see Martha Tingey Cook, "Pioneer Bands and Orchestras of Salt Lake City" (Master's thesis, Brigham Young University, 1960).

37. Much of the confession had to do with drinking to excess. The Cedar City (Utah) band likewise had a problem with drinking (see Lorenzo Brown Journal, 5 March 1857, typescript in HBLL). And Ballo's band sometimes accepted drink as a reward for its serenades; see Joshua Midgley Journal, microfilm of holograph in HDC, 13 June 1857: "after we had Plaid a few tuns mor we got a little Licker witch was veary kindly received by us."

38. "Treasurers Report for the Nauvoo Band Carriage" (June–July 1850), Salt Lake City Band Papers, HDC.

39. See the accounts of the day in *DN,* 27 July and 10 August 1850.

40. Letter from Daniel H. Wells, *DN,* 19 October 1850.

41. This occasion was recalled by band member Joshua Midgley in Thomas Griggs, Journal, 21 November 1902, holograph in HDC.

42. The information in this and the succeeding paragraph is taken from the Deseret Dramatic Association Minute Book, 20 February 1852–14 June 1853, HDC. For a general study of the Deseret Dramatic Association see Ila Fisher Maughan, "History of Staging and Business Methods of the Deseret Dramatic Association, 1852–1869" (Master's thesis, University of Utah, 1949).

43. Gunnison, *The Mormons,* p. 37.

44. Remy and Brenchley, *Journey to Great Salt Lake City,* 1:213–14.

45. George Spilsbury Diary, photocopy of holograph in HBLL, 14 January 1855.

46. Horace G. Whitney, "Domenico Ballo," *Contributor* 1 (1880): 31–35.

47. "Organic Rules for Building a Music Hall," Salt Lake City Bands Papers; Spilsbury Diary, 17 and 19 February 1855.

48. By June the foundation was complete, and band members laid the wall adobes in October. See Spilsbury Diary, October 1855; "Music Hall," *DN,* 27 June 1855.

49. Historian's Office Letterpress Copybook, manuscript in HDC, 29 March 1855.

50. See Jonathan Grimshaw's report of the tour in *DN,* 29 August 1855.

51. Elizabeth Wood Kane, *Twelve Mormon Homes Visited in Succession on a Journey through Utah to Arizona* (Salt Lake City: Tanner Trust Fund, 1974), pp. 98–99.

52. See Doctrine and Covenants 124:1. Campbellite Disciples of Christ Churches, for example, from whom so many early Saints had been harvested, still debated in the 1850s about the use of organs in their services. See Louis Cochran and Bess White Cochran, *Captives of the Word* (Garden City, N.Y.: Doubleday, 1969), pp. 155–58.

53. Cf. Burton, *City of the Saints,* p. 286: " 'profane,' i.e. operatic and other music is performed at worship, as in the Italian cathedrals, where they are unwilling that Sathanas should monopolize the prettiest airs." The distinction between "sacred" and "profane" tunes in American religious music was dubious, especially among the folk hymns that dominated the shape-note tunebooks. Virtually all of these had "profane" melodic counterparts in American and British folklore. Moreover, many religious journals printed Christianized lyrics to popular ballads.

54. *TS* 6 (1 May 1845): 895. See also Henry Mayhew, *The Mormons: or Latter-day Saints* (London: National Illustrated Library, 1852), p. 44.

55. *DN*, 25 January 1851 and 15 February 1855.

56. Daniel Tyler Diary, photocopy of holograph in HBLL, 15 October 1853.

57. Christopher J. Arthur Journal, typescript in UHS.

58. *OPH* 13:360.

59. These songs are mentioned in *DN*, 20 June 1855, 12 November 1856, 26 June 1861, and 25 March 1857. On the Mormon Creed and its songs see Michael Hicks, "Minding Business: A Note on the Mormon Creed," *Brigham Young University Studies* 26 (Fall 1986): 125–32.

60. See *DN*, 19 March, 2 April, and 22 October 1856.

61. *TS* 6 (1 February 1845): 799; *Nauvoo Neighbor*, 5 February 1845. "The God that Others Worship" made its way into the Mormon hymnbook and was even sung by choirs (see *DN*, 5 August 1857).

62. *DN*, 16 September 1857.

63. See Charles Brent Hancock, *The Hancock and Adams Families* (n.p., n.d.), copy in HBLL, p. 26.

64. Ibid., p. 33. Songs to Joseph appeared during his lifetime as well, the earliest of which appears to have been Joel H. Johnson's 1831 "To Joseph Whom I Love" (see Joel H. Johnson, Songbooks, holograph in HDC).

65. A copy of an 1851 version called "The Indian Student," with music by "Mrs. L. L. D. J. of New Orleans," is in the Library of Congress. The popularity of this song among the Mormons may be estimated by the numerous songs written to its tune. Other than Taylor's song, some of these adaptations are: "O give me back my God again," "The Emigrant's Lament," "My Old White Stone," and "Farewell my true and faithful wife." See *Wasp*, 31 December 1842; *DN*, 4 March 1857; and Daniel Tyler Diary, 20 August 1853.

66. Another version of "Come to Me," composed by Levi Hancock, appears in his holograph poetry book, HDC. "The Indian Hunter" was sung at the Nauvoo Music Hall; see Aurelia Spencer Rogers, *Life Sketches of Orson Spencer and Others, and History of Primary Work* (Salt Lake City: Cannon, 1898), p. 30.

67. See Augusta Joyce Crocheron, *Representative Women of Deseret* (Salt Lake City: J. Graham, 1884), pp. 1–2; the Nauvoo Brass Band part book of Robert T. Burton in HBLL; and Calder, Letterpress Copybook, miscellaneous orders in 1859.

68. James McBride Autobiography, typescript in HBLL.

69. *DN*, 22 January 1853.

70. *WWJ* 4:353 (21 October 1855).

71. Laura McBride Smith, quoted in Robert Sayers, "Sing Anything: The Narrative Repertoire of a Mormon Pioneer," *Journal of the Southwest* 29 (Spring 1987): 76–77.

72. *DN*, 3 April 1861.

73. See Whitney, "Domenico Ballo."

5

Going Forth in the Dance

Visitors to Mormon territories during Brigham Young's lifetime were often surprised at the vivacity with which the Saints exercised themselves in balls and soirées. Likewise, many converts to Mormonism in this period marvelled at how freely the elders of their new faith indulged in dances. But church leaders' attitudes toward dancing were rarely so untroubled as outsiders and proselytes at first believed them to be. Joseph Smith seems hardly to have countenanced dancing, Brigham Young vacillated between praise and scorn for it, and after Young's death the church's attitude toward the practice remained ambiguous as the Saints struggled with the hoary problem of being in the New World but not of it.

Americans had wrestled with the propriety of dancing since colonial times. Puritans, for whom good morals devolved in part upon good manners, could look upon dancing as a social grace, one which inculcated balance and harmonious movement. Practiced by men with men or women with women on days other than the Sabbath, dancing was often enjoyed by pious folk. At the same time, dancing, especially "mixed dancing" (men with women), brought down the wrath of churchmen who thought it a masquerade for sensual allurement. Southern society, with its predominantly mercantile origins, seems to have accepted mixed dancing more readily than did Northerners, whose heritage was decidedly more religious. But during the Great Awakening and the spread of American revivalism dancing became a vulnerable target for preachers trying to quell carnal amusements. Evangelists boasted of converting dancers and dance musicians; they often convinced the latter to destroy their instruments as an act of true repentance. This antipathy toward dance colored the attitudes of many early Mormons.[1]

Most Mormon leaders of the 1830s had grown up with negative feelings toward dancing and there is every indication that these feelings persisted. The daughter of an early Mormon apostle recalled that dancing was roundly condemned in this period of Mormonism and was considered a "near unforgivable" sin, one for which the sinner could be "cast out."[2] Church records confirm that a year and a half after the Kirtland Temple dedication, the local high priests disfellowshipped twenty-two members who had attended a local dance. The high council demanded that they, along with nine others who were also eventually found out, confess to their wickedness or be excommunicated. On 1 November most of the offenders repented to the council; the rest were threatened with excommunication, although the threat appears not to have been carried out.[3] A few years later a Mormon woman in the British mission was excommunicated for the sin. After being persuaded to do so by her non-Mormon husband, Alice Hadock briefly indulged in a dance at a local tavern. Some pious Mormons reported having seen her to the church authorities. She was cut off and never returned to the church.[4]

As Mormon Nauvoo settled into its inevitable status as a "river town," dancing crept into the church. In spring 1843 apostle Heber C. Kimball organized a society for youth, partly in order to keep them away from riverboat dances. At the founding meeting, Kimball denounced some young people for "frequenting balls and such places, which, he said, would generally lead to many evil practices, and would draw away the mind from more innocent amusements."[5] But later that year dancing made inroads even into the domicile of the Prophet, although by all accounts this went against his wishes. Joseph's home in Nauvoo, known as "The Mansion House," had been designed as a fair-sized hotel, which, because of the notoriety of its owner, attracted many boarders. To keep these boarders from spending their money on riverboat amusements— and to provide the Smiths with an income—the Mansion House began offering weekly dances in the winter of 1843–44. Joseph apparently disputed with Emma over the dancing, and said, according to a confidant, "everything against it he could."[6]

But the love of dancing prevailed, not only among gentiles but also among the local Mormon youth. Joseph never denounced the dances publicly, preferring to register his disapproval by sitting upstairs in his room during the parties and privately warning his friends not to let their children, especially their daughters, attend the affairs. He was particularly piqued by the presence of "blacklegs" at the dances and by their tales of the seduction of Mormon girls on steamboats docked near the Mansion House.[7] Nevertheless, he refused to stop the soirées, and this refusal surely suggested a tacit approval of dancing in the community, an implied sanction which only made the parties more popular.

In February 1844 an anonymous letter to the *Times and Seasons* called for an official statement on the propriety of Saints' attending the Mansion House dancing parties. An editorial, also anonymous, responded in moderate tones that dancing was a "science," a gymnastic exercise which tended to "invigorate the system." Echoing revivalist rhetoric, the editorial noted the acceptability of dancing among the ancient Israelites, but countered, "when we can see such a dance, we shall join in it heartily. [But] we do not consider that the dancing that is now practiced is of that kind." The editorial concluded with the rather ambiguous observation that "as an abstract principle . . . we have no objections to [dancing]; but when it leads people into bad company and causes them to keep untimely hours, it has a tendency to enervate and weaken the system, and lead to profligate and intemperate habits . . . injurious to society, and corrupting to the morals of youth."[8]

Further complicating the question of the local dances' propriety was the common knowledge that church musicians accompanied them. Having taken care to court the talents of these musicians, Joseph undoubtedly did not wish to deny them a supplement to their already meager livelihood. Perhaps to avoid slighting the musicians, Joseph visited one of the Mansion House dances and even called upon one of the players that night to dance a hornpipe for him.[9] Although this certainly constituted no breach of Puritan heritage (i.e., of solo or unmixed dancing for "invigorating the system"), the incident probably implied a sanction of the whole proceedings to the onlookers and only further confused the Saints as to the Prophet's attitude toward these balls.

Joseph's affection for other amusements, especially wrestling and telling jokes, was renowned. But when cataloguing the social pastimes of the Prophet, Joseph's friend Benjamin Johnson did not mention dancing.[10] It is likely that Smith associated the practice with what he called the "foolish errors . . . weakness of youth and . . . corruption of human nature" that plagued his adolescence and from which he hoped to distance himself. Ironically, the assassination of Joseph and his brother Hyrum further aggravated the problem of dancing at Nauvoo and helped drive a wedge between Joseph's widow and church leaders.

When they were brought to Nauvoo from Carthage, the mutilated corpses of the Smith brothers were laid out in the Mansion House dining room—the site of the dance parties—to be prepared for viewing and burial. During the time the bodies were in state in the dining room, some blood seeped through the coffins and stained the floor. When Emma resumed holding dances in the dining room that fall, Heber Kimball fiercely protested "all this frolicking and dancing over the blood of the prophet, where it was drenched in the blood from the coffin."[11] Though he failed to mention the issue of Joseph's blood, Brigham Young spoke as did Kimball, issuing an "epistle" from the Twelve Apostles exhorting the people that "balls, dances, and other vain and useless amusements be neither countenanced nor patronized; they have been borne with, in some instances heretofore for the sake of peace and good will. But it is not now a time for dancing or frolics but a time of mourning, and of humiliation and prayer." As an alternative to dancing he proposed the Saints go to concerts.[12]

Like most Mormons of his time, Young grew up with the notions that fiddling and dancing constituted "a step in the direction of Davy Jones." Brigham conceded later in life that the strictness of his father's mandate against these evils simply made him want to dance and hear fiddles all the more.[13] Thus, in the last days of Nauvoo, only weeks after the apostles' sermons against attending the local balls, Young began to permit and even encourage dancing—including mixed dancing—in, of all places, the newly completed Nauvoo Temple. In the winter of 1845–46, Young initiated all-day ritual sessions in the temple, at the close of which instruments were taken from their cases to accompany square dances in the building's upper story.

Young legitimized the dances in three ways. First, he said that those who built the temple should be able to recreate themselves in it however they wished. Second, he said that, without gentile influences, the Saints in the temple could "worship God in the dance, as well as in other ways." Third, he likened dancing to the New Testament apostles' practice of "shaking the dust off their feet" as a testimony against those who would not receive them.[14] How tentative Young really felt about dancing, however, became clear within days of his express sanction of the practice, when he summarily prohibited any further dancing in the temple, "lest the brethren and sisters be carried away by levity."[15]

In diaries and accounts of the Saints' journey westward one finds countless references to dancing. Young seems to have tolerated, and even encouraged, dancing as a means of relaxation and, perhaps more urgently, of keeping warm at night.[16] On 14 January 1847, at the Saints' winter stopover in Nebraska, Young delivered a written revelation to the Saints which, for the first time, formally sanctioned Mormon dancing in the name of the Lord: "If thou art merry, praise the Lord with singing, with music, with dancing and with a prayer of praise and thanksgiving."[17] Young in turn ritualized this divine dancing at their newly built hall nine days after the revelation was given. On the afternoon of 23 January 1847, after making a short speech, Young called members of the church hierarchy into the middle of the floor, arranged them in squares, had them uncover their heads, and began to pray that God would accept the evening's offering of dance, a procedure which, according to one of the apostles, "was set as a pattern" of how to "dance before the Lord." As the band began to play, another attendant noted in his diary, "the whole house appeared to me to be filled with the melodious sounds of the inspired harps of Heaven."[18] This evening's offering appears to have given rise to the neo-biblical way in which the Saints for some time thereafter referred to dancing—"going forth in the dance."

Subsequent preachments on dance during the trek west were often guarded. In March Young ordered church leaders to stop dancing and devote more attention to prayer and ordinances. In April the apostles wrote to the Saints in St. Louis to "let dancing alone; else it would prove a snare and a trap in which the enemy would catch many souls." And in late May Young warned those who were "giving way" to dancing that they were to "cease their folly and turn to the Lord."[19]

But the "pattern" had been set by Young, and the Mormon love of dancing blossomed early in Utah. It was employed in celebrations of all kinds, holidays, birthdays, weddings, building dedications, during intermissions of plays, and most often perhaps, in simple impromptu soirées. The style of this pioneer dancing was eloquently described by a witness: "None of your minuets or other mortuary processions of gentles in etiquette . . . but the spirited and scientific displays of our venerated and merry grandparents. . . . executed with the spirit of people too happy to be slow, or bashful, or constrained."[20]

Young discussed the subject of dancing on many occasions, almost always with evident pride in the Saints' ability to consecrate a sinful practice from the world outside. Mormons had long boasted of their faith's unconventional ways, and dancing was considered, in the words of one Saint, a way of "shucking off some traditions."[21] Early in the trek westward, Brigham Young advanced the notion that dancing and other amusements were sinful only to those with impure hearts. With characteristic excess, Young said that, to the wicked, even praying was sinful. But to good Saints, especially those who helped build the structures in which dancing was enacted, no evil could be imputed for dancing; they had earned the right to dance by their righteous labor.[22]

Young's critique of sectarian policies toward fiddling and dancing were frequent, verbose, and often comical. A sampling of these diatribes, from the 1850s and 1860s, suggests their scope and typical tone:

1852: In many places [Christian] folly and superstition are so great that they would consider they had committed the sin of blasphemy if they happened to hear a *violin*. . . . In the first place, some wise being organized my system, and gave me my capacity, put into my heart and brain something that . . . fills me with rapture at the sound of sweet music. *I* did not put it there. . . . It was the Lord, our heavenly Father, who gave the capacity to enjoy these sounds, and which *we* ought to do in His name, and to His glory. But the greater portion of the sectarian world consider it sacrilege to give way to any such pleasure as even to listen to sweet music, much more to dance to its delightful strains.

1854: Many preachers of the day have said that fidling & music Came from Hell. But I say that . . . their is not a fiddler in hell or any music of any kind. Music belongs in heaven to cheer God, Angel, & man. . . . the Devel has Stolen music & many other things that was ordained of God for the Benefit of man & has turned it to an evil use but music & danceing is for the Benefit of the Holy ones.

1860: Every decent fiddler will go into a decent kingdom.

1862: Tight-laced religious professors of the present generation have a horror at the sound of a fiddle. There is no music in hell, for all good music belongs to heaven. . . . Every sweet musical sound that can be made belongs to the Saints and is for the Saints.[23]

The vigor of Young's attacks on sectarian traditions suggests how prevalent such traditions must have been in the church. Protestant dogma hardly could help but linger in a church so intent on converting and gathering Protestants. Like Young, many members had been raised amid intolerance for fiddling. Indeed, some of the most prominent Mormon musicians (e.g., the Hancock brothers) destroyed their fiddles before joining the church; others continued to play, but felt guilty about it.[24] Even in light of Young's love of fiddle music, many church leaders remained cautious. One apostle claimed in 1848 that he took more pleasure in Brigham's own sermons than in "hearing a million dollars worth of fiddle strings worn out."[25]

But the rise of dancing in the church, Young's praise of the fiddle's sweetness and divinity, and perhaps even the rumor that Joseph Smith had played some fiddle[26] seem to have allayed performers' sense of guilt and allowed them to consecrate their instruments to God, a practice that can be traced at least to the Nauvoo period. During one of the Nauvoo Temple dances, for example, the Danish fiddler Hans C. Hanson made a speech in which he confessed to the folly of playing for the wicked (he apparently included the Mansion House dances). He swore henceforth to play only for the Saints. When he went on a mission, he said, he would even leave his fiddle with the Saints for their use.[27] Young, however, took Hanson along in the first company of pioneers and kept him near his own wagon, to play for dances along the way.

As dancing became more popular in Deseret, fiddlers and other dance musicians were praised for their work. The *Deseret News* called the quadrilles, reels, and jigs played at a twenty-fourth of July celebration "the healing balm of music's holiest strains."[28] More important, the dance musicians found steady wages, though remuneration took various forms. Usually players were paid in goods—meat, flour, or molasses, with a bushel or more of wheat being a typical night's wages for a single musician. Those who could play "by note" (many of them members of the Nauvoo and

Ballo bands) could demand cash for their services because they could read the latest sheet music from the East Coast.[29] Except for those dances sponsored by Brigham Young, in which musicians appear to have donated their talent, dancers usually had to pay their way into public balls, either with barter or coins (ten cents was a typical admission price).[30]

Aside from fiddles, other instruments—accordions, concertinas, bagpipes, flutes, and so on—also accompanied dances. Other, less conventional means were also used: solo singing, whistling, and even comb playing.[31] The need for instruments created during this time a small but steady music industry in the territory. Violins and viols of all sizes began to be made by regional craftsmen, many of whom were Scandinavian immigrants.[32] In Great Salt Lake City merchants imported wagonloads of instruments, music sheets, and books for an eager public. The Mormon's love of dancing also created a powerful demand for music lessons and the established players took in pupils by the dozen.

At least one of the church apostles actually considered the new surge of dancing a fulfillment of ancient prophecy, and the *Deseret News* rewrote a verse of Psalm 133 in describing one dance: "Behold! how good and how pleasant it is for brethren, or young saints to DANCE together in unity."[33] But Young maintained that the people must not elevate dancing to a sacred rite. He observed that, "when compared with the eternal realities of our holy religion, [dance is] like chaff to the sterling wheat; the one contains the essentials of life, the other is comparatively valueless."[34] He tried to keep the connection between religion and dance tenuous: "When we come to the things of God, I had rather not have them mixed up with amusement like a dish of sucotash."[35] Fearful that a kind of Shakerism might infest the church, Young reprimanded attempts to make dancing an ordinance of the faith or of the temple, although he clearly had provided the essential rationale for such attempts.[36]

Conversant as he apparently was with liberal arguments being put forth in the States for making dancing a part of public education, Young argued that dancing was best used to provide invigorating exercise.[37] At the same time he would brook no excess of physical stimulation. Bishop Newel Whitney expressed in a homespun way the evolving church position toward exceptionally fervent dancing by remarking that "when we dance we should do it as much by the spirit as we would pray. . . . we must not get giddy, nor transcend the bounds of reason and right, or we will get out of the way, and have to fall back and hunt up a position of right again."[38] A Mormon lyric of this period, set to the tune of "God Save the King," invoked God thus:

Let mirth & jollity,
Joy and hilarity,
Bow at thy nod.
When we engage to play,
As we do now this day,
Let not our spirits stray,
From thee, our God.[39]

Young himself in a more colorful way decried what he thought was the excessive merriment of some of the Saints who danced, deriding church elders who would "dance as niggers. . . . they will hoe down all, turn summersets, dance on their knees, and haw, haw, out loud."[40] The desire to maintain decorum while at the same time getting the full "healthful" benefit created among the Mormons a style that Richard Burton found remarkable in his 1861 visit. He observed that " 'positions' are maintained, steps are elaborately executed, and a somewhat severe muscular exercise is the result."[41]

With excessively vigorous dancing discouraged, the Saints turned to dancing masters to teach acceptable steps. Soon, many Saints became obsessed with dancing *well.* Despite his reservations about overindulgence in the dance, Young enlisted trained dancers to travel throughout the settlements in order to teach steps and calls with proper priesthood supervision.[42] John Hyde, an English proselyte who left the church after immigrating to Utah, lamented the rise of these Mormon dancing schools. He complained that dancing masters were demanding their wages in advance, while general schoolmasters in the territory often went unpaid. "Their children *ought* to learn to read," he wrote, "but they *must* learn to dance." He went on to observe that, in the winter of 1854–55, dancing schools were held in virtually all of Great Salt Lake City's nineteen schoolhouses, "and necessarily so much more attention to dancing involved so much less attention to study."[43] Mormon apostle Orson Pratt, whose son became one of the most notable local musicians, complained similarly about the attention being given to dance education, whatever its healthful effects may have been: "Think of the time consumed in learning how to take every step properly, when it might be used to a hundred times more profit. . . . If our minds are neglected, I do not care how graceful the body may be, the usefulness is not there."[44]

Young agreed, and as part of the church reformation begun in 1856 he endeavored to stop all dancing parties and theatricals in the territory. The results of this ban appear to have delighted him, for he wrote to one of the apostles in January 1857 that, since proscribing the amusements, "the peace and contentment among the saints is Greater than you have ever witnessed, they appear more willing to do as they are told to abide counsel."[45] The ban seems to have eased gradually within the year. By Christmas 1857 Young allowed faithful Saints to dance, but "those that drink whisky, will lie, steal & commit adultery, betray their Brethren, act the hypocrit, & so on amoung this People have no liberty from me to dance & furthermore I forbid them from Dancing."[46]

Some Mormons wished the ban to continue, perhaps in the spirit of the "Great Revival" of 1858, which sought to repress dancing throughout the nation. David Calder revealed a more basic wish in his call for the ban to continue. He wrote to a friend in the fall of 1858 that "if there are no . . . dances nor theatre during winter, it will nearly kill [the local gentiles]. Hope it will freeze them out of the territory."[47] But the Mormon passion for dancing prevailed and dancing resumed, if indeed it had ever fully ceased. On the return of dancing and theatricals the *Deseret News* acidly observed in 1859 that "if any particular good or benefit has accrued to the community or those who have gone forth in the dance, [we] have not been advised."[48] Yet in 1860 the paper returned to the celebration of dancing, calling the practice "the poetry of motion" and even "a feast to the mind."[49] And in February of that year one Mormon summed up his impressions of a dance at the Social Hall: "A more heavenly feeling I never enjoyed."[50]

Two occasions for scandal worried the Mormon faithful: drunkenness and seduction. The fight of church leaders against mixing liquor with dancing apparently had scant success in early Utah. Dancing schools seem to have attracted imbibers.[51] And diaries of the period contain many accounts of parties marred by drunken dancers or of Mormon girls who had their hearts broken by young men stealing out for a drink between tunes. In St. George (southern Utah), the problem grew especially grievous, in part because the dance floor of the opera house sat over the local wine cellar and aromas pervaded the whole edifice.[52]

Church leaders generally attributed the problem of seduction to "round dancing." Square dancing, of course, allowed for little intimacy because partners were continually changing hands. The waltz, mazurka, polka, and other round dances, however, allowed the male partner's hand to rest for long spells on a female's waist. Like most of their sectarian contemporaries, Mormon leaders abhorred the "lewdness" of a practice in which a couple simulated a public embrace. During the 1850s and 1860s, and particularly after the completion of the transcontinental railroad in 1869, modern dance fashions flowed into Utah and appeared in the dancing schools of both Mormon and gentile masters.[53] In his last years (1870–77), Young tried to remove such dances from Deseret, although, with typical diplomacy, he allowed for one or two round dances to be played at each dance party, for the benefit of foreign-born immigrants who might not be able to appreciate American-style square dancing.[54]

Young's policy, of course, virtually assured that every dance held in the territory would have at least some round dancing. Furthermore, second-generation Mormons, the principal patrons of the dances, hungered for the elegance of the waltz, attracted to its relatively relaxed manner of execution, its refreshing three-beat meter (as contrasted with the near-constant twos and fours of the square dances), and, of course, its enhanced occasion for romance. According to one participant, these sanctioned waltzes were not so intimate as the waltzes of the gentiles: instead, they were "straight forward . . . [with] none of your clasping close and young ladies reclining in the arms of young men."[55] Nonetheless the church hierarchy found the round dances threatening even as their children found them attractive. The attitude of the latter is expressed in a Mormon song from about 1870:

> To balls and parties I oft go,
> For dancing I admire,
> And waltzing is the thing, I own,
> Of which I never tire.
> And should my partner squeeze my hand
> I know what I'm about;
> It pleases him and it don't hurt me,
> I'm the merriest girl that's out.[56]

In addition to discouraging round dances, Young also tried to eliminate late-night dancing, which depleted health, he felt, rather than fostering it. Several Mormon diaries contain accounts of dances which lasted into the early hours of the morning or even till daybreak (though these were sometimes to avoid freezing during bitter weather).[57] An early visitor to Utah noted as well that the Mormons' "private balls and soirées are frequently extended beyond the time of cock-crowing by the younger members, and the remains of the evening repast furnishes the breakfast."[58] In the 1870s Young called upon the Saints to begin dances in the afternoon in order that they might end in the early evening. The plan failed, though, since generally only women could attend during daylight hours—the men stayed at work.[59]

The *Juvenile Instructor,* the journal of the church's Sunday schools, praised Young's determination to suppress dancing. While conceding that dancing could promote health, the magazine nevertheless attacked current Mormon practice in language identical to that being used in the nation at large. No longer the "simple, innocent, sociable gatherings of brethren and sisters" that once pervaded the territory, the new balls had been "perverted into fashionable, formal, extravagant" affairs; dances had become worldly and fatiguing seductions rather than the wholesome amusements they were designed to be. The *Instructor* then appealed to the Mormons' sense of loyalty by insisting that "every young person who has . . . pride or ambition [to be a good Saint] will have no other feeling than gratitude towards President Young for his care and solicitude for their welfare. They will not consider it any deprivation to be prohibited from dancing during the whole of the night, or from indulging in round dances."[60]

But a young patron of dances in southern Utah recalled that, not only did all the girls there continue to waltz and polka with their heavy-booted suitors, but they sometimes skipped school in order to rest and conserve strength for late-night dancing.[61] And some dance musicians themselves, if the diary of one of them gives any indication, spent more time at balls than at Sunday School.[62] Outraged by this continual flouting of education, Young tersely told an Idaho congregation in 1873, "Instead of going 'right and left, balance all, promenade,' go to work and teach yourselves something. Instead of having this folly, I want to have schools and entertain the minds of the people and draw them out to learn the arts and sciences."[63]

As one might expect, the greatest champions of education in the territory were often the most resistant to attacks on modern fashion. They consequently entertained somewhat liberal views toward round dancing. The short-lived *Utah Musical Times,* for instance, carried an editorial in 1878 that, using terms which unmistakably referred to round dancing, praised what it termed "the art of dancing." It condemned "certain over-righteous persons" who would find fault with any sort of dancing, except for that which was indulged to excess. Indeed, the only suggestion the editors made respecting current practice in Utah was that balls should be seasoned with more concert music, with a ratio of about one hour of listening to two or three hours of dancing.[64]

Meanwhile, the *Deseret News* published on 16 January 1877 the sternest attack on "mixed dancing parties" ever delivered in Utah. It cited police records to the effect that several girls had been "ruined" by attending such gatherings and alerted parents to the growing evil of the waltz's intoxicating embrace. The editorialist then discussed a New York authority who questioned the judgment of parents who allowed their children to frequent dances. The editorial closed with the warning that allowing girls to attend mixed dances was consenting to "a danger worse than death." "Every girl who has not utterly lost her self-respect," it added, "should recognize that in scenes of [this] kind she will certainly sacrifice it and perhaps her innocence also."

Young's death in August 1877 brought the well-bred hymn writer John Taylor to the head of the church. Some may have expected the succession to moderate church policy toward round dancing. But Taylor, who probably had written the old *Times and Seasons* editorial on dancing, quickly redoubled church opposition to round dancing on the grounds of both modesty and "hygiene" (although the menace of the latter went unexplained). Within two months of assuming the reins (and coincident with a national Catholic backlash against round dancing), Taylor issued an epistle on "Dancing Parties and Amusements." In it he reiterated Young's warning that round dances tend to demoralize (as well as Young's allowance for one or two a night) and made a fresh call for bishops and for the young men's and young women's associations of the church to police their affairs.[65]

At the same time the *Deseret News* sermonized on its own against the practice. It responded to the argument (adapted from Brigham Young's statements on dancing in general) that only the impure could be tainted by round dancing with the simple observation that these "whirling, giddy, seductive" dances were in their very form immodest. Then, allowing that there may be some who could round dance without immoral thoughts, it called for those innocent practitioners to abandon the waltz for the sake of their weaker brothers and sisters.[66] Many who found the dances innocuous complained at such a sacrifice, though they seldom balked at making at least a pretense of abstinence. One local church leader—later an apostle—responded to his stake president's call to abandon round dancing with profound sorrow, since, as he wrote, he "prefer[red] to engage in the round dance rather than to sit down to an elaborate and sumptuous banquet." Only those who had mastered round dancing, he argued, could know what robust pleasure it could afford.[67]

Ironically, it was just when the church was suffering its most intense persecution from moralists for its practice of polygamy that it joined its persecutors in moralizing against round dancing. At the same time the church leaders heatedly defended plural marriage and went into hiding to escape prosecution, they also allied themselves with non-Mormons in the national outrage against the waltz, mazurka, and polka. Perhaps bending over backward to assure the gentiles of their high morality, Mormon leaders echoed the anti–round dance rhetoric of their sectarian persecutors.[68] Indeed, *The Contributor* approvingly cited a gentile who called the waltz "the dance of death" itself.[69] But more important to church leaders than the moral argument was the very question of obedience. In 1884 apostle George Q. Cannon wrote for the *Juvenile Instructor* an editorial rebuking those who questioned church counsel on round dancing, insisting that the charge not to waltz should be received as unquestioningly as God's command not to eat the fruit of the tree of knowledge.[70]

Throughout the territory committees formed to supervise dances and "get [them] under the control of the Priesthood."[71] Dance parties came to be judged "official" or "unofficial" by local bishops or committeemen, who were instructed to scrutinize the steps and assure that no immodesty was transacted. To hold an impromptu, renegade dance became a transgression, and violators were tried for their membership.[72] Regulations were drawn up of which the following were typical: dances must be overseen by bishops, must not be organized to make money, must begin and end with prayer, must not last past midnight, and must not allow liquor or "swinging with one arm around the ladies" (upon possible penalty of expulsion from the ball).[73]

In the end, it was the fear that young Mormons might balk at such regulations and desert the church-sponsored balls in favor of gentile parties that brought church leaders gradually to allow round dancing as a matter of course. In 1890 the old counsel to allow two round dances to be played at each dance was reformulated: now each *person* at a dance was allowed to dance two round dances a night, a new situation that displeased some apostles.[74] By 1900 only two local congregations (Bear Lake, Utah, and Juarez, Mexico) still prohibited round dancing. Many young Mormons had insisted on their right to dance according to the latest fashion. The First Presidency acknowledged that it was losing its influence over this matter and reaffirmed its position that it would be better to allow round dances than to drive young people into the company of the wicked. At least one apostle told the priesthood leaders of Juarez that "[I] have not seen the great sin in waltzing" and suggested that the church would either have to forbid the practice altogether or sanction it: "I want to predict that the time will come when this stake of Zion will admit of Waltzing or else the other stakes of Zion will discontinue it."[75]

The apostle's prediction came true as even the most recalcitrant congregations gave up their bans on waltzing. Allowing round dances among Zion's youth was an expediency adopted for the sake of keeping the youth within the fold. In the ensuing years debates over new dance forms overwhelmed the long-standing round dance controversies. The conflict between steadfastness and expediency would continue to trouble the Mormons' goings forth in the dance.

NOTES

1. On American dancing see Joseph E. Marks, *America Learns to Dance* (New York: Exposition Press, 1957). On Puritans and dance see Percy Scholes, *The Puritans and Music in England and New England* (London: Oxford University Press, 1934), pp. 58–80. On the general Protestant attitude toward dance see Martin E. Marty, *Protestantism* (New York: Holt, Rinehart and Winston, 1972), pp. 230–31. For other treatments of Mormonism and dance see Davis Bitton, " 'These Licentious Days': Dancing among the Mormons," *Sunstone* 2 (Spring 1977): 16–27; Leona Holbrook, "Dancing as an Aspect of Early Mormon and

Utah Culture," *Brigham Young University Studies* 16 (Autumn 1975): 117–38; "Dancing—A Pioneer Recreation," in Kate B. Carter, ed., *Treasures of Pioneer History*, 6 vols. (Salt Lake City: Daughters of the Utah Pioneers, 1952–57), 2:345–404; Ruth E. Yasko, "An Historical Study of Pioneer Dancing in Utah" (Master's thesis, University of Utah, 1947); and Karl E. Wesson, "Dance in the Church of Jesus Christ of Latter-day Saints, 1830–1940" (Master's thesis, Brigham Young University, 1975).

2. Helen Mar Whitney, *WE* 12 (15 September 1883): 58.

3. *HC* 2:519–20.

4. "Experiences and Memories of James Jepson, 1816–1882," typescript in HBLL, p. 1. Even into the 1850s, one British Mormon claimed, "We had lain the world aside and we were not thinking of our worldly pleasures . . . & we had no dancing in those days for pleasure, but we were very happy in the enjoyment of the gospel" ("Biographical Sketch of the Life of Priscilla Merriman Evans," typescript in HBLL).

5. "A Short Sketch of the Rise of the Young Gentlemen and Ladies Relief Society of Nauvoo," *TS* 4 (1 April 1843): 155.

6. Heber C. Kimball, *TS* 5 (1 November 1844): 694.

7. See Joseph Smith Diary, 15 January 1844; and Helen Mar Whitney in *WE* 11 (15 November 1882): 90; and 12 (1 September 1883): 50. See also her remarks in *WE* 11 (1 March 1883): 146; and 12 (1 November 1883): 82.

8. *TS* 5 (1 March 1844): 459–60.

9. Horace G. Whitney, "Nauvoo Brass Band," p. 135.

10. See Zimmerman, *I Knew the Prophets*, pp. 19–20.

11. *TS* 5 (1 November 1844): 694.

12. *TS* 5 (1 October 1844): 669. This advice helped spur the building of the Nauvoo Music Hall.

13. *DN,* 12 March 1862, and *JD* 2:94.

14. See *WE* 12 (1 September 1883): 50 and *HC* 7:557, 561, 564.

15. Elden J. Watson, ed., *Manuscript History of Brigham Young, 1846–47* (Salt Lake City: Published by the Author, 1971), p. 9.

16. *William Clayton's Journal*, p. 116 (30 April 1847). Keeping warm remained a powerful impetus to the dance in Mormon culture. See especially the account in *OPH* 15:42.

17. Doctrine and Covenants 136:28.

18. Charles Kelly, ed., *Journals of John D. Lee, 1846–47 and 1859* (Salt Lake City: University of Utah Press, 1984), p. 56, and *WWJ* 3:123 (see also 3:124, 126).

19. See Watson, *Manuscript History of Brigham Young*, pp. 537, 546, 555.

20. Thomas L. Kane, *The Mormons*, pp. 30–31.

21. Kelly, *Journals of John D. Lee*, p. 95.

22. Ibid., p. 71. See also Watson, *Manuscript History of Brigham Young*, pp. 520–21.

23. Respectively, the citations are from *JD* 1:48, *WWJ* 4:239, *JD* 8:178, and *JD* 9:244.

24. See the autobiographical "Life of Levi Hancock," holograph in HDC, in

which Levi recalls that after a revival his brother Solomon "took his violin and broak it and I burned it." See also Martha Cox Autobiography, typescript in HBLL, pp. 2–3.

25. *WWJ* 3:319.

26. See John Hyde, Jr., *Mormonism: Its Leaders and Designs*, 2nd ed. (New York: W. P. Fatridge, 1857), p. 119.

27. See *WE* 12 (1 September 1883): 50.

28. 26 July 1851.

29. See for example Charles Olsen Autobiography, passim.

30. See for example "Biographical Sketch of John Nielsen," typescript in HBLL, p. 31.

31. See *OPH* 1:220–21 and 8:456.

32. See for example "Autobiography of James H. Martineau," typescript in HBLL, p. 11, and "Sketch of Dell Cox," typescript in HBLL, passim.

33. *WWJ* 3:126 and *DN*, 17 May 1851.

34. *JD* 3:107.

35. *JD* 9:194 (9 February 1862).

36. Young said on one occasion that the only "lawful" place to dance was in a temple or similar sacred house (*WWJ* 3:309).

37. Ibid. See also his sermon in *DN*, 11 January 1851: "Dancing is only to exercise the body, to enable it to attend to things of greater importance."

38. *WE* 14 (1 July 1885): 18.

39. Ca. 1867, typescript in Taylor Papers.

40. Young did add, "I don't mean this as debasing the negroes by any means." See *William Clayton's Journal*, p. 196 (29 May 1847). Brigham's brother Joseph, himself a fervent dancer on occasion, warned an 1848 congregation against being overtaken by "the spirit of dancing" (*WWJ* 3:318–19).

41. Burton, *City of the Saints*, p. 253.

42. See *OPH* 2:492–93; 15:337. See also Brigham Young's positive remarks on learning dance steps, quoted in Roberta Reese Asahina, "Brigham Young and the Salt Lake Theater, 1862–1877" (Ph.D. diss., Tufts University, 1980), p. 183. The shame felt by those who could not dance may be sensed in the diary of a pioneer who after displaying "blunders by the dozen" in his dancing, wrote that "the ring of the music had vanished from my mind, but it leaves many unpleasant . . . thoughts, of the dance and human frailties in general" (W. H. Dusenberry Diary, excerpts in *OPH* 1:238).

43. Hyde, *Mormonism*, p. 120.

44. *JD*, 3:293.

45. Young to John Taylor, 26 January 1857, Taylor Papers.

46. Robert Glass Cleland and Juanita Brooks, eds., *A Mormon Chronicle: The Diaries of John D. Lee, 1848-1876*, 2 vols. (Salt Lake City: University of Utah Press, 1983), 1:139.

47. Calder to Bro. Stenhouse, 15 October 1858, Calder Letterpress Copybook.

48. 28 December 1859.

49. "The Ball Room," *DN*, 26 December 1860.

50. Joseph Beecroft Journal, 17 February 1860.

51. See Larson and Larson, *Diary of Charles Walker,* 1:105 (cf. 1:158).
52. "Life Sketch of Mary Ann Mansfield Bentley," typescript in HBLL, p. 14.
53. See the account of introducing the waltz into a Mormon village, *OPH* 8:473. See also the episode involving Diantha Clayton, who waltzed with a gentile in 1850, Allen, *Trials of Discipleship,* pp. 253–56.
54. See Charles Olsen Autobiography, p. 62.
55. Martha Cox Autobiography, p. 34.
56. *OPH* 7:397.
57. See *OPH* 15:42.
58. Gunnison, *The Mormons,* pp. 74–75.
59. See Margaret Robertson Salmon Autobiography, excerpts published in *OPH* 11:256.
60. *JI* 11 (15 February 1876): 42.
61. Martha Cox Autobiography, pp. 34–35.
62. See "Sketch of Dell Cox," p. 63. A fiddler and fiddlemaker in Orderville, Utah, Cox records that from 5 March to 31 December 1876 he attended fifteen Sunday schools and sixteen dances.
63. *JD* 16:170. See also the *Juvenile Instructor* editorial asking that young Mormons stop dancing so much and devote themselves to "intellectual enjoyment," *JI* 17 (15 January 1882): 24.
64. "Music and Dancing," *Utah Musical Times* 2 (1 February 1878): 169–70.
65. *DN,* 28 November 1877. Cf. "The Festive Season," *DN,* 13 November 1877.
66. 3 October 1877.
67. Rudger Clawson, Memoirs, photocopy of typescript in UHS, pp. 22–23.
68. See "Round Dancing," *DN,* 3 October 1877 (citing Catholics); "Denouncing a Fashionable Evil," *DN,* 29 May 1878 (Episcopalians); the article by "L. Y. D.," "Dancing—When a Demoralizing Practice," Herbert J. Foulger Diary, manuscript in HDC. Cf. the moderating of a Methodist attack on dancing, *DN,* 27 January 1875.
69. *Contributor* 8 (January 1887): 115. See also "Recreations and Amusements," *Contributor* 10 (January 1889): 81–84.
70. *JI* 19 (15 February 1884): 56.
71. W. D. Johnson to L. John Nuttall, 15 January 1884, Nuttall Papers, HBLL. See also John Taylor's 1882 instructions in James R. Clark, *Messages of the First Presidency of the Church of Jesus Christ of Latter-day Saints,* 6 vols. (Salt Lake City: Bookcraft, 1965–1975), 3:121–22.
72. See Nels Anderson, *Desert Saints: The Mormon Frontier in Utah* (University of Chicago Press, 1966), p. 424.
73. See Russell R. Rich, *Land of the Sky-Blue Water: A History of the L.D.S. Settlement of the Bear Lake Valley* (Provo: Brigham Young University Press, 1963), p. 108. Some of the information in the following paragraph derives from this source, pp. 104–12.
74. See the diary entries for 6 December 1890 and 3 January 1891 in Melvin Clarence Merrill, ed., *Utah Pioneer and Apostle Marriner Wood Merrill and His Family* (Salt Lake City: Published by the Editor, 1937), pp. 134, 136–37.

75. For these statements and a discussion of the First Presidency's feelings on the matter, see the priesthood meeting minutes in Juarez Stake Records, 18 May 1901 and 10 December 1906, microfilm of holograph in HDC.

William Wines Phelps, early Mormon poet and adapter of hymn texts. Courtesy Library-Archives, Historical Department of the Church of Jesus Christ of Latter-day Saints.

A mid-1860s portrait of a Mormon brass band led by Ebenezer Beesley in Salt Lake City. Courtesy Library-Archives, Historical Department of the Church of Jesus Christ of Latter-day Saints.

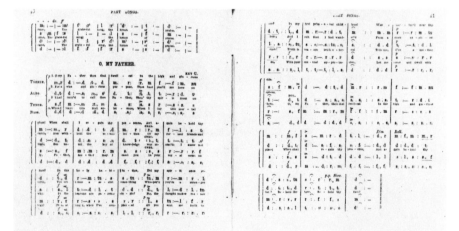

Pages from David Calder's 1862 Tonic Sol-fa songbook, showing the new notation endorsed by Brigham Young—here applied to one of Young's favorite songs, "O My Father." Courtesy Harold B. Lee Library, Brigham Young University.

An unidentified Mormon band on a horse-drawn carriage typical of those used for pioneer parades. Courtesy Harold B. Lee Library, Brigham Young University.

"Professor" Charles John Thomas, Mormon hymn composer, orchestra leader, and choir conductor. Courtesy Harold B. Lee Library, Brigham Young University.

A page from a soprano partbook in C. J. Thomas's collection, showing a verse and chorus from Thomas's own "Saints' National Anthem." Courtesy Library-Archives, Historical Department of the Church of Jesus Christ of Latter-day Saints.

John Tullidge, Mormon hymn composer, vocal trainer, and music critic. Courtesy Library-Archives, Historical Department of the Church of Jesus Christ of Latter-day Saints.

A small orchestra that played at the Salt Lake Theatre, 1865, after Brigham Young agreed to pay them for playing. The three violinists are (left to right): Ebenezer Beesley, David Evans, and George Careless. Courtesy Library-Archives, Historical Department of the Church of Jesus Christ of Latter-day Saints.

The first page of one of the many "home compositions" published in the 1870s in Utah. Courtesy Harold B. Lee Library, Brigham Young University.

The Tabernacle Choir, New Year's Day, 1884, with conductor Ebenezer Beesley (full-bearded) sitting in the front. The book that many members are holding is the first published book of anthems for the choir. Courtesy Library-Archives, Historical Department of the Church of Jesus Christ of Latter-day Saints.

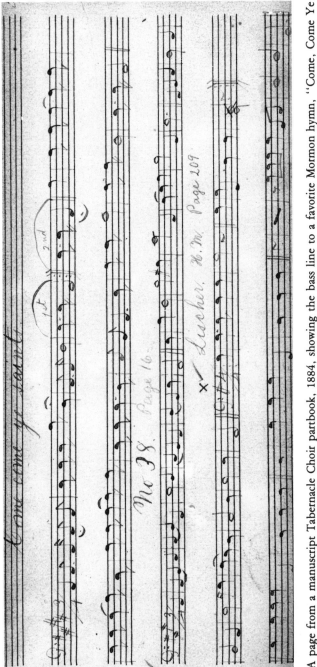

A page from a manuscript Tabernacle Choir partbook, 1884, showing the bass line to a favorite Mormon hymn, "Come, Come Ye Saints." Singers would read the words from their pocket-sized hymnbooks. Courtesy Harold B. Lee Library, Brigham Young University.

Evan Stephens (arms outstretched) astride the train that carried the Tabernacle Choir on its controversial 1911 East Coast tour. Courtesy Library-Archives, Historical Department of the Church of Jesus Christ of Latter-day Saints.

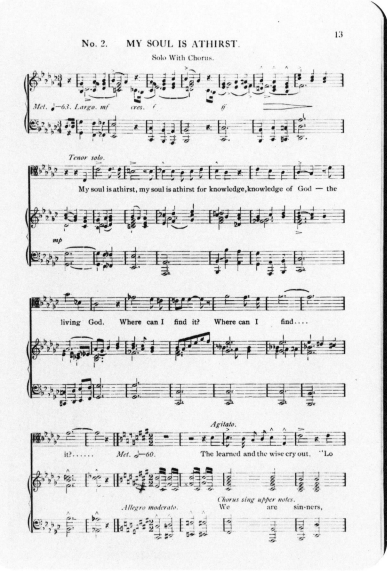

A characteristic sample of Evan Stephens's music, a page from *The Visions*. This number depicts Joseph Smith praying to know which church to join. Courtesy Library-Archives, Historical Department of the Church of Jesus Christ of Latter-day Saints.

Tony Lund, popular Mormon music teacher and director of the Tabernacle Choir during its early radio days. Courtesy Library-Archives, Historical Department of the Church of Jesus Christ of Latter-day Saints.

Tracy Cannon, hymn composer and longtime leader of the Church Music Committee. Courtesy Library-Archives, Historical Department of the Church of Jesus Christ of Latter-day Saints.

A radio broadcast of "Music and the Spoken Word" with Spencer Cornwall directing the Tabernacle Choir, many of whose male members are seen here wearing military uniforms. Courtesy Library-Archives, Historical Department of the Church of Jesus Christ of Latter-day Saints.

Five apostles practicing male-arrangements of Mormon hymns during the preparation of the 1948 hymn-book. Harold B. Lee, adviser to the Church Music Committee, is at the piano. Standing are (left to right): Mark E. Petersen, Matthew Cowley, Spencer W. Kimball, and Ezra Taft Benson. Courtesy Library-Archives, Historical Department of the Church of Jesus Christ of Latter-day Saints.

A page from Leroy Robertson's Oratorio from the Book of Mormon. Courtesy Marriott Library, University of Utah, and Marian Robertson Wilson.

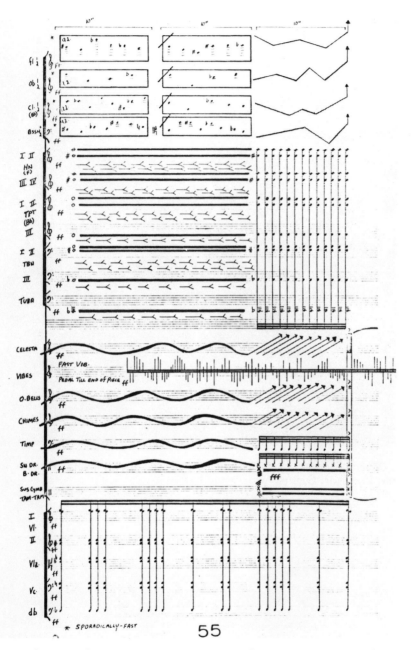

55

A page from David Sargent's oratorio *Apostasy and Restoration*. Courtesy of the composer.

The Osmond family with presidents Jimmy Carter and Spencer Kimball (bottom right) in the Tabernacle. Courtesy Wide World Photos.

6

The Immigrant Professors

On the evening of 6 March 1862, four months before Lincoln signed the federal anti-bigamy law, Brigham Young sat with several of his wives in his new theater, listening to the choir and band perform a dedicatory piece. The text of the new anthem (written by one of Young's wives) was titled "God Bless Brigham Young." The orchestra conductor, Charles John Thomas, had composed the music in the style of a patriotic air and had dubbed it "The Saints' National Anthem." Like "The Star-Spangled Banner," which preceded it on the program, it drew wild applause (though Thomas observed that the fiercely patriotic Saints would have applauded the anthems "no matter how they had been played, or by whom"[1]). The air not only summarized the Saints' feelings about their spiritual leader and artistic patron, Brigham Young, it introduced many people in the city to the work of Thomas. Fondly known as "C. J.," the conductor and composer was the first of a line of immigrant music professors who would try to edify the Mormon nation with European-style concert music.

While proselyting in Britain in 1840, the Mormon apostles visited theaters, royal pageants, and elaborate Protestant musical services. Young and his frontier-bred colleagues wrote enthusiastically about what they heard. Wilford Woodruff, for example, wrote in his diary, concerning the Concerts d'Hiver at the Theatre Royal: "It manifested the greatest perfection in music of any thing known. . . . By having a view of it it gave us a knowledge of the art of man, & what could be perfected with instruments of music."[2]

Such "perfection" struck the apostles as necessary for Zion—a place that must advance in culture until it became the kingdom of God on earth. Joseph Smith had taught that salvation consisted of eternal progress, chiefly mental progress.[3] Brigham Young repeated this theme throughout his life, continually berating those converts whom he deemed "first-rate Methodists" (i.e., Mormons who felt ill-inclined to improve their secular learning).[4] Seeking the sophistication he had admired in Britain, Young encouraged C. J. Thomas not only to enrich the Saints' amusements, but also to refine their tastes.

By choosing the thirty-year-old Thomas to conduct the all-volunteer orchestra of his theater, Brigham Young may also have hoped to appeal to the vast British public in Mormondom and to impress the attentive East Coast press, who scrutinized developments in Great Salt Lake City on a weekly basis. A London-trained conductor at the helm of the city's theater would enhance the reputation of the city among gentiles. Thomas had wide experience in theater music. He made his first public appearance at nine years old playing French horn at Newcastle-upon-Tyne's Theatre Royal, studied harmony with Covent Garden's composer–violinist John Thirlwall, and toured with Karl Anschutz's Italian opera company in the early 1850s, shortly after converting to Mormonism.

Young organized the theater orchestra less than three weeks after Thomas's arrival in the valley. Thomas took over Ballo's band at the same time and, according to the *Deseret News,* manifestly improved it.[5] Moreover, two weeks after Young heard Thomas conduct the Fourteenth Ward choir alongside Calder's singing school group and the Tabernacle Choir, the Mormon leader dropped James Smithies as conductor of the Tabernacle Choir and called Thomas to that post.[6] Because Young felt that only free service would sanctify musical entertainment, Professor Thomas led the orchestra, band, and choir without pay. The only remuneration for his work was the occasional use of the theater (to hold benefit concerts for himself) and the endorsement of Young when acquiring private students.

The orchestra also played free. The year before the theater was built a speaker at the Social Hall paid homage to the orchestra's long-standing devotion to music making with the observation that "no class of public servants are so justly entitled to favor as Musicians; they are expected always to be in tune, on all public occasions in the true Mormon style, without purse, or even city scrip."[7] This "Mormon style" prevailed under Thomas without protest except for the bitter complaint of the first violinist David Evans, who in an 1864 Deseret Dramatic Association meeting hoisted himself up on his crutches and denounced Young to his face for economic oppression.[8]

The principal outposts of Mormon music remaining outside of Thomas's control were the old Legion bands and David Calder's Deseret Musical Association. The former held little appeal for someone of Thomas's experience. The Legion fife and drum corps, led by the church's first band director, Dimick Huntington, had declined into a quaint relic of the old days: apparently they lacked anyone who read music "by note" and had few who even played well by ear.[9] The better players of Pitt's band had been absorbed into the orchestra, leaving them little time for other sorts of playing. Only Calder's group thrived. Brigham Young materially aided Calder, continuing to give the singing school free use of his schoolroom for rehearsal and of his theater for benefit concerts to raise money for sheet music, gowns, and accompanying instruments.[10] In turn the Deseret Musical Association endeavored to aid Young's campaign for progress by ignoring the old shape-note tunebook anthems and folk hymns and offering the Saints popular glees, pseudoclassical anthems, and occasionally borrowed liturgical pieces (Rossini's *Stabat Mater*). Above all, Calder began to feature new vocal works by Professor C. J. Thomas, many of them accompanied by Thomas's theater orchestra.[11]

Yet, even after the two musical leaders joined forces, the Deseret Musical Association remained solely Calder's enterprise. Whereas Thomas presided over groups that could consecrate and exploit the "perfections" of gentile music, Calder had a method of training children, and Mormonism placed a high value on progeny. Clad in white, the Deseret Musical Association's members played on the public heartstrings far more than Thomas's players or singers could. In an era obsessed with novelty the spectacle of hundreds of children singing concert music provoked their audiences to an almost revivalistic fervor. It impelled Eliza Snow, for example, to write that Calder's group inspired "thoughts of Eden's fresh bowers of love" and that it was an earthly foreshadowing of heaven's choir.[12] Ironically, Calder's zeal to educate Zion's youth and to strengthen their lungs weakened his own system so much that he could hold no rehearsals for his October 1863 concert and during the concert itself had to prop himself with the music stand to avoid collapsing.[13] Although he overcame the illness, five of his own children contracted consumption and died before winter was over.

Accustomed to nothing but praise under the sponsorship of the Mormon prophet and territorial governor, Calder soon encountered a curious new foe: the music critic. The *Deseret News* carried a thorough critique of Calder's unrehearsed 7 October 1863 concert. Written by one "Musicus," the review pronounced the concert a qualified success, but faulted the horn section for playing flat. It also suggested ways the chorus could improve its tempi (and its vibrato) and lamented that some of the players "lacked energy."[14]

"Musicus" turned out to be another recently immigrated "professor," John Tullidge, who had come to Utah in hopes of reforming Mormon singing practice. His resumé included these achievements: he had sung in a British Methodist choir at three and led one by age ten, had been principal tenor of the York Philharmonic concerts (about 1840), had taught at singing schools in York, and had received the endorsement of the Camidge family (organists and composers who dominated music at York for a century). In 1856, about five years after his journalist son

Edward converted to Mormonism, Tullidge founded a singing school for Latter-day Saints in Liverpool and began to compose settings for Mormon hymn texts.

A letter Tullidge wrote to promote his work to apostle Orson Pratt revealed his musical self-assuredness: he wrote of being sent by God to earth to play music, of hearing huge symphonies in his mind from infancy and of being guided by Providence through his musical training. Then, after quoting public notices of praise for his work in Wales, Tullidge explained how he had "trampled down all difficulty and opposition, that stood in my way to retard my progress in every kind of musical knowledge" and now stood ready to help reform and educate Mormon musical habits.[15] On the advice of the British mission president, Tullidge immigrated to Utah in 1863. Because Great Salt Lake City's chief musical posts were occupied, the fifty-six year old launched himself on a part-time career as Mormondom's first music critic.

While the *News* in 1862 and 1863 printed lengthy and sometimes caustic reviews of local plays, it treated musicians with care, printing notices such as this: "To speak approvingly of either or any of the performers in contradistinction to the others, would be doing a wrong, for all did well and there was nothing wanting to render the entertainment as complete as the most fastidious could have expected or desired."[16] Tullidge felt that such unqualified praise threatened Salt Lake City's further progress in the art. He believed that his training not only enabled but compelled him to critique the local musicians meticulously. His reviews generally contained a preemptory air of flattery for whatever ensemble he was considering, sharp words for one or more performers on the given program, and detailed suggestions for allaying faults—all in terms too technical for most of his readers to understand.

Many readers disliked Tullidge's reviews. In one particularly strident critique of the theater orchestra, Tullidge had rebuked the group for ignoring Haydn, Mozart, Beethoven, and their "contrapuntic" works. When challenged on his assessment, Tullidge countered by saying that he must continue to endure "spiteful remarks" in the pursuit of his "mission" as a music critic.[17] This self-defense notwithstanding, some Mormons apparently thought that Tullidge was, in effect, questioning the judgment of Brigham Young's musical appointments. Probably as a consequence of the ill will his writings had provoked, Tullidge apparently found no work as a singing teacher. To raise money, Tullidge held a benefit concert in his own honor in October 1864, but filled less than a quarter of the seats in a local meetinghouse.[18] The *News*, meanwhile, printed no more of Tullidge's reviews for six years.

With the successes of the Deseret Musical Association, David Calder came to realize the strength of the Mormon musical market. The popularity of the theater and dancing, along with Young's crusade for cultural advancement, enhanced the public demand for instruments, music lessons, and even sheet music—though few as yet could actually read it. Young himself directed Calder to order from New York's Firth and Pond performance copies of Haydn's *Creation* and "Spring" Symphony, Mozart's Twelfth Service, Mendelssohn's "As the Hart Panteth," Andreas Romberg's "Song of the Bell" (*Lied von der Glocke*), and Handel's *Messiah*.[19] By 1863 Calder also stocked Hawkins's *History of Music, Our Musical Friend,* and other journals (ordered in quantities of one hundred apiece), and multiple copies of dozens of sentimental songs. At the same time he amassed an inventory of strings, reeds, guitars, accordions, and various keyboard instruments. Calder had the distinct advantage of being able to order from Brigham Young's own office. And when it became clear that Calder's major competitor was a racketeer who could not deliver on the orders he was taking, Calder ended up with a monopoly of Utah's early musical trade.[20]

In 1864 a diminutive young British violinist named George Careless reached the Salt Lake Basin. He had been trained at London's relatively new Royal Academy of Music, where he had completed the four-year course in three years under tutors such as Manuel Garcia. He also had played under the batons of Luigi Arditti and Wilhelm Ganz. Sometime after Careless was converted by Mormon missionaries in 1850 a church elder, William Staines, persuaded him that he must devote his musical skill to Zion by immigrating to Utah. (This was, of course, the customary advice given to all Mormon artisans in the mid-nineteenth century.) He arrived there only to find music in Utah controlled by a handful of fellow countrymen. His wages limited to those of a private teacher, Careless vowed to attempt making a living at music for two years, unless he starved first.[21]

A few months after he arrived in Utah (so Careless maintained throughout his life) Young called Careless privately to his office and asked him to "lay a foundation for good music" in Deseret. Careless replied to Young that he would "do the best I can with the material I can get," to which Young quipped, "Oh, you will have to make [the material]." A discussion of style ensued between the two men. Young asked Careless to foster "sweet music"—his term for sentimental popular songs and rollicking dances—while Careless insisted that Mormon music sometimes must be vigorous and bold. Young conceded the point and told Careless he was "all right."[22] However accurate Careless's story may have been, Young did send C. J. Thomas to southern Utah in 1865 on a mission to found singing schools, direct bands, and teach basic harmony, and appointed Careless director of the theater orchestra and overseer of the choir in the Tabernacle.[23]

Professor Careless continued to refine the Mormon capital's musical establishment. Finding the orchestra's playing ragged, Careless cut nine members from the sixteen-member group and threatened to resign if Young did not allot money to pay the remaining seven players three dollars a night. The Mormon leader reluctantly did so, torn between his belief that all talents should be devoted freely to the church and his hope to enhance the city's musical renown. At Careless's first meeting with the church choir in the old Tabernacle the conductor found the building dark and cold. The meager group of singers sported candles in order to read their oblong partbooks and keep warm. Careless demanded more choir members, heat, and light for their Friday night rehearsals. Again Young acquiesced.[24]

The remaining years of the 1860s saw radical alterations in the texture of Mormon life. Young continued to inveigh against technological and cultural backwardness among his people, insisting that God inspired all progress. Yet while he forged links with the outside world, Young also redoubled his efforts to keep it at bay. At the same time that he was building a huge telegraph system in the territory and courting the railroad barons who were laying track across the continent, Young was avidly preaching for polygamy and against abolitionism, and calling for an ever more potent theocracy in Mormondom. The railroad, Young knew, would bring both progress and peril to the Saints.

The new railroad in Utah—much of it built to the serenading of Mormon bands[25]—enabled the Salt Lake Theatre to book popular artists from the East Coast and to bring the first opera company to the territory. But in their attempt to make Great Salt Lake City a cosmopolis of the West, the theater managers realized that the orchestra and local singers were ill prepared to perform with so little rehearsal the complicated scores required by visiting troupes. The theater singers depended primarily on their ears or Tonic Sol-fa notation to learn the simple anthems the conductors routinely composed for the shows. In 1869, when approaching Parepa Rosa for some concert dates in the Rocky Mountains, the theater managers warned the singer of the situation. Rosa would have to bring her own chorus and instrumentalists because "our orchestra except the *Leader,* are only good amateurs, and would not be competent for Opera on so short notice, neither have we such chorus singers as you might require, that is to say, people who can rend [*sic*] at sight."[26]

As the orchestra's deficiencies became clear, the players justly feared for their jobs. "Dull times," in the dramatic circles' parlance, had already forced the managers to lay off orchestra members from time to time; importing musicians from across the continent would surely threaten the players' income and perhaps provoke Young to restore his no-wage policy.[27] The players called for a local musician's union, which, on the one hand seemed a logical extension of the Mormon spirit of cooperation, but on the other hand seemed dangerously factious. Careless fought the idea, and when unionization became inevitable he resigned his post. The theater managers immediately wrote to C. J. Thomas and offered him his old post back.[28]

Although Thomas advertised his players as the "Enlarged and Efficient Orchestra," the deteriorating theater music under Thomas drew criticism. Letters critical of the music appeared in the *News* and the new *Salt Lake Herald*. The *Herald* editorialized that it could indeed "suggest improvements" for the orchestra but that it would not, because it was too late in the season to make any difference. Thomas replied to both papers that the playing had suffered only because the management had fired players due to failing receipts: some of the instrumental parts could not be played and that left holes in the music. John Tullidge entered the fray by suggesting that Thomas should write his own arrangements of the music from piano scores, instead of relying on standard sets of parts. And the *Deseret News* published this attempt at tactfulness: "A NEW TUNE WANTED.—We have been asked by several parties to ask that a new tune be played by the Theatrical Orchestra, by way of relief. How is this professor? Can you oblige?"[29]

The theater post Thomas had resumed was scarcely the one he had left in 1865. To their credit the musicians were better trained, more committed, and anxious to work. But the theater itself was worn out by frequent use and occasional rowdiness. Wealthier patrons reportedly refused to attend because the seat cushions were soiled. Many would-be patrons were stranded at home when horse diseases plagued the county. Local productions began to command smaller and smaller houses. In 1873 a melodeon where "brazen women dance lewd dances" began to draw some adult business away from the modest family playhouse.[30] The theater tried to compete by booking minstrel shows, magic acts, jugglers, and pantomimists, but by the winter of 1873–74 the musicians were again laid off and Brigham Young sold the theater.[31] Perhaps worst of all, rumors spread that the theater had poltergeists, rumors which some thought were confirmed when in January 1873 John Tullidge, who was working as Thomas's copyist, inexplicably fell down the theater staircase in the middle of the night and died. A scene painter claimed to feel a ghost enter his room at the moment of the death, and Tullidge's box of manuscript compositions mysteriously vanished that night.[32]

The Civil War era had been a great epoch of American popular music, one which saw the virtual birth of mass culture in the New World. The Saints had celebrated the rise of popular music in their culture as a sign of progress, but they continued to consider concertizing only an amusement, like pitching quoits or wrestling.[33] An 1862 program for the

Theatre suggests the light character of the music typically being performed: the staple patriotic pieces ("Hail Columbia" and "Star-Spangled Banner"), two polkas, three waltzes, a varsoviana, and the songs "Within a Mile of Edinburgh Town" and "My Wife's a Winsome Wee Thing."[34] As the Civil War deepened, songs such as "When This Cruel War Is Over" and "When Johnny Comes Marching Home Again" entered many Mormon gatherings. Moreover, as with dancing, the notions of moderation and propriety governed Mormon attitudes toward concertizing. Although Young encouraged singing and fiddling (for dancing's sake) for their physical benefits, some Mormons considered lingering at concerts for the sake of listening to sentimental and comic songs a species of idleness. At the New Year's Ball of 1853 James Ferguson, one of the founders of the Dramatic Association, explained that the true purpose of concerts was "amusingly to instruct." But, he added, they must not become "a primary object with us" and should only be considered "pastimes."[35] Eleven years later the *News* warned that indulging in too much vocal or instrumental music would be "unquestionably injurious."[36]

After the Civil War, America's great cities began holding music festivals, colossal gatherings of singers and instrumentalists into "monster" choruses and orchestras. The sponsors of these festivals, or "jubilees," as they were often called, sought to outdo one another and establish for their patron cities the glory that inevitably accompanied the gigantic. Reading of these events in the city papers and in the *Juvenile Instructor,* George Careless and his fellow professors felt it not only a civic but a sacred duty to enact such festivals in the Mormon capital.

In the 1870s the eighty-five-voice Tabernacle Choir became the nucleus of several "monster choruses," as Careless temporarily imported choristers from outlying settlements during the church's semiannual conferences held in the new Tabernacle. (This new building was a strange, oblong domed structure described by one of the apostles as resembling "Noah's ark turned bottom side up."[37]) In 1873, for example, the Tabernacle congregation enjoyed a hoir of 304 assembled from fifteen settlements.[38] In 1876 Careless mounted the first western territory performance of the centerpiece of many jubilees, Handel's *Messiah*. Except for Careless's wife, apparently, none of the combined forces for the work had ever heard it before, other than the "Hallelujah" chorus, which had been sung in Utah at least since 1853. Thus, because the work was so little known, the performance necessitated a great deal of learning by note. The phenomenon of an oratorio in the frontier metropolis attracted crowds to the Salt Lake Theatre for two nights, and was considered by John Tullidge's son Edward the birth of "supreme" musical culture in Mormonism.[39]

By the 1870s many Mormons, including Brigham Young, had been converted to the idea of music as a "science." Young himself observed that unless the arts were turned into sciences, they would never become "permanent" and "stable," but would remain "uncertain."[40] An 1870 article called the current musical endeavors of the Saints part of a "transition state" in Mormondom's music, while another, two months later, described the "dawning of a brighter day" occurring in Mormon musical life.[41] By 1875 a British tourist, noting the Mormons' musical progress, predicted that "if there is something wrong in this society, it will be eradicated by the elevation of the general tastes of the people,—and what elevates the taste as does music?"[42]

A symbolic event in the attempt to elevate Mormon tastes was the collaboration of Calder and Careless on a musical journal, the *Utah Musical Times* (1876–78). The two professors explained in their first issue that they had founded the *Times* to continue the work of popularizing classical music among a people already little inclined to it. Each issue contained an editorial, with subjects ranging from Tonic Sol-fa to novel-reading; reports on national and international music festivals, including Wagner's first *Ring* cycle at Bayreuth; reviews of local church concerts and entertainments, and visiting music troupes; articles on Handel, Haydn, Mozart, bagpipes, and "Musical Sound vs. Noise"; a page of ads for local music teachers; and, of course, endorsements of Calder's music business. The *Times* castigated the solo singing of the Original Georgia Minstrels ("very deficient") and the playing of "Blind Tom" Bethune ("not sufficiently attractive to interest an audience during a whole evening's entertainment").[43] It also, quite expectedly, endorsed the Curwen Tonic Sol-fa method and pleaded that it be fostered in local congregations to help alleviate the people's lack of musical sophistication.[44] The most frequently cited notice in the journal came to be "The First Presidency on Music," a paean to the potentials of Mormon music, which compared its destiny to that of Hebrew and Catholic traditions.[45] But exactly two years after it began, the journal folded. The only reason given was that other public and private duties compelled the editors to abandon the work.

In 1879 David Calder visited a rehearsal of C. J. Thomas's small male chorus, the Union Glee Club. Speaking on behalf of Brigham Young's successor, John Taylor, he announced that the First Presidency wished the group to become the core of a comprehensive musical society that would unite all Mormon musicians in a common bond. Calder explained that this society would "counteract the efforts which are continually being made by the anti-Mormon residents of this city, in their musical associations, to induce our young brethren and sisters to become members of those outside societies. [The presidency of the church] can see a great and growing evil in the acquaintances and associations thus formed by our young people, and, it is believed, if we organise a first-class musical society of our own, the desire of our young brethren and sisters for musical culture would thereby be gratified, and the temptation for them to join with those not of their own faith would be removed."[46]

Thomas assented and, along with Careless, joined the twenty-five-man board of directors of what became known as "Zion's Musical Union." After approving a constitution the board deliberated on what work would best exemplify the society during the church's jubilee year and surprisingly chose Gilbert and Sullivan's *The Sorcerer*.[47] Gilbert and Sullivan works were then very popular in Salt Lake City. The Theatre recently had been filled for at least ten performances of *H.M.S. Pinafore* (composed just after *The Sorcerer*)—six by Careless and four by the Sunday School—just one year after its premiere at the London Opera Comique. But, as performed by Zion's Musical Union, *The Sorcerer* proved a severe disappointment to both Mormons and gentiles in the city. The *Salt Lake Herald* reported that the whole city spoke ill of the production and added its own assessment: "There should be more life in so large a chorus; the solos of all can be bettered materially, and if a good, square criticism were entered into, from a professional standpoint, many severe things could be said."[48] Thomas, who had rehearsed and conducted the entire production himself, resigned the Union's conductorship.[49] Having more or less neglected the show in order to produce his own series of local concerts with the "Careless Orchestra," Careless was dropped from the board of directors; he also resigned his directorship of the Tabernacle Choir, vehemently denying that he had been fired by Taylor.[50]

In the 1880s classical music grew more popular among certain social classes in Mormondom. Yet many Mormons continued to resist the art. At the founding of Zion's Musical Union the Sunday School's *Juvenile Instructor* admitted it was "partially true" that "the Saints generally have no appreciation for anything in the line of music above simple melody, that the opera and oratorio possess no charms for them." It also attributed this low taste to the persecutions and harassment inflicted on the church: Mormons had little opportunity to advance themselves because the gentiles hindered them. But the article also forecast an imminent elevation of taste, thanks to the prevalence of inexpensive instruments and good teachers in Utah.[51]

In 1884 the Saints brought Adelina Patti, "the greatest singer in the world," to a crowd reputed to number 7,000 in the Tabernacle. Patti's reception was generally lukewarm, though one of the apostles described the performance as "beyond description."[52] For her part, Patti said that the Tabernacle was "as easy to sing in as any parlor."[53] The church's First Presidency met privately with Patti and even toasted her with champagne, although they seemed more impressed by her $60,000 car than her music.[54] A year earlier the city had hosted the renowned New York Philharmonic conductor Theodore Thomas in a festival at the Tabernacle. Thomas's all-classical concert, even with its 250-voice choir coordinated by Professor C. J. Thomas, disenchanted much of its audience. Apostle Abraham H. Cannon called it "very fine" but added "it was classical, and therefore very few appreciated it."[55] Salt Lake Theatre managers Hiram Clawson and John Caine were more severe: "The fine music was so far beyond the comprehension of the public that a feeling of something like dissatisfaction was created. Concerts held here hereafter in this city should give more popular music or they will not be patronized so well as such talent deserves." In 1886 the managers summed up the situation thus: "Candor compels us to state, that the public here do not patronize those high-toned concerts as they deserve to be. The number who 'gush' at such entertainments cannot fill the house."[56]

Throughout the remainder of the 1880s the prospects for musical progress seemed to worsen. Calder had died in 1884, Thomas had returned to England for a mission in 1885, and Careless was disspirited for several years after his wife succumbed that year to an overdose of morphine.[57] The influx of trained musicians was subsiding; British conversions and immigration were dwindling to a small fraction of what they had been in earlier days. Just as devastating to the cause of Mormon music was the passage of the Edmunds anti-polygamy law in 1882, which had been enacted almost entirely to crush the Mormons by outlawing not only new plural marriages but also any existing polygamous cohabitation. By 1886 scores of church leaders had been arrested and hundreds of others, including John Taylor, had gone into hiding or moved to Canada or Mexico. Although most professional musicians, including Thomas, Calder, and Careless, appear to have been monogamous, the men's sections of choirs and the whole of some orchestras dwindled as the "cohabs" among them (those accused of "unlawful cohabitation") fled or were jailed.

Barely two weeks after the Edmunds bill was signed into law by President Arthur, a twenty-eight-year-old Welsh bachelor sang for the Sunday School Board in the Salt Lake Council House. After two songs the board members began clapping so wildly that applause was henceforth forbidden in their meetings.[58] The object of their adulation was Evan Stephens, who had come to the city to study with the Tabernacle organist, Joseph J. Daynes, and to propose to the Sunday School board that he be allowed to teach singing-by-note free to ten children from each Sunday school class in the city. His only condition was that he be granted the full receipts of one jubilee concert with them, with the proceeds of other concerts to go to a fund for printing new Mormon tracts.[59] After some mild debate, the board accepted the offer.

Stephens's earliest "Grand Concerts" with the children (among the first ever to have electric lighting in the Tabernacle) featured the Welshman in a mock prima donna performance in drag.[60] But the vocal quality of the 450 children overrode any offense that might be taken at the female impersonation. Wilford Woodruff, soon to succeed John Taylor as church president, recorded that "it was the Most interesting Exhibition I ever witnessed in my life" and predicted that Stephens's methods would soon turn out "scores [if] not hundreds of our Children who would be Capable of teaching Music."[61] A member of the Sunday School board recorded that Stephens's project was "by far the most extensive . . . of any effort hitherto tried to infuse into the youthful a thorough knowledge of the divine art."[62] Stephens further ingratiated himself by turning several concerts into benefits for local hospitals and for the Sunday School Union itself. By virtue of his growing notoriety Stephens rapidly attracted hundreds of paying students at the modest rates of seventy-five cents per student for a course of thirteen lessons.

During the 1882–83 season, during which Stephens's choirs numbered between 250 and 600 members, the Tabernacle Choir had only 101 singers enrolled: 39 sopranos, 13 altos, 15 tenors, and 34 basses.[63] After Careless's resignation in 1880 the choir had voted Thomas Griggs to become its new conductor, even though he was then away on a proselyting mission. Ebenezer Beesley, primarily known as a hymnwriter, bandmaster, and music arranger, became acting conductor. The diary of one chorister summarized the general response to Beesley's first rehearsal with the choir: "Beesley leads the choir. George is missed very much."[64] To the surprise of the choir, when Griggs returned in 1881 he refused to unseat Beesley and chose instead to become the group's treasurer. Beesley remained in control of the choir for a decade.

In 1884 the Logan *Utah Journal* wrote that the Tabernacle Choir had greatly improved its technique and "promises to become as good as that of our Logan choir. When it does Utah will possess two splendid choral organizations."[65] In the face of such mediocre assessments Beesley struggled to redeem his choir's reputation. He complained at his group's having to prepare so much music for church conferences, calling it an "ordeal," yet also faulted many of his singers, who, he said, lacked sufficient talent to be members of the official Mormon choir. Ordering that auditions be held for all singers, he inaugurated recruiting drives to attract better voices and established a perpetual benefit fund for the choir in order to sweeten the prospect of membership.

Unfortunately, Beesley's attempt to elevate standards coincided with the federal crusade against "cohabs." By February 1885 most of the prominent male singers in the choir dropped out. Subsequent rolls reveal astounding absenteeism. By 1886, despite recruiting efforts, the choir membership still hovered around one hundred. And, according to another local musician, blunders continued to mark the choir's performances.[66]

That same year, Evan Stephens left Salt Lake City to study at the New England Conservatory, then in its twentieth year. The active musical scene at Boston converted Stephens to opera, while his classes with George Chadwick augmented his skills in harmony. He reputedly won first place in a school composition contest with a piece judged to be a model for ''American'' style.[67] But after ten months he abruptly cut off his studies with Chadwick allegedly because the Boston composer arrived at class with the scent of liquor on his breath. Stephens returned to Salt Lake City and founded his own opera company, which in 1889 performed *Bohemian Girl, Daughter of the Regiment,* and *Martha.*[68] That same year, upon organizing a ''monster chorus'' for the visit of Patrick Gilmore, director of some of the East Coast's largest jubilees, Stephens dubbed the four-hundred-voice choir the Salt Lake Choral Society. In 1890 the group began to mount its own festivals, which included solos and choruses by Weber, Schumann, Rossini, Verdi, Wagner, Donizetti, Dudley Buck, and, of course, Arthur Sullivan. Comparing the Choral Society with the Tabernacle Choir, some church authorities suggested that Stephens take over Beesley's position—and bring his best choral society singers with him.[69]

As the decade closed the church was beset by a tempest of rhetoric on the question of polygamy. Anti-Mormons continued to campaign against it and some young Mormons were drifting away from ''The Principle,'' as plural marriage was called, and from religious fundamentalism generally. At the same time many of their elders defended the old ways and defied the government to tamper further with the church's practices. The older Saints' resistance to federal pressure was driven in part by a lingering belief among some of them that Christ might come in 1890 or 1891, a belief rooted in several prophecies pronounced by Joseph Smith. Church leaders, however, even some of Joseph's most passionate disciples, were beginning to see the Millennium as more distant and to prepare to abandon—at least publicly—their advocacy of plural marriage. Leading apostles began preaching against the belief that the world would end by 1891.[70] In October 1890 Woodruff announced the church would no longer sanction polygamy. The same month, he released Beesley from his duties and called Stephens to lead the Tabernacle Choir.[71]

In the spring of 1891, the *New York Eagle* published a catalogue of Salt Lake City's musical enterprises. In the heart of Mormondom, the newspaper explained, one could find four music stores, two drum corps, a forty-member mandolin club, an orchestra, one of the largest organs in the world, a huge choir and choral society, virtuosic soloists and teachers, and, most important, a public willing to patronize them all.

Citing the *Eagle*'s catalogue, the *Deseret News* noted that "a people among whom the divine art is so extensively cultivated cannot be as coarse, brutal and depraved as many editors and preachers represent the 'Mormons' to be." The *News* went on to insist that musical advancement in Mormondom was emblematic of the Saints' determination to advance themselves: "It will be found that the tendency of 'Mormonism' is not only to encourage musical progress, but to stimulate advancement in every department of practical and scientific education."[72] With the outside world reconsidering the Saints, and the Saints reconsidering themselves, the fruits of Deseret's immigrant professors nourished Mormondom's hope for its own continuance.

NOTES

1. *DN*, 2 March 1912. In the theater dedicatory prayer Daniel Wells blessed the musicians, praying God to "enable them to discourse sweet melody to the enlivening of the soul and cheering the depressed spirit, and to the delight and benefit of thy saints" (*DN*, 12 March 1862). On Young's direct involvement with the theater orchestra see Asahina, "Brigham Young and the Salt Lake Theater," pp. 182–83.

2. *WWJ* 1:581 (21 December 1840).

3. See, for example, Stan Larson, "The King Follett Discourse: A Newly Amalgamated Text," and related articles in *Brigham Young University Studies* 18 (Winter 1978).

4. *DN*, 18 November 1863.

5. "Ballo's Band," 20 July 1862. For a description of Thomas as a conductor see the remarks of Mrs. M. G. Clawson, quoted in Sterling E. Beesley, *Kind Words the Beginnings of Mormon Melody: A Historical Biography and Anthology of the Life and Works of Ebenezer Beesley, Utah Pioneer Musician* (N.p.: Published by the Author, 1980), pp. 248–49.

6. *OPH* 15:490. For an anecdote on the Tabernacle Choir's double duty as a theater chorus and church choir, see Alfred Lambourne, *A Play-House* (n.p., n.d., ca. 1914), pp. 21–22.

7. Anonymous address, ca. 1 March 1861, in Deseret Dramatic Association Minutes. For a list of the orchestra members at this time—most of whom appear to have been young bachelors—see Asahina, "Brigham Young and the Salt Lake Theater," p. 258.

8. See Deseret Dramatic Association Minutes, 20 April 1864, and Annie Adams Kiskadden, "The Life Story of Maude Adams and Her Mother," *The Green Book Magazine* 11 (July 1914): 8.

9. See "Newlywed Joins Handcart Company," *OPH* 14:542, and the reminiscence of Frederick Beesley, typescript in Sterling Beesley Papers, HBLL.

10. For some of the many public endorsements of Calder see *DN*: "Musical," 6 April 1864; "Music—Its Culture and Influence," 8 February 1865; and "Leisure Hours—Mental Improvement," 28 December 1865.

11. To add to the auspiciousness of their concerts, Calder had programs with the texts of songs printed and distributed to the patrons. A typical Association program included twenty pieces: five songs or glees by the combined forces; three dances and a patriotic air by the orchestra; two duets and a trio; and seven solos, ranging from "Return of the Salmon River Gold Digger" to the cavatina from *Robert Le Diable.* See *Songs, Duets and Glees to be sung at the Concert of the Deseret Musical Association, to be given at the Theatre, Great Salt Lake City on Wednesday Eve., Oct. 7, 1863* (Great Salt Lake City: Deseret News, 1863), copy in HBLL.

12. "That Concert," *DN,* 2 March 1864.

13. Calder to John M. MacFarlane, 15 October 1863, Calder Letterpress Copybook.

14. "The Concert," *DN,* 21 October 1863.

15. *Millennial Star* 19 (14 March 1857): 170–72. See also the extensive review of Tullidge's career in Edward Tullidge, *History of Salt Lake City* (Salt Lake City: Star, 1886), pp. 772–73, 962.

16. "Professor Thomas' Concert," *DN,* 5 August 1863.

17. See the reviews of *DN,* 2, 16, and 30 March 1864.

18. See "That Concert," *DN,* 19 October 1864.

19. See Calder to George Q. Cannon, 13 February and 12 March 1863, Calder Letterpress Copybook.

20. On Calder's competitor, H. L. Raymond, see "To the Patrons of Music," *DN,* 27 April 1864.

21. George D. Pyper, "In Intimate Touch with George Careless," *JI* 59 (March 1924): 115–18. For another survey of Careless's career see Bruce David Maxwell, "George Careless, Pioneer Musician," *Utah Historical Quarterly* 53 (Spring 1985): 131–43.

22. See the eulogy given Careless by Edward P. Kimball, published in Howard Hoggan Putnam, "George Edward Percy Careless: His Contributions to the Musical Culture of Utah and the Significance of His Life and Works" (Master's thesis, Brigham Young University, 1957), p. 95, and the slightly different account in Susa Young Gates and Leah D. Widtsoe, *The Life Story of Brigham Young* (New York: Macmillan, 1930), p. 247.

23. Although Robert Sands appears as conductor of the choir in newspaper notices of the choir 1865–69, Careless seems to have maintained he was the actual overseer during this period. See the discussion in Putnam, "George Careless," pp. 30–31.

24. See Pyper, "In Intimate Touch," *JI* 59 (April 1924): 174; and 59 (May 1924): 233.

25. See Joseph Barton Diary, holograph in HDC, pp. 6–7.

26. See the page following the letter of John T. Caine to James Linforth, 23 September 1869, Deseret Dramatic Association Letterpress Copybooks, HDC. Fitz Hugh Ludlow, *The Heart of the Continent* (New York: Hurd and Houghton, 1870), p. 366, describes Mormon concertizing thus: "They played . . . quite as well as the ball-room bands of most Eastern towns no larger than Salt Lake City, if we except those whose population has become

somewhat Teutonized; and what they lacked in quality, they made up in quantity.''

27. On bad business at the theater see especially Thomas McIntyre Journal, 2 June 1867.

28. Secondary accounts such as Orson F. Whitney, *History of Utah*, 4 vols. (Salt Lake City: George Q. Cannon, 1892–1904), 4:350, claim Young called Thomas back. The first approach, however, seems to have come from the theater managers, Hiram Clawson and John Caine. See Clawson to Thomas, 10 March 1871, Deseret Dramatic Association Letterpress Copybooks.

29. *DN*, 16 and 21 July 1871, and *Salt Lake Herald*, 20 July 1871. These clippings and others from the 1870s appear in the scrapbook kept by Thomas, HBLL. See also ''Our Theatrical Orchestra,'' *Salt Lake Herald*, 13 January 1872, and the notice in *DN*, 26 June 1872. Similar complaints had been lodged against Thomas six years earlier. See Therald Francis Todd, ''The Operation of the Salt Lake Theatre, 1862–1875'' (Ph.D. diss., University of Oregon, 1973), p. 210.

30. See George Reynolds to Brigham Young, 5 February and 7 March 1873, Deseret Dramatic Association Letterpress Copybooks.

31. For a comprehensive listing of theater performances see H. L. A. Culmer, comp., ''Record of Performances for Forty Years in the Salt Lake Theatre from its Opening March 5, 1862 until March 7, 1902,'' holograph in George D. Pyper Papers, UU.

32. George D. Pyper, *Romance of an Old Playhouse* (Salt Lake City: Seagull Press, 1928), pp. 194–95, and Virgil H. Camp, ''John Elliott Tullidge: The Influence of His Life and Works on the Musical Culture of Utah'' (Master's thesis, Brigham Young University, 1957), p. 30. Tullidge's death followed that of W. W. Phelps (1872) and preceded by a month that of William Pitt.

33. See ''Cultivation of Music,'' *DN*, 28 September 1854, and ''The Concerts in the Tabernacle,'' *DN*, 17 December 1862.

34. See the program in *DN*, 31 December 1862. Compare the program of the Parowan Harmonic Society, *DN*, 22 February 1865, which contained thirteen popular pieces and one classical piece (a movement from Haydn's Mass in B-flat).

35. *DN*, 22 January 1853.

36. ''Amusements—Their Use and Abuse,'' 16 November 1864.

37. George A. Smith to Hannah P. Butler, 28 January 1869, Historian's Office Letterpress Copybook. See also the accounts of the Boston World Jubilee in *DN*, June 1872, passim.

38. *DN*, 8 October 1873. See also the call ''To the Choir Masters and Choristers of the Territory,'' *DN*, 23 October 1872. For good summaries of choir activity throughout the territory, see *OPH* 4:133–80 and 15:490–526.

39. *History of Salt Lake City*, p. 777. Due to a powerful thunderstorm, the attendance of the second night was poor.

40. *JD* 13:306.

41. *DN*, 11 May and 13 July 1870.

42. William Minturn, *Travels West* (London: S. Tinsley, 1877), p. 141. Along the same lines, see ''Cultivation of Music,'' *DN*, 23 June 1875.

43. *Utah Musical Times* 1 (15 May 1876): 45, and 1 (15 July 1876): 77. "Blind Tom" (Thomas Bethune), however, was much sought after by the Salt Lake Saints—see George Reynolds to Thomas Warwick, 30 April 1873, Deseret Dramatic Association Letterpress Copybooks.

44. *Utah Musical Times* 1 (15 December 1876): 153; 1 (15 January 1877): 169; and 2 (1 December 1877): 137.

45. 1 October 1877. The piece probably reflects the views of the editors only, since not only is no member of the church hierarchy actually cited, but there was at that time no "first presidency" of the church. (The quorum of Twelve Apostles was then governing the church in the wake of Young's death.)

46. Union Glee Club Minutes, 10 March 1879, HDC.

47. See the notices on the Society in *DN*, 15 May and 17 June 1877.

48. 9 March 1880.

49. *DN*, 8 March 1880, and 21 June 1881.

50. See his letter to *Salt Lake Herald*, 19 August 1880. On Careless's hopes to elevate Utah's musical tastes with his orchestra in this period see "A First-Class Orchestra," *DN*, 20 September 1878.

51. 1 April 1879.

52. Abraham H. Cannon Journal, 2 April 1884, photocopy of holograph in HBLL. On the Tabernacle's career as a concert hall see Robert C. Mitchell, "Desert Tortoise: The Mormon Tabernacle on Temple Square," *Utah Historical Quarterly* 35 (Fall 1967): 279–91.

53. M. B. Leavitt, *Fifty Years in Theatrical Management* (New York: Broadway Publishing, 1912), p. 406.

54. *WWJ* 8:234, 239. Although Mormons today are known for abstinence from alcoholic drinks (including champagne), this practice has evolved slowly. See Thomas Alexander, *Mormonism in Transition: A History of the Latter-day Saints, 1890–1930* (Urbana: University of Illinois Press, 1986), pp. 258–71.

55. Journal, 15 June 1883.

56. David McKenzie (secretary to the theater managers) to Carl Strakosch, 30 August 1883; McKenzie to E. H. Wartegg, 27 February 1884; and Clawson and Caine to Henry Wolfsohn, 20 December 1886, all in Deseret Dramatic Association Letterpress Copybooks. (Compare the letter complaining about pianist Joseffy's lack of "variety," 25 August 1884.)

57. See "Lavinia Careless: Death from Morphine," *DN*, 16 July 1885.

58. George Goddard Journal, 3 April 1882, holograph in HDC.

59. Though many secondary accounts say that the Sunday School approached Stephens, superintendant George Goddard makes it clear in his journal, 10 April 1882, that Stephens approached the board first.

60. See the 1883 broadside "Grand Concert," in HDC.

61. *WWJ* 8:134.

62. Goddard Journal, 24 October 1882.

63. These figures and other information in this paragraph are from the TC Minutes, HDC.

64. McIntyre Journal, 22 August 1880. For a compendium of primary sources on Beesley see Sterling Beesley, *Kind Words*.

65. *Utah Journal,* 12 April 1884. On the Ogden choir see Melvin Ray Sorenson, "The Ogden Tabernacle Choir: Its History and Contributions to the Cultural History of Utah" (Master's thesis, Brigham Young University, 1961).

66. TC Minutes, 9 April 1886.

67. See Annie Wells Cannon, "Evan Stephens, the Children's Musical Friend," *Relief Society Magazine* 13 (April 1926): 178.

68. The Chadwick story was often told by J. Spencer Cornwall throughout the latter's life; see, for example, the personal interview with Cornwall cited in Dale A. Johnson, "The Life and Contributions of Evan Stephens" (Master's thesis, Brigham Young University, 1951), pp. 15–16.

69. See the recollection of John James in Johnson, "Life and Contributions," p. 89.

70. See, for example, Abraham Cannon Journal, 7 October 1889, 5 October 1890.

71. See Benjamin F. Cummings, Jr., "Shining Lights: Professor Evan Stephens," *Contributor* 16 (September 1895): 659.

72. Quoted in "A Musical People," *DN,* 27 April 1891.

7

Homemade Music

In 1832 Joseph Smith announced that God wanted the church to "stand independent above all other creatures beneath the celestial world."[1] Determined to fulfill this dictum, Smith and his fellow churchmen struggled to build Zion through self-reliance and community cooperation, traits that drew both praise and protest from outsiders. During and after the trek to the Rocky Mountains, Brigham Young called upon the Saints to import cultural goods to build up Zion. But as conflicts with the gentiles intensified he began to preach a rigorous self-sufficiency and to nurture a territory-wide obsession for "home" production of all kinds. The home production movement extended to virtually everything within the culture: home fashion, home literature, and even home music. Despite Young's eagerness to bring European and American art music into Utah via Mormon immigration, church musicians wished to prove their zeal for Mormon nationalism by transcending reliance on borrowed music of every sort, from hymn tunes to theater music and parlor songs. David Calder and George Careless expressed this doctrine of musical self-sufficiency in their "home journal," the *Utah Musical Times*: "We believe in home-made music as we believe in home-made cloth. Each, to us, is a source of strength and union."[2]

Mormon songs and hymns appear to have depended entirely on borrowed tunes until John Tullidge produced his *Latter Day Saints' Psalmody* in 1857. Since his conversion to Mormonism, Tullidge had objected to the Mormon sacred music he encountered. He found the melodies in use confused and unscientific, especially those tunes borrowed from Wesleyan practice. "As for the harmonies," he wrote, even "the Arch-enemy himself could scarcely have produced such a concourse of discords." The "freshness and vigor" of the Mormon spirit, he insisted, demanded something better than "that dolorous, whining class, so incompatible with praise from full and grateful hearts."[3]

Tullidge's objections to tune borrowing were both aesthetic and practical. The unusual meters of many hymns in the Manchester hymnbook made it difficult to set them appropriately with any but a very few tunes. In such cases, to give variety to their music, Mormon choristers often picked tunes that did not suit these hymns metrically, creating in Tullidge's mind "a constant jingling with words and music." Moreover, Tullidge despised borrowings from secular music not only because the tunes could be "barbarous . . . insipid and uninspired," but because "we cannot help adverting to the original words from which the composition has been separated," many of whose texts consisted of "obscenity and low slang twang." Tullidge was well aware that many British observers scorned the crudity of Mormon hymn texts generally, and he hated to see some of those texts' rough-hewn origins manifest in the tunes.[4]

Tullidge's *Psalmody* contained original settings for thirty-seven hymns and one anthem, "How Beautiful Upon the Mountains." As tunebooks went, the volume was impressive, with Italian tempo markings and keyboard accompaniments that supported the vocal harmonies without merely doubling the voices. Many of the pieces changed meter between the verse and chorus, even when this was not demanded by the text. Overall Tullidge favored simple quadruple and compound duple meters with tempi that were almost always buoyant. Unlike much of the Mormon hymnody then being practiced in America, Tullidge's tunes invariably used complete seven-note scales—none of them in minor modes—in broad and often angular lines.

Tullidge insisted that his tunes were suitable for "untrained congregations" to sing. But in fact many of them required controlled, accurate singers. The melodies reflected a rather sophisticated, if not altogether sacred, vocal tradition, particularly in the disjunctness of some of its lines, as in his setting of "O My Father." Although formerly he had written elaborate Latin-texted pieces for Catholic choirs,[5] many of the tunes in his collection had an air of British theater about them, as in the collection's opening song, "Hail to the Brightness," with its rapid syllabic setting. These somewhat difficult melodies bespoke Tullidge's idealism about what Mormons could and should sing. They also provided excellent texts (and pretexts) for his singing school classes. Despite his pretensions to the contrary, Tullidge evidently believed that one needed proper education in order to sing proper Mormon music.

Whether Tullidge's countryman C. J. Thomas used the *Psalmody* is not known, although Thomas directed a number of Mormon choral concerts in London, 1858–60.[6] For at least one of those concerts Thomas used four of his own compositions, including a setting of a new Mormon hymn about Michael the archangel, whom Young personally regarded as the spiritual Father of mankind:

Sons of Michael, he approaches!
Rise, the Eternal Father greet.
Bow ye thousands, low before him;
Minister before his feet.[7]

In setting this hymn Thomas manifested his theatrical background: the tune was boldly declamatory, with each brief line of its text starkly punctuated by rests.

Other hymn tunes that survive from this period of Thomas's life, particularly those written after his 1860 move to New York, show him paring down his settings to bring them into the range of less experienced choirs and perhaps even of congregations. Unlike Tullidge he gave the hymn settings formal tune names, most of which held distinctly Mormon connotations: "Nephi," for example, and "Moroni," even "Mormon" itself. Curiously, the three hymn tunes bearing these names (which represent Book of Mormon characters from the same clan) reflect a certain melodic family relationship.

Whether such musical correspondences were the results of calculation or just happenstance is not clear, especially given the nature of Thomas's method of composing. His daughter reported that his pieces often came to him in the form of melodies which he would jot down in solfege on his sleeve while he was out walking. Tunes also came to him in the night and he kept pencil and paper by his bedside at all times. Some of his earliest compositions thus composed reputedly became popular among London theaters. Regrettably, these and most of Thomas's early works were lost during his sojourn in southern Utah, 1865–71.[8]

What remains of his later instrumental music reveals a body of work that was vigorous, though relatively undistinguished, relying on mundane melodies draped over primary harmonies. However, the vocal works Thomas composed while director of the Tabernacle Choir show much greater flexibility of phrase design, along with an occasional harmonic quirkiness, as in his anthem "The House of the Lord," written in C-flat major, modulating to F-flat major in its center section. Probably his most interesting extant work, the so-called "Saints' National Anthem," displays some interesting shifting accents which suggest changing meters that are often at odds with Eliza Snow's text.

Such subtleties, along with the sense of spontaneity borne of self-education, seem largely absent from Careless's extant work, although the latter is, on the whole, more polished and studied than is Thomas's. Careless wrote prodigiously for the Salt Lake Theatre orchestra, partly because the fluctuating membership of the group made reliance on standard sets of parts from the East impossible and partly because Brigham Young had become increasingly strident in his opposition to mercantile or cultural trade with gentiles (notwithstanding the successful musical business being run by his clerk, David Calder). Hence, Careless wrote dozens of incidental pieces for the plays shown in Deseret, most of them dancelike and regular in their phrasing and harmony.

As the transcontinental railroad tracks approached Utah from both east and west, Young's hopes for more immigration of foreign Saints were countered by his fear of gentile pollution. To offset the potentially baneful effects of the railroad, church leaders intensified their sermons on independence. In 1868 Young called upon his people to "manufacture that which we consume, to cease our bartering, trading, [and] mingling . . . with all the filth of Babylon."[9] That same year Young founded Zion's Cooperative Mercantile Institution to help solidify Mormon trade. In response, proponents of free enterprise in the territory founded the *Utah Magazine* to disseminate their views.

Ironically, the magazine strongly encouraged the "home manufacture" of music. As had the music of Pitt and Ballo, the music of Thomas and Careless circulated through parts copied from one band's notebooks to another's. Choral music likewise proliferated through manuscript part books, as well as through the Tonic Sol-fa notation published and popularized in Utah by Calder. In 1869, however, *Utah Magazine* imported a cache of musical type from the East Coast and engaged John Tullidge to supervise the publication of new pieces.

Tullidge urged Latter-day Saint composers to send him new, expressly Mormon works, especially hymn settings. He proposed even more vigorously than he had twelve years earlier that the church's rapid expansion and relatively self-contained culture demanded its own distinctive hymnody (or "psalmody," as he usually referred to it). His own 1857 *Psalmody,* Tullidge wrote, was indeed too simple: "for Zion a more extensive and classical work is of course necessary." He envisioned congregations being led by confident choirs in this difficult music, which would be composed by himself, Thomas, Careless, Calder, and the young Tabernacle organist Joseph Daynes. The typeset pieces to be published in *Utah Magazine* would form a "choice stock" from which a new *Psalmody* could be assembled.[10]

But virtually none of the music the *Magazine* published over the next seven months was appropriate to such a psalmody. Indeed, of the fifteen pieces published in the magazine, only four could be characterized as sacred, and only two of these (including Tullidge's 1857 setting of "An Angel from on High") treated texts in the LDS hymnbook. The other pieces consisted of sentimental glees and piano dances. And all of these pieces were subject to the editorial control of Tullidge, who urged composers to stick to primary harmonies and binary and ternary ("duplex" and "triplex") forms. He also demanded perfect part-writing, pieces free from consecutive perfect fifths and other theoretical errors. Genius was not enough, he averred; musical science must govern "home composition." Yet, at the same time he condemned any trace of "non-originality" in the music he published.[11]

Regretably, Tullidge's bluntness alienated some of the best Utah musicians. Of A. C. Smyth, he coolly wrote that "with a little study he will make a good composer," and in Joseph Daynes's anthem "Praise Ye The Lord" Tullidge discerned "much genius and many mistakes." The bitterest contention involved C. J. Thomas, who complained when Tullidge altered his music and failed to preface Thomas's name with the title "Professor." The omission of the title Tullidge attributed to a printer's oversight. The alteration of two notes in the music was necessary though, in Tullidge's words, to remove "a very great fault"—parallel fifths—and "to render the resolution perfect." He continued dryly: "We are always much pleased with the Professor's compositions, and shall always be glad to receive any favor from him; and we will also say that if he would send his pieces correct we should deem it sacrilege to alter them."[12] After other readers complained about Tullidge's policy of altering the music they had submitted to the *Utah Magazine,* he explained that, although he wished to foster musical inspiration in Utah, he was bound to correct any errors he detected. Those whose work he improved upon, he added, should not complain. Rather, "they must compare our alterations with the original for their instruction."[13]

If Tullidge's apparent arrogance were not enough to quell his influence, the excommunication of the magazine's proprietors for apostasy was. *Utah Magazine* increasingly had become a forum for the "New Movement" led by William Godbe and Elias Harrison, a movement that challenged Brigham Young's authority to dictate in affairs of territorial trade. Thus, the journal became anathema among the orthodox. While his son Edward heatedly defended the principles of the New Movement, John Tullidge quietly bowed out of the magazine and spent his last years arranging and copying parts for Professor Thomas at the Salt Lake Theatre.[14]

While Tullidge and his musical colleagues sought to create a distinctive Mormon music out of "scientific" musical principles, unschooled Saints continued spinning uniquely Mormon songs from well-known gentile models.[15] W. W. Phelps had set the pattern for transfiguring outsiders' hymns and songs and he continued to be prolific well into the 1860s, producing in his old age some of his fieriest lyrics—"too hot for publication" he remarked of one of them.[16] He appears to have felt it his peculiar obligation to keep the essential millennial fervor of Mormonism alive amid the Civil War. Consider lyrics such as these—in his beloved dactylic meter—from the cynical "The United States' End":

The United States is as dim as the gloom
Of a meteor's flash, or the gleam of a flame;
And the death knell and wail, from the hearth-stone and tomb,
Put an end to the Echo of "Freedom and fame."

The trumpet of war sounds to arms! rush to arms!
And two nations,—'Once One'—shout for "Victory or death";
While their armies, for armies, with Lucifer's charms
Use the "new Patent method" to draw their last breath.

And in a more hopeful song, "Israel Reigns," Phelps wrote these somewhat cramped verses to the tune of "Dixie":

'Tis sweet to know that the Lord has spoken—
And a joy to watch the token—
Ev'ry day; ev'ry day; ev'ry day,
    Israel reigns.

'Tis sweet to see the light of Zion,
And to hear Jehovah's lion—
Clear the way; clear the way; clear the way,
    Israel reigns.[17]

Dozens of Mormon authors followed in Phelps's path, writing hundreds of song texts during the 1860s and 1870s. Whereas the trained composers and literati had the backing of Brigham Young's aspirations to enhance Zion, the folksingers and novelty writers traded on Young's constant endorsement of the virtues of simplicity and plainness. Hence, in this period several books of hymn and lyric collections were published, simple works not for worship per se, but for the private devotion and delight of the Saints.

The blind Welshman John Davis compiled twenty-one song texts into his 1868 *Beehive Songster*, noting in the preface that he aimed solely to be simple and plain, and explaining that the critical reader "may as well leave him alone, and use his power of criticism on efforts of a higher order, by which he may display himself to greater advantage." Davis's work centered on the themes of self-reliance ("A Co-operative Community" and "The Bees of Deseret"), the growing fame of Mormonism ("All Are Talking of Utah"), and the railroad, perhaps the favorite topic of the day, which Davis celebrated in these pseudo-apocalyptic lines, to the tune of "Caerfilly March":

The Iron Horse draweth nigh
With his smoke nostrils high,
Eating fire while he blazes,
Drinking water while he grazes.

> Then the steam rushes out,
> Whistles loud, "Clear the route,"
> For the Iron Horse is coming
> With the steam in his snout.[18]

Away from Zion's core, Salt Lake City, folk song thrived in perhaps a greater abundance, especially in southern Utah, where song was one of the few means to soothe the harshness of desert life. Among the best known of the southern Mormon song adapters was Charles Walker, who wrote texts such as "The Grecian Bend," a satire of modern fashions; "The Last Greenback Dollar" (yet another Mormon reworking of "The Last Rose of Summer"); a critique of the pace of life in St. George, Utah, called "St. George and the Drag-on"; and earthy desert lyrics such as:

> All tourists declare 'tis the Land Desolation,
> And marvel how white folks can live here and thrive;
> They know not how we starved while at work on half rations
> 'Twas grit that kept body and soul just alive.
> The grub that we ate was in no way inviting,
> Hard flapjacks of caneseed with boiled lucern greens;
> And burnt pungent treacle in which ants were fighting,
> While flies buzzed by millions for lack of wire screens.[19]

Such songs provoked debate for their candor but spread wildly through the Mormon colonies. One in particular, written by Walker's colleague George Hicks, drew both admiration and reproach for its bluntness:

> I feel so weak and hungry now, there's nothing here to cheer
> Except prophetic sermons, which we very often hear.
> They will hand them out by dozens and prove them by the book—
> I'd rather have some roasting ears to stay at home and cook.[20]

Throughout the territory, hero songs about Joseph Smith continued to abound. But this repertoire was augmented by songs about Brigham Young. Both men, as one song explained, were members of "The Royal Family":

> We'll see Joseph Smith and Hyrum
> Dressed in white upon Mount Zion.
> . . . . . .
> We'll see Brigham Young and Heber
> Singing praise to their Redeemer.
> . . . . . .
> We'll see Apostle Paul and Peter,
> There will be nothing sweeter.
> Oh, how glorious 'twill be!
> Dressed in white and crowned with glory
> With the royal family.

On one hand songwriters celebrated Young as God's "chosen seer" and "The Lion of the Lord" (a nickname Phelps had given him in Nauvoo). On the other hand, some singers felt freer to poke fun at Young than they ever had with Joseph. One of the better known of such satirical songs had the chorus:

> Brigham, Brigham Young—
> 'Tis a miracle he survives
> With his roaring rams, his pretty little lambs
> And his five and forty wives.[21]

Increasingly, Mormons used homespun song to help transmit the lore of their faith to their children. But they also turned to more formal means: the Sunday school song. Throughout the United States Sunday schools were beginning to occupy a central place in Protestant church life. In the process, they engendered their own style of sacred song, rooted in the "gospel song" style. The term "gospel song" derived from Philip Bliss's 1874 collection *Gospel Songs,* a collection of light hymns composed for revival meetings. Such songs often used bouncy rhythms, repeated pitches, an infectious verse-chorus pattern, and melodramatic metaphor (such as those found in Bliss's titles: "Pull for the Shore, Boys," "Hold the Fort for I Am Coming," and "Let the Lower Lights Be Burning"). While such songs clearly had descended from the old camp-meeting songs, their style caught the imagination of the post–Civil War generation, primarily through the Dwight Moody evangelistic crusades, whose musical leader Ira Sankey wrote hundreds of gospel songs. Sankey's brand of revival songs first appeared in his 1875 collaboration with Bliss, *Gospel Hymns,* the first in a sixteen-volume series of evangelistic songsters reputed to have sold around fifty million copies. The power of these songs was suggested in a contemporary's apt description of them as "grappling hooks of heaven."[22]

American Sunday school leaders after the Civil War used a similar music in their work, partly because they liked it, and partly because they hoped it would prove accessible to children. Although some Protestant leaders urged caution in using gospel songs in Sunday schools, the style proved irrepressible.[23] It was in this period, as the railroad was about to reshape Mormon society, that the Deseret Sunday School Union was founded. In this new church auxiliary the national movement toward gospel songs converged with the Mormon call for home composition.

In August 1873, seven months after John Tullidge's death, the Union's *Juvenile Instructor* began using musical type to publish C. J. Thomas's pieces for the upcoming the Sunday School Union musical jubilee. This jubilee had been organized to rouse public interest in the organization and to raise money to publish a children's hymnbook. Before the event took place Thomas's *Instructor* pieces were bound into a *Jubilee Song Book* in an edition of fifteen hundred. Demand ran so high that two more editions, of four thousand and five thousand respectively, came out by summer. The success of this jubilee music book encouraged the Sunday School Union leaders to proceed with a larger collection, exclusively consisting of texts and tunes by "home talent."[24]

Soliciting new works from its patrons, the *Instructor* began publishing a song page in every issue, printing in conventional musical type (not Tonic Sol-fa) the songs to be collected in the future hymnbook. The texts of these pieces tended to be less crisp and clever than those of Mormonism's folksingers and novelty writers and generally fell into four categories: songs for opening or closing meetings, holiday songs, hymns in praise of Utah or of Sunday school itself, and didactic works (on the sabbath day, the golden rule, etc.). Unlike the bulk of Mormon hymns in use since the 1830s and 1840s, these songs contained little theology and only sparse references to Zion and the impending Millennium. Instead they tended to express simple sentiments such as those in Joseph Townsend's "Little Lispers":

> What can little bodies do
> Like us little lispers,
> Full of life, and mischief too,
> And prone to noisy whispers?
>
> Oh, we here can come to school
> And, with merry voices,
> Sing about the golden rule
> Till every heart rejoices.[25]

Sacred ballads also appeared in the *Instructor,* works such as "The Iron Rod," Joseph Townsend's adaptation of a Book of Mormon vision. As sung by children the opening lines of its chorus must have struck outsiders as singular: "Hold to the rod, the iron rod / 'Tis strong and bright and true."[26] But the most popular of the sacred ballads was A. C. Smyth's setting of George Manwaring's "Joseph Smith's First Prayer." The extent to which *Instructor* editors seem to have helped aspiring home authors may be seen by comparing the first stanza of Manwaring's "finished" song written into his notebook—

> 'Twas on a lovely morn in spring,
> The sun was shining bright,
> When Joseph saw the woodland shade
> And humbly kneeling there he prayed
> For wisdom and for light.

—with the published version credited to him:

> Oh, how lovely was the morning:
> Radiant beamed the sun above,
> Bees were humming, sweet birds singing,
> Music ringing through the grove,
> When within the shady woodland
> Joseph sought the God of love.[27]

Ebenezer Beesley, former student of both Thomas and Careless, edited most of the *Instructor* music throughout this period. Under his direction the published music varied in style and mannerism—in part because variety was another virtue extolled by the arbiters of Mormon doctrine. (Brigham Young, for example, had urged that the Saints strive to keep their houses, furnishings, and fashions varied: "here is one's taste, and another's taste, and this constant variety would give beauty to the whole."[28]) But the music generally emulated the style of Sunday school music dominant throughout the nation, replete with dotted-eighth cum sixteenth-note rhythms, swaying choruses, and occasional echoes of minstrelsy, as in the syncopated line endings of Beesley's own "Kind Words Are Sweet Tones of the Heart." Beesley's music dominated the musical pages, as did, to a lesser extent, that of A. C. Smyth and Evan Stephens. Of the three, Stephens showed the greatest breadth in his writing, from bombastic anthems to unadulterated Sankey-style imitations. Stephens had the added distinction of writing most of the texts he set.

In order to hasten the banishment of Protestant hymnbooks from Utah's Sunday schools, George Manwaring suggested the Union begin selling 6" x 9" cards with a song on each side for the children to practice. In 1877–78 at least twenty-four cards (altogether containing forty-five songs) were issued in editions of five thousand each, beginning with Manwaring's own "We Meet Again." While not all of the songs sported home texts, every one had music written by a composer from Utah. Like the *Juvenile Instructor,* the music cards included songs of varied styles, from relatively solemn sacrament hymns to bouncing gospel songs like Stephens's "To-day" and "The Cause of Truth" (on card nos. 24 and 21, respectively). But although they sold for only one and a half cents apiece, the cards failed to supplant the sectarian books in many areas, and *Instructor* editor and First Presidency member George Cannon complained at the Saints' sloth and cultural disloyalty.[29] His urgency was prompted by a strong belief that home music was needed to help "preserve [the children] from apostasy."[30]

Partly to complement the light religious music being published in the *Instructor,* Calder and Careless began their *Utah Musical Times,* including in each issue one or two sacred choral pieces, usually dignified Mormon hymn-text settings. These settings were firmly rooted in old-style British and American hymn practice: the first two lines of a stanza were declaimed homophonically by all four voices, while the third (or sometimes fourth) line gave way to counterpoint or, more frequently, a reduction of voices to three or two. Then, in the fourth line the texture returned to that of the hymn's opening. Although they were often much simpler than Tullidge's hymns, the settings published in the *Utah Musical Times* were still clearly designed for choirs and often depended for their effects on dramatic dynamic contrasts that would be difficult for a congregation to render.

In addition to publishing these new pieces the *Times* argued its case for home composition thus: "A nation without its characteristic music would be a nation without patriotism. The people who have to depend on others for their songs are very apt to depend on others for their liberties."[31] Such rhetoric reemphasized Mormons' view of their community as a veritable nation. It also made it clear that Mormon music was meant to be as much a manifestation of nationalism as French, German, or Italian music.

Before the *Times* was a year old, Joseph Daynes's rival music company began publishing its own monthly, the *Utah Musical Bouquet*. Unlike Calder and Careless's prose-saturated journal, each issue of the *Bouquet* consisted of nothing but printed music and a single page of theory instruction. The music was also far more varied in style and genre than that in the *Instructor* or the *Musical Times*, with a typical issue containing a sentimental parlor song, a waltz or mazurka for piano, a part song, and possibly a harmonized hymn tune (without text); sacred and secular pieces appeared in about equal measure, with secular prevailing. The predominant composers in the *Bouquet* were Daynes, Beesley, and C. J. Thomas, who in 1877 stopped publishing in the *Instructor*. In addition to the monthly *Bouquet*, Daynes issued occasional sheets of his own music, most notably the stately funeral march he had composed for the rites of Brigham Young.[32]

The following year Eliza Snow cofounded a church auxiliary designed in part to extend musical training to the very young. Intended originally to enlist only boys, the Primary Mutual Improvement Association decided to add girls "to make it sound as well as it should." First Presidency member Joseph F. Smith was eager that the organization promote good music and notified Snow that "we might better afford what expense might be incurred in furnishing uniform, musical instruments, etc., for the cultivation of the children in Zion, than what we are expending in converting people abroad where elders spend years in converting a very few."[33]

In 1880, when the Primary Association officially became a churchwide organization, Snow had a tunebook printed at the *Instructor* office for the Primary's use. The forty-page work contained fifty-nine settings of Mormon and non-Mormon hymns, only thirteen of which had been or would be printed in the *Instructor* itself. The songs ranged from "Am I a Soldier of the Cross?" and "How Firm a Foundation" to didactic songs like "Don't Kill the Birds" and the minstrel favorite "Love at Home." Although the tunebook did not merit a second edition, it put forth in print a number of hymn settings and gospel songs that would end up among the most popular and durable in Mormonism, including "Do What Is Right" (tune: "The Old Oaken Bucket") and "We Thank Thee, O God, for a Prophet."

Still laboring over their proposed hymnbook, the Sunday School Union organized a churchwide music contest in 1882 to inspire composers and lyricists to produce fresh works in eleven categories. Hundreds of entries were submitted and C. J. Thomas, George Careless, and Ebenezer Beesley reviewed the works both for their musical quality and to guard against "objectionable" texts. After the review the Sunday School superintendant expressed satisfaction at the people's willingness to "aid by their feeble efforts a cause so noble." In May 1883 a total of $200 was awarded as prize money to thirty-two previously unpublished works submitted pseudonymously. Seven of the prize-winning works were immediately collected by Beesley into a forty-five-page publication for his Tabernacle Choir, who were until then still relying on manuscript part books.[34]

Evan Stephens swept the awards, taking both first and second prize in four of the categories and first prize in two others. Because of this, at least one disgruntled entrant, John Lewis, charged that Stephens had tampered with the judging—and indeed Stephens had helped screen some of the hundreds of entries.[35] But Stephens was exonerated by the Sunday School Board, leaving his place in the home music movement as secure as ever. Indeed, because he was essentially self-taught, Stephens perhaps best exemplified the spirit of self-reliance to the onlooking Saints. He had begun composing songs and hymns by ear in his early teens, and, he explained, "spoiled much paper in . . . grand choruses, like Handel's, only not properly put together; grand fugues, without a regular chord in them."[36] In 1879 the *Instructor* praised Stephens for his self-teaching, his "high order of talent," and his published compositions, many of which, it noted, had become "very popular" in the church.[37] The next year Stephens produced an operetta in Logan, composed entirely by himself—the first of its kind by a home talent.

When he began teaching the Sunday School Union singing classes in 1882 Stephens relied almost exclusively on his own music, and in 1883 he published *A Primer and First Reader of Vocal Music,* an almost entirely secular songbook for the use of his pupils. Its preface shows Stephens at his most self-conscious: "Nothing but a desire to follow out my *own* mode of teaching could have induced me to publish this little work. It seemed to me that I could not do my pupils justice by following other works (though they all have good points); so, in justice to them and myself, I commit myself to the mercy of the public as an 'Author,' fully prepared to bear both just and unjust criticism (if indeed the little book proves worthy of any notice at all).'' The book included twenty-six works, most of them apparently by Stephens, presented in a mixture of Tonic Sol-fa notation and "the old notation," neither of which, he later admitted, he could totally endorse.[38]

In January 1884 the *Deseret Sunday School Union Music Book* went on sale. It contained eighty-six songs with music and two without. Only two of the songs had come from the Sunday School Union music competition, and none had appeared on the old music cards. As its preface proudly announced, the work included such a varied mix of styles that virtually everyone, regardless of taste, could find something useful in it. Apparently they did: its first edition of five thousand had sold out by year's end and another five thousand were immediately issued. By the time the second edition was exhausted, about one copy for every four Mormon children enrolled in Sunday school had been sold.[39]

The success of the home songbook was an important step toward keeping Mormondom's core intact, for that core was in danger of erosion. In the 1870s churches were dedicated throughout Utah (especially in Salt Lake City) by Catholics, Episcopalians, Presbyterians, and Methodists, and in the 1880s by Baptists and Lutherans. The territory also became the target of proselyting crusades by the Methodists and the American Home Missionary Society. The establishment of gentile churches disrupted the Saints' theological isolation; but the proselyting, while somewhat threatening to the youth, proved little more than an annoyance. More important, Mormon Utah became the focus of federal anti-polygamy campaigns, which drew a thick cloud of fear over the Saints' refuge.

Throughout this period Mormon folksingers intensified their celebration of polygamy's joys and perils. In 1876, for example, when the Cincinnati Convention created a platform plank vowing to thwart Mormon polygamy, Charles Walker responded testily:

> Should the "Plank" be of oak
> May it all end in smoke,
> And the ashes decay and get rotten.
> May its author do well
> On his journey to hell
> And sink, sink and sink till forgotten.[40]

But anti-polygamy resolutions prevailed. Those who were imprisoned had a favorite song about the penitentiary, a place they dubbed "Limbo." It began:

> All you cohabs still dodging round,
> You'd better keep in under ground,
> For if with number two you're found,
> They'll pop you into Limbo![41]

Meanwhile, as Mormons satirized their persecutors, gentiles (and even some Mormons) spoofed polygamy in songs such as the racist, pseudo-minstrel piece "The Mormon Coon":

> I got a big brunette, I got a blonde petite,
> I got 'em short, fat, thin, and tall,
> I got a Zulu pal and big old Cuban gal;
> They come in bunches when they hear me call.
> Now I got a homely few, but I got 'em pretty too,
> I got 'em black as the octoroon,
> I can cut a figure eight, I must ship 'em by freight,
> For I am a Mormon coon.[42]

The Saints' need to consolidate their ideals in the face of federal persecution and the incursion of other faiths into Zion led church musicians to propose the making of a definitive Mormon hymnal. The exiled president John Taylor received a letter in August 1885 from Beesley, Daynes, and Thomas Griggs asking permission to compile and publish a definitive tunebook for all the hymns in the standard hymnal, then in its eighteenth edition, as well as to include "a number of choice anthems both original and selected." Taylor surprised them by replying that he had several other applications to do the same and felt that the time was not right for such a work. Although Taylor did not name the other applicants, their identity may be fairly guessed by his subsequent appointment of George Careless and Evan Stephens to join Beesley, Daynes, and Griggs in producing the book. Besides their common zeal for home composition, the five men shared a common post: one was the Tabernacle Choir's accompanist, another its conductor, one its former and another its future conductor, and one a conductor who had been elected but never served.[43]

Not surprisingly then, the work they produced, named after Tullidge's *Latter Day Saints' Psalmody,* leaned heavily toward elaborate choir hymns and away from congregational songs. The compilers' preface to the first edition of five thousand copies rightly called the work a "labor of love and principle" that was, with few exceptions "the production of 'our mountain home' composers." Virtually all of the tunes and settings had appeared in print before, but their assemblage here was auspicious. Exactly one fifth of the collection's settings were by Careless (twenty-two more than by the prolific Daynes, who had forty-four in the book). Stephens is credited with thirty-nine; Beesley, eighteen (along with three arrangements of anonymous tunes); and Griggs, thirteen (plus two arrangements). Several composers contributed several settings apiece, including A. C. Smyth (nine) and John Lewis (five), while nine of the settings were taken from Tullidge's pathbreaking 1857 collection. None of the non-Mormon composers credited in the *Psalmody* were of the "gospel song" stripe: Handel had three settings; Haydn, Mozart, and Mendelssohn were given two each; and Auber, Boyce, and Rossini, to name a few, each had one setting. Forty-nine of the works were anonymous. Many of these last reflected the old folk-hymn tradition, even though they adapted melodically and harmonically the cultured European tradition espoused by the book's compilers. C. J. Thomas, once the favored composer of the Mormon elite, was on a proselyting mission in England during the entire compilation. Hence, only one of his hymns, "Sons of Michael," appeared among the 330 in the new *Psalmody*.

Most of the apparently new settings in the *Psalmody* were rooted in Careless's choral hymn style. Other influences were less obvious, as in the case of Daynes's setting of Phelps's 1856 poem "If You Could Hie to Kolob," for which Careless's theater music became the model. (Daynes's opening line borrows note for note from Careless's waltz for the play *Cinderella*.) Some of the older settings were edited to resemble Careless's style. Tullidge's tune to "Awake and Sing the Song," for example, was much improved by the *Psalmody*'s composers and rechristened with the tune name "Bishop." Indeed, how far the *Psalmody* improved upon Tullidge's work generally may be seen by comparing Daynes's setting of the anonymous English paraphrase of Isaiah, "As the Dew from Heaven Distilling," with the setting Tullidge had made thirty years earlier.

The musical typesetting for this massive 330-piece work took nearly two years, resulting in the costliest book yet produced in the territory. (Taylor had died four months after the typesetting began, so the work required Wilford Woodruff's presidential approval, which it received in spring 1889.) In its sophistication, handsomeness, and sheer mass, this 1889 compilation struck some observers as nothing short of miraculous. But unquestionably the work was the child of a lengthy and strenuous gestation.[44]

It took six and a half years for the first edition of the *Psalmody* to sell out.[45] By then the *Deseret Sunday School Union Music Book* and its successor, the *Deseret Sunday School Union Song Book* (1891), had gone through a total of six editions representing thirty thousand copies.

By appealing directly to the growing legions of Mormon children, the Sunday School Union had gained a powerful influence over Mormon music—despite the attempts of the better-trained musicians to elevate and codify its musical standards in the form of choral hymns and anthems at the expense of what Evan Stephens called "cheese-cloth music" (gospel songs).[46]

After more than five decades of calls to gather to Zion, Mormonism had opened itself both to the most exalted and most mundane musical products of sectarian religion. As the emerging American mass culture confronted the idealism of Mormonism's musical professors it produced a curious hybrid, a hymnody alternately profound in its solemnity and jaunty in its triviality. And while the two strains somehow coexisted well, the latter captivated the sentiments of the vast and diverse Mormon populace, which, by July 1897 (the jubilee of the Saints' entry into the Salt Lake Valley), was 255,000 strong.

For that jubilee sixty-five-year-old Charles Walker composed one of the most moving of the old-style Mormon folk adaptations. Sung to the tune "Marching to Georgia," Walker's summation of the pioneering of Deseret contained these eloquent lines:

> O'er trackless wilds and sagebrush,
> O'er many a turbid stream,
> Through wild and somber canyons
> Now where locomotives scream,
> With weary limbs and bleeding feet
> They urged their jaded team
> As they came marching on to Utah.
>
> Their sufferings and their hardships
> Time will not let me tell;
> Of stampedes, raiding Indians,
> Their horrid midnight yell,
> The sad and lonely funerals,
> Without the dirge of bell,
> As they came marching to Utah.
>
> With faces pinched by hunger
> They trod the desert wild,
> The famished mother failing
> To nurse her newborn child;
> Yet 'midst these dire privations
> God looked on them and smiled
> As they came marching to Utah.[47]

A few days before Walker composed these lines Evan Stephens complained to the Tabernacle Choir that the Saints were losing interest in their own history and cultural identity. Home compositions were still being written, "but who are learning or singing them? . . . What are the young folks doing?"[48] His questions were symptomatic of the times. The sacred nation portrayed by Walker had reached its second and third generations and seemed to be slipping into the mainstream of American life. The need for a musical commonality with the outside world sharply challenged the hope for a Mormon national music.

In virtually all of its forms, of course, Mormon home composition had been imported. While Mormon-sounding names on sacred songs tended to legitimize them to the Saints, the music and sentiment of most of the songs continued to emanate from the larger Christian culture, the seedbed of Mormon proselyting. Ironically, the deliberately "indigenous" Mormon tunes and settings of this period actually seemed to draw less on the church's roots than did the feisty and vivid lyrics sung by its folksingers to borrowed tunes.

Still, Mormon culture came to value many forms of music in its midst, if for no other reason than that the diversity reflected the variety of God's own creation. And however distinguished or flawed may have been the fruits of the home music movement in nineteenth-century Mormondom, the movement did provide the basis for a change from a predominantly oral musical culture into a culture of musical print. Putting music on the page allowed the religion to establish at last an orthodoxy of tune, a canon of music to match its canon of words.

NOTES

1. Doctrine and Covenants 78:14.

2. "Singing in Sunday Schools," *Utah Musical Times* 2 (1 May 1877): 25.

3. The quotations in this and the following paragraph are from Tullidge's letters to the editor, *Millennial Star* 19 (21 February 1857): 116–17, and 19 (19 March 1857): 170–72; also 20 (2 January 1858): 11–12.

4. For a typically caustic review of the Mormon hymnbook of this period see *Edinburgh Review* 202 (April 1854): 186–87. For a milder assessment see Mayhew, *The Mormons*, pp. 42–46.

5. See the comments by his daughter in *OPH* 15:102.

6. See William Earl Purdy, "The Life and Works of Charles John Thomas: His Contributions to the Music History of Utah" (Master's thesis, BYU, 1949), pp. 10–13.

7. To put this hymn in context see David John Buerger, "The Adam-God Doctrine," *Dialogue* 15 (Spring 1982): 14–58.

8. See Purdy, "Life and Works," pp. 52–53. Cf. the C. J. Thomas and George Careless part books, HDC.

9. *JD* 12:284–89.

10. See the weekly editorials in the *Utah Magazine* 3 (May 1869). Studies of Thomas and Careless have been mentioned previously. On Daynes see

Marion Peter Overson, "Joseph J. Daynes, First Tabernacle Organist: His Contribution to the Musical Culture of Utah and the Significance of His Life and Works" (Master's thesis, Brigham Young University, 1954).

11. "Our Home Composers," *Utah Magazine* 3 (3 July 1869): 139.

12. "Musical Correspondence," *Utah Magazine* 3 (2 October 1869): 347–48.

13. "Musical Correspondence," *Utah Magazine* 3 (23 October 1869): 392.

14. See Ronald W. Walker, "The Commencement of the Godbeite Protest: Another View," *Utah Historical Quarterly* 42 (1974): 216–44.

15. Mormon folk song from this and later periods has been amply surveyed in the collections in the Fife Folklore Archives (Utah State University, Logan, Utah), the Austin and Alta Fife recording collection and the Lester Hubbard recording collection (both at UU), and in the books published from them: Austin and Alta Fife, *Saints of Sage and Saddle: Folklore among the Mormons* (Bloomington: Indiana University Press, 1956); Lester A. Hubbard, comp. and ed., *Ballads and Songs from Utah* (Salt Lake City: University of Utah Press, 1961). See also the articles on the subject cited in those works as well as in Thomas E. Cheney, ed., *Mormon Songs from the Rocky Mountains: A Compilation of Mormon Folksong* (Salt Lake City: University of Utah Press, 1981). For a sampling of recorded songs see *New Beehive Songster,* vol. 1 (University of Utah Press Record 175-3). On the problems of defining "folk" music see Bruno Nettl, *An Introduction to Folk Music in the United States,* rev. ed. (Detroit: Wayne State University Press, 1962), pp. 1–7.

16. This statement and the verses below are from Phelps to Brigham Young, 17 February 1863, holograph in HDC.

17. "Jehovah's lion" refers to Brigham Young, to whom Phelps sent this song on New Year's Day 1862. The cover letter explains, "I present this hymn to you for the purpose of singing 'Dixie' in that spirit that sounds like heaven, and swells the soul to thoughts that breathe, by words that burn, with sense and sound. Let your children sing it and may God grant them the music of paradise" (Phelps to Young, 1 January 1862, holograph in HDC).

18. "Ieaun" [John Silvanus Davis], *The Bee-Hive Songster* (Salt Lake City: Daily Telegraph Office, 1868), pp. 11–13.

19. Larson and Larson, *Diary of Charles Walker,* 1:xvi.

20. Cheney, *Mormon Songs,* pp. 118–20.

21. On these songs see Hubbard, *Ballads and Songs,* pp. 393–95 and 408–14; also Cheney, *Mormon Songs,* pp. 176–78.

22. Charles L. Thompson, *Times of Refreshing: A History of American Revivals from 1740 to 1877* (Chicago: J. S. Goodman, 1877), p. 352. For a summary account of the gospel song phenomenon, see Foote, *Three Centuries of American Hymnody,* pp. 264–71.

23. See R. G. Pardee, *The Sabbath-School Index* (Philadelphia: J. C. Garrigues, 1868), pp. 221–23, and Ernest Trice Thompson, *Presbyterianism in the South,* 3 vols. (Richmond: John Knox Press, 1973), 2:333–34.

24. No copy of the *Jubilee Song Book* appears to have been found. But see "Thanks and Facts," *JI* 9 (1 August 1874): 182; "Sunday School Matters," *JI* 9 (29 August 1874): 206; and "New Hymn Book," *JI* 9 (19 December 1874): 312.

25. *JI* 14 (15 November 1879): 264. The song also appears on the seventeenth Sunday School Music Card.

26. While to gentiles an "iron rod" suggested an instrument of punishment, to Mormons it was a symbol of the Word of God. See I Nephi 8 and 15.

27. See Manwaring's Notebook, holograph in HDC, and *JI* 13 (1878): 72.

28. *JD* 11:305.

29. See "Music Cards," *JI* 12 (15 May 1877): 120, and the editorials in *JI* 12 (1 November 1877): 246, and 13 (1 February 1878): 30. HBLL has a bound set of twenty-four cards, apparently all that were issued.

30. "Deseret Sunday School Union Meeting," *JI* 18 (15 May 1883): 150.

31. "Singing in Sunday Schools," *Utah Musical Times* 2 (1 May 1877): 25.

32. Issues of the *Bouquet* may be found in HBLL.

33. Rogers, *Life Sketches*, pp. 209–10. For a history of the Primary Association see Carol Cornwall Madsen and Susan Staker Oman, *Sisters and Little Saints: One Hundred Years of Primary* (Salt Lake City: Deseret Book, 1979).

34. Ebenezer Beesley, comp., *A Collection of Hymns and Anthems Set to Music by Home Composers* (Salt Lake City: Juvenile Instructor Office, 1883). See the part books in the Sterling Beesley Collection; also, in the same location, a marked copy of *Thomas's Sacred Music* (New York: W. A. Pond, 1866), apparently once in Ebenezer Beesley's possession. Independent of the Sunday School Union's efforts but symptomatic of its spirit was the publication of Joel H. Johnson's 327-page *Hymns of Praise for the Young.* See "Sacred Song," *DN,* 27 May 1882.

35. On the awarding of prizes see *JI* 18 (15 June 1883): 186–87.

36. Stephens in "Shining Lights," p. 655.

37. *JI* 14 (1 April 1879): 78.

38. See Abraham Cannon Journal, 24 and 31 October 1890.

39. On editions and enrollment see *Jubilee History of Latter-day Saints Sunday Schools* (Salt Lake City: Deseret Sunday School Union, 1900), pp. 40–41, 48.

40. Larson and Larson, *Diary of Charles Walker,* 1:429. Walker records this as a poem. But the evidence is overwhelming that no practical distinction was ever made between songs and poems in nineteenth-century Mormondom.

41. Thomas Broadbent Autobiography, typescript in HBLL, 29 October 1889.

42. See Levette J. Davidson, "Mormon Songs," *Journal of American Folklore* 58 (October–December 1945): 291–92; Cheney, *Mormon Songs,* pp. 183–84; Hubbard, *Ballads and Songs,* p. 420.

43. See Beesley et al. to Taylor, 7 August 1885, and Taylor to Beesley et al., 10 August 1885. Both of these are printed in Sterling Beesley, *Kind Words,* pp. 433–34.

44. See, for instance, "About Music," *DN,* 5 April 1890.

45. See Griggs Journal, 7 June 1894 and 29 July 1895.

46. Griggs Journal, 24 October 1901.

47. Larson and Larson, *Diary of Charles Walker,* 2:847.

48. Griggs Journal, 12 July 1897.

8

Modern Hymnody and the Church Music Committee

As America entered the twentieth century, the crosscurrents of fashion were sweeping through the hymnody of all faiths. Mass revivalism kept gospel songs before the public. Dozens of them became "standards," transdenominational hymns of which a professing Christian could not be ignorant. But some denominational leaders and many seasoned church musicians continued to scorn the style of gospel hymnody. To provide a musical alternative they created new hymns in a sturdier, more elegant European style, much like the products of the Oxford movement of the mid-nineteenth century. A spirit of aestheticism countered the populist spirit of gospel songs.

Mormon music felt the strength of both the gospel songs' popularity and the church music reformers' passion. But it also felt the lingering undercurrents of homemade music. Mormons in the twentieth century have struggled with the dilemma of maintaining a solid musical identity without continuing to alienate the rest of Christendom. In an era of rapid change and fluctuating ideals, aestheticism and populism have vied to determine the musical identity of Mormonism. For much of the century a committee of church musicians has overseen the struggle.

By 1908 the *Deseret Sunday School Union Song Book* had reached its tenth edition, leaving something over 100,000 copies in circulation (more than one for every four Mormons on the church's rolls). Its unparalleled success prompted Mormon Sunday school leaders to contemplate an even larger collection, rivaling the *Psalmody* in size. The church Sunday school board asked choristers throughout the church to submit lists of their ten favorite hymns not then contained in the *Song Book*. From the tally of about a thousand songs submitted, one hundred were finally added to the new 1909 book, *Deseret Sunday School Songs*, including many sacrament songs to accompany the new emphasis on administering the sacrament in Sunday school meetings and also what the book called the "higher grade of devotional hymns demanded by so many of our musicians."[1]

The content of the new Sunday school book was partly inspired by the 1908 Chicago publication of a songbook compiled by a group of Mormon mission leaders. This songbook took its name from early Mormonism's fleeting ideal: *Songs of Zion.* The church's membership outside of the Rocky Mountain region had topped sixty thousand that year and it became increasingly evident that "mission field" congregations could afford neither the expense nor the confusion of multiple hymnals. (In some areas choristers had to call out numbers from different books to represent the same hymn.) As early as 1899 a *Missionary Song Book* had appeared in the vast Southern States Mission, edited by Evan Stephens, containing words only to many of Stephens's works, songs from the hymnal and Sunday school book, and also a sampling of Ira Sankey favorites, designed to appeal to prospective converts. The 1908 *Songs of Zion,* with printed music to 264 songs, at last provided a correlation of other church songbooks for the convenience of Mormons outside of the Rocky Mountain Zion.

In 1912 the official words-only hymnal, *Sacred Hymns and Spiritual Songs,* reached its twenty-fifth edition, and its companion, the *Psalmody,* reached its fifth. That same year *Songs of Zion* had already reached its fourth edition, apparently making it the fastest-selling Mormon hymnal ever. The Sunday school collection still thrived, but the words-only *Sacred Hymns* was losing its appeal in the face of so many music-typeset works in print. Meanwhile, the *Psalmody* still appealed primarily to musicians, although it had added sentimental gospel songs like Palmer's "Memories of Galilee" ("Each Cooing Dove"); Christian favorites such as "Rock of Ages" and "I Need Thee Every Hour"; and new Mormon songs like John McClellan's "Mother" and Evan Stephens's "Our Mountain Home So Dear." The *Songs of Zion*'s appeal to the full spectrum of church members' tastes foreshadowed the spirit of the 1920s, a decade of churchwide consolidation and synthesis led by new church president Heber J. Grant.

Mormon president Joseph F. Smith died ten days after the 1918 armistice was signed. His successor, Grant, was a devout yet highly pragmatic and progressive businessman, the first church president born in Utah, and likewise the first not to live in polygamy while heading the church. Unlike Smith, whose interest in music seemed wholly utilitarian, Grant possessed a curious fascination with the art and the personal challenges it provided for him. Virtually tone-deaf, Grant had struggled for years to learn how to sing Mormon hymns by rote. Throughout his life Grant boasted of the virtues of perseverance, citing his own determination to learn to sing (the efficacy of which remained dubious to many observers). He frequently visited church musicians in order to sing for them, and often spoke on the power of sacred music to develop morals. He also aired his strong opinions of various hymns, insisting the Saints refrain from all "anti-doctrinal" works. Grant said of the well-known revivalist song "Just As I Am" (as one singer recalled): "I want you to go home and get that piece of music and write on it 'condemned.' I don't want you to tear it up or burn it, but I want you to write 'condemned' on it." And of another popular revival song, "Sometime, Somewhere"—which was in the Sunday school songbook— he told another musician, "that isn't anywhere, don't sing that song."[2]

In September 1920 Grant called apostle Melvin Ballard to select and head a committee of twelve musicians whose principal duties were to regulate musical affairs in the church, institute technical training for musicians in local congregations, foster greater knowledge of music literature, and undertake a radical revision of the *Psalmody* along the lines of *Songs of Zion.* The nine-man, three-woman committee Ballard chose contained, among others, the Tabernacle Choir conductor and his assistant, three Tabernacle organists, the manager of the Salt Lake Theatre, and the two surviving patriarchs of Mormon music, George Careless and Evan Stephens.[3]

The church had transfigured itself since the heyday of the immigrant professors. It gradually had abandoned polygamy and communitarianism for a place in the larger landscape of American life. It had proven its ability to prosper without economic isolation, erecting chapels and temples, and even acquiring important church history sites—making itself the lawful caretaker of many of its once-disputed shrines. Church leaders were restructuring the institution after the pattern of business and civil bureaucracies.[4] This was nowhere more evident than in the appointment of the music committee, a group of trained musicians who could scrutinize the musical habits of a church with over half a million members.

Although Mormons had gained some repute among outsiders for the quality of their singing, the committee busied itself trying to improve sacred music performance among their people. Within a few months they had visited and evaluated dozens of congregations, instituted mandatory training in vocal technique and solfege, started preparing handbooks for choristers and organists, and begun to "wage [a campaign] against poor, battered, and out-of-tune instruments in our places of worship."[5] Latter-day Saint choirs had lost some of the primacy they gained in the previous century. Nevertheless, the committee hoped to better the quality of Mormon choral singing by publishing a series of anthem books. In March 1921 the Deseret Book Company attempted to focus the committee's interest on the hymnbook by warning them that all copies of the previous *Psalmody* edition would be sold out by mid-summer.

Busy with its other, seemingly more pressing tasks, the committee proceeded on the *Psalmody* revision with careful deliberation. In September 1921 they settled certain matters of format: they would abandon the *Psalmody*'s three-stave settings and would print *all* verses of each hymn with its music, in order to do away with the need for the old words-only hymnbooks. The revision would try to eliminate three things: hymns rarely sung, doctrinally unsound texts, and bad music. After holding several contests for new texts and music the committee produced a revision outline in November 1923, which proposed to eliminate eighty-five works from the *Psalmody* and give almost as many texts new or revised music.[6]

Grant and the First Presidency approved this plan eleven months later, at which time the committee ambitiously began transcribing, editing, and composing new music. While it appears that most committee members performed these services without pay, they urged that all composers in the church be paid for the use of their work, hoping that money would help stimulate home composition.[7] Evan Stephens became the chief beneficiary of this policy. Not only did he win the prestigious sacrament hymn contest ($25), he also arranged to be credited $5 for each of the 56 new hymn settings he would compose, and $1 for each of 164 transcriptions.[8]

During the next few years it became clear that the emerging hymnal would be less a revision than a wholly new work. Tracy Cannon,[9] who was emerging as a leader within the committee, assigned hymn texts to committee members for new settings throughout 1924 and 1925, at which time the committee decided to abandon the title of "psalmody" and name the new work *Latter-day Saint Hymns*.[10] In August 1926—almost six years after it was begun—the work remained unfinished, leading Cannon to report that the hymnbook was "progressing about as usual." Finally in January 1927 the work was ready for the Deseret Book Company to begin plating. Only after it was ready in April, apparently, did the committee ask the First Presidency for its formal approval of the book to be published under the committee's name.

The contents of *Latter-day Saint Hymns* revealed how strongly the spirit of musical reform governed the music committee. Only one Bliss song, "Let the Lower Lights Be Burning," appeared and there were no songs by Ira Sankey or the popular Fanny Crosby. The book also showed how much Evan Stephens's gospel-song-cum-grand-opera-chorus style had taken hold of Mormon hymnody. Whereas George Careless had 63 hymn settings in the new book (compared to 66 in the last edition of the *Psalmody*) Stephens had composed 84 (20%) of *Latter-day Saint Hymns*'s 421 settings, many of them treating his own texts or the lyrics of apostle Orson Whitney.[11] Stephens hymns such as "Midway of Life," "Wrinkled Brow of Time," "O Balmy Mountain Air!" and "Tenderly Wipe the Bitter Tears" were especially ostentatious new works, clearly designed as choral showpieces rather than as congregational songs.

Stephens had chided the Saints a few years earlier for being "a little too much impressed by the rhythmic swing of so-called 'gospel hymns,' out of which error I trust we will gradually emerge.'' But his own music was disposed to propulsive dotted-eighth-cum-sixteenth-note rhythms reminiscent of the gospel hymn style. This trait was necessary to the creation of a specifically Mormon music, he explained, because it breathed ''optimism and not pessimism,'' unlike Catholic music with its ''gloomy solemnity.'' In his music, which he thought exemplary for aspiring Mormon composers, ''the somber must not predominate, but be used only as a means of contrast to heighten the effects of the bright.''[12]

Just as the musical style had veered from the somber stateliness of the *Psalmody*'s most reverent works, so the texts had all but abandoned the millennialism and communitarianism of the church's initial wave of hymn-text writing in the 1830s and 1840s. The new texts dwelt primarily on personal spiritual experience, sentimentality over life's trials, and occasionally, the grandeur of the Mormon landscape. The variety of moods in this early-twentieth-century body of writing ranged from the standard revivalism of Bertha Kleinman's

> Why should I wonder, O Sun of my day,
> With doubt like a wilted husk gone to decay?

to the ornateness of Whitney's

> Roll on my days, responsive to Thy rule,
> This tongue Thine oracle, this pen Thy tool,
> Designed to soar, or doomed to lowly plod,
> Amanuensis of the mind of God.

Besides adding such new lyrics, the committee revised a number of old texts as part of the new ''good neighbor'' policy between the church and the States. Phelps's hero-song about Joseph Smith (''Praise to the Man'') contained the words ''Long shall his blood . . . stain Illinois''; the committee changed them to ''Long shall his blood . . . plead unto heaven.'' The committee also softened some of the striking promises made to the Saints in the song ''O Ye Mountains High'': ''on the necks of thy foes thou shalt tread'' became ''without fear of thy foes thou shalt tread''; and ''The Gentiles shall bow 'neath thy rod'' became ''And thy land shall be freedom's abode.'' There was doctrinal retrenchment as well: the second line of the hymn ''Sons of Michael'' was altered from ''Rise, the Eternal Father greet'' to ''Rise, the ancient father greet,'' and even the paramount expression of early Mormonism, ''The Spirit of God Like a Fire Is Burning,'' had two of its verses removed, apparently for their excessive temple imagery.[13]

Aside from producing this new hymnbook, the music committee in the 1920s undertook to promote sophisticated music in the church, the community, and the nation at large. They authored articles on technique and aesthetics for church magazines, sponsored classes (usually taught by committee members) at the church-owned McCune School of Music,[14] opposed plans to reduce music programs in the public schools, supported efforts to bring more nationally famous musicians to Salt Lake City, and endeavored to promote proper use of the phonograph and radio for elevating people's tastes. At the same time they arranged deals with Columbia and Victor records to make recordings of Mormon hymns.[15]

With the deaths of Stephens (1930) and Careless (1932) the old guard passed from the scene and the committee's younger members, led by Tracy Cannon, came to preside over official Mormon music. In 1934 the committee prepared a self-study in order to clarify its mission and prerogatives. It was, first, to develop sacred music in the church, not just by publishing home music but by endorsing and teaching the techniques of sophisticated "selected" music that would promote an "exalted fellowship" and a "holy communion with the Infinite." Second, it would provide appropriate secular music for the Saints' entertainment and delight. Third, it would make local church choirs the "chief musical organization[s]" of the church. Fourth, and perhaps most controversially, it would try to have pipe organs installed in all Mormon chapels, stopping the proliferation of pianos and electric organs.[16]

In 1936 the committee's alarm over electric organs had been aroused to the point that they tried to stop any more from being installed in Mormon chapels, and even proposed the church start building its own pipe organs. The Paris-trained Tabernacle organist and Church Music Committee member Alexander Schreiner prepared a set of organ books for use on these pipe organs in 1937, mainly to counteract the popular organ pieces that were being played in church by some Mormon organists, love songs such as "Pale Hands I Love" and "I Love You Truly." But that same year the First Presidency overruled the committee's rejection of Hammond organs for church use and authorized their widespread installation in church buildings—a decision the committee would oppose for over thirty years.[17]

In 1936 the committee persuaded the First Presidency to authorize certain musicians to travel throughout the church to train its members in the canons of sacred music and to counsel them to "avoid the sentimentality of popular ballads, the distraction of love songs in church, the contradictions of sectarian songs which we cannot believe."[18] By 1939 over five thousand church organists and choristers had taken classes from these itinerant teachers, and Cannon happily announced that the "students are developing an enlarged consciousness of the vastness of the field of musical expression."[19]

The committee took two important steps in hymnody in the 1930s. First, in September 1933, they began broadcasting radio dramatizations of "hymn stories," narratives of faith-promoting events surrounding the writing of beloved LDS hymns. These broadcasts led to a series of articles in the *Improvement Era* and to the 1939 publication of George Pyper's *Stories of Latter-day Saint Hymns* (copies of which Pyper and Heber J. Grant autographed and presented to all Tabernacle musicians). Second, they began to contemplate a new hymnbook that would supersede both the Sunday school book and *Latter-day Saint Hymns*, downplay gospel hymnody and the Evan Stephens style, and draw heavily on classic European Protestant tradition.

Latter-day Saint Hymns, or the "green book," as it was commonly called because of the color of its cover, had sold relatively poorly and was little used because of the continuing popularity of Sunday school songs.[20] Despite the music committee's efforts, the Sunday School Union held de facto control of Mormon hymnody. Many of the music committee's members as well as other prominent Mormon musicians also held positions on the Sunday school board and took the opportunity to try to consolidate the two vying songbooks into one. The music committee discussed publishing a single, unified hymnbook as early as 1936 and issued a call for new hymns in 1939.[21] J. Reuben Clark, who was more or less directing the church in Heber Grant's old age and disability, urged the committee to proceed, but was money-wary in the wake of the Depression. He insisted that a new hymnbook should not be produced when the publishers and merchants still had stacks of the old on their shelves.[22]

Delaying its work on that account, the committee sponsored a church-wide "hymn-of-the-month" singing program, designed to shrink backstocks of *Latter-day Saint Hymns*. By drawing all of these monthly practice hymns exclusively from the green book, the committee hoped that the Mormon congregations who still lacked them would buy up the books.[23] The plan seems to have worked. Two years later the committee settled on a plan to compile two hymnbooks, one for children and one for adults, primarily to make a clear separation between legitimate adult devotional music and the large body of Sunday school music that was clearly intended for children but still being sung by adults.[24] Both books, they hoped, would be out in 1947, the centennial year of the Saints' entry into the Salt Lake Valley.

Although Mormons, more than most American religious bodies, continued to focus on their own heritage, they could not escape the ecumenism of the times, which was born of the need to unite for peace during World War II. The broad appeal of certain hymns, coupled with the unwieldy profusion of denominational hymnbooks in the nation, led several religious parties to cooperate in the production of hymnbooks. In 1940 the church sponsored a festival to be broadcast from the

Tabernacle, under the rubric of "Your Hymns and Mine." Featuring choirs from the denominational churches of Salt Lake City, the evening was introduced by J. Reuben Clark. The First Presidency member told the crowd that all Christian churches, Mormon and non-Mormon, agreed on the essentials of faith and should unite against the evils of war. "Out of the efforts of all of us," he added, "these mountains and valleys . . . shall come to be the home of sacred music."[25] In consonance with such sentiments, the Church Music Committee, chaired by Tracy Cannon after Melvin Ballard's death in 1939, sought to unite Mormon hymnody with the broader Christian tradition, relying less on home music and revival songs and more upon the sophisticated high church traditions of Europe.[26]

During World War II, Mormon musician and scholar Sterling Wheelwright drafted one of the first and most erudite of a number of scholarly theses on Mormon musical history. In his "The Role of Hymnody in the Development of the Latter-day Saint Movement," Wheelwright scrutinized the course Mormon hymnody had taken since its origins. He wrote that twentieth-century Mormon hymnody had "faltered" and lost the "social relevancy" of its earliest days.[27] In March and April 1943 he met with the Church Music Committee to explain his findings and to plead for a return to what he considered the intimate and meditative hymnody of the early Mormons, a position that only served to bolster the committee's opposition to triviality in church music. Tracy Cannon endorsed the scholar's conclusions and asked all members to read the work and use its precepts in preparing the new hymnbooks.[28]

Partly to restrain the committee's aesthetic independence, the First Presidency in 1944 appointed a committee of four apostles—Harold B. Lee, Joseph Fielding Smith, Spencer W. Kimball, and Mark E. Petersen—to oversee the project.[29] This apostolic group submitted to the First Presidency the music committee's preliminary selection from the existing hymnbooks in October 1944, noting that many of the best hymns in Mormon tradition were borrowed outright from Protestant sources and that indeed more than one-third of the hymns in the existing collections contained neither words nor music written by Mormons. "This has argued," they wrote, "for the desirability of obtaining from similar sources other equally splendid songs that are not now included in our song literature."[30] But while this new "executive committee" supported the professional Church Music Committee's hopes to elevate worship music, it sometimes also dampened those hopes. Lee and his colleagues, for example, fought to keep a hymn despised by Grant, "Sometime, Somewhere," in the hymnal, and to restore Phelps's original words ("stain Illinois") to "Praise to the Man."[31] Meanwhile, although Grant's health was virtually spent, the First Presidency sought to govern the new work in an unprecedented way. Most significant, the Presidency insisted that the collection not omit any verses of standard Mormon hymns, since Grant had long felt that some of the best stanzas were the last ones.[32]

Having its own concerns about hymn texts, the music committee solicited new works from church poets, sponsored a hymn contest through the *Deseret News,* and freely revised the lyrics of venerable Protestant hymns—not to transform them, in the radical ways early Mormon poets had, but to conform them to current doctrinal orthodoxy.[33] Several of the hymns they wanted to include, however, apparently failed to meet even minimal standards of propriety, including "Fairest Lord Jesus" and "All Hail the Power of Jesus' Name," which contained the inexplicably objectionable line "let angels prostrate fall." Many of the best new lyrics came from Frank Kooyman, who had been repeatedly asked by the committee to compose as many hymns as he could for the work. His texts, though they could not compare to the best of the borrowed hymns, were contemporary and fresh. Their simple diction was blended with scriptural allusions, as in the closing hymn "Thy Spirit, Lord, Has Stirred Our Souls":

> Thy Spirit, Lord, has stirred our souls
> And by its inward shining glow
> We see anew our sacred goals
> And feel thy nearness here below.
>
> . . . . . .
>
> Did not our hearts within us burn?
> We know the spirit's fire is here.
> It makes our souls for service yearn;
> It makes the path of duty clear.
> Lord, may it prompt us day by day
> In all we do, in all we say.[34]

As for the hymnwriting contest, out of 590 entries the text by executive committee member Joseph Fielding Smith won. But his winning hymn, "Lord Thy People Rise to Praise Thee," was deemed by the music committee not fine enough to be included in the hymnal.[35]

The hymn texts collected for this mid-century hymnal tended to confirm Wheelwright's judgments. Mormonism's enduring hymn texts had sprung spontaneously from the Saints' fervent faith and the resulting bouts with outsiders. Now much of the conflict had stilled and the fever that surrounded nineteenth-century Mormon works had cooled. Whatever their strengths or weaknesses, the new hymn texts arose from the Saints' response to formal administrative calls. Mormon composers likewise, while often superbly educated, were losing interest in hymnwriting as an expression of Mormon self-reliance. As the musical descendants of Careless and Stephens turned to larger, often secular forms and increasingly balked at the styles of their elders, it became clear that an awesome void had been left in home music.

The music committee tried to fill this void by sending twenty-two of their best new texts to Mormon composers with a request for new settings. The committee stipulated five criteria for these settings. First, a dignified hymn style was to be maintained (hence, no gospel songs). Second, the melody was to be strong, original, and appealing, and composers were instructed to "try always to avoid triteness." Third, all common part-writing errors and "any signs of musical illiteracy" must be absent from the music. Fourth, composers were to ask themselves always, is this a hymn the Saints will sing without "undue promotion"? Fifth, composers should imitate the durable old hymns, incorporating as much as they could of those hymns' "vital elements" into the new music.[36] Along with this solicitation, the committee brought together a number of Bach chorales, hoping to include them in the book. Some committee members (notably Schreiner) in turn wrote neo-Bachian settings of their own for the newly accepted texts.[37]

In 1945 Cannon wrote a frank letter explaining the committee's attitude toward music for the new hymnal. He admired the British hymns, he wrote, but "it is a long way, I fear, from the dignity of these hymns to the triviality of some of the music we sing." He admitted that it would be a slow, possibly never-ending transition to such dignity and that Mormons generally would never find the same appeal in them that the committee did. Remarking that some of the lighter songs were being abolished from the new collection to give the book "a better standard of musical expression," he acknowledged the ill will this could arouse: "That we shall be criticized by some people who love the songs we have eliminated goes without saying but I am sure we are making a good step forward, without being altogether too drastic since, as I said, we cannot make transitions to a higher plane of expression very fast in a democratic body of people."[38]

When the collection was completed in fall 1946, only twenty-two Evan Stephens songs remained among the work's nearly three hundred different hymns, some of which had been arranged for male or female chorus. The committee had added majestic Protestant hymns such as "A Mighty Fortress," "Praise to the Lord, the Almighty," "Christ the Lord Is Risen Today," "All Creatures of Our God and King," and "Break Forth, O Beauteous, Heavenly Light," none of which had previously appeared in LDS hymnals. Works by committee members occupied a relatively small portion of the collection, and many of them were patterned after the old hymns they had borrowed. Leroy Robertson published the most and arguably the best in the hymnbook with twelve; Schreiner had eleven; and Cannon a mere five.

George Albert Smith, who succeeded Heber Grant as church president at the close of World War II, kept the collection in his office for over a year and a half, along with phonograph recordings of the new hymns.[39] This long deliberation tried the patience of music and executive committees alike. Harold B. Lee, who was especially anxious to get the hymnal out for the centennial, wrote a series of urgent letters on the project to his superiors, but seems not to have succeeded in expediting the hymnbook's publication.[40] The work was at last approved in summer of 1948, on the condition that six hymns be restored to the collection and that the title be changed from *Latter-day Saint Hymns* to *Hymns: The Church of Jesus Christ of Latter-day Saints* because Smith wanted the church's full name in the title.[41] An edition of seventy-five thousand was ordered, with typography and midnight-blue cover to be patterned after a favorite hymnal of the music committee's, the Christian Science hymnbook.[42] To give the book added authority in replacing other collections, the preface written by the music committee was signed by the presidency of the church.

Public response to the work was lukewarm. The Deseret Book store manager reported that he was "bombarded" with complaints about the small size and poor binding of the book.[43] Several church authorities questioned the hymn selection and even some of the attributions.[44] Tracy Cannon himself would only go so far as to say that "there are many good points about the book and some that are not so good." Insisting that, since so many copies were already circulating, criticisms among committee members should be kept private, Cannon and his colleagues resolved to defend the new book as better than any yet produced.[45] Nevertheless, they undertook a hasty but substantial revision, dropping twelve hymns, shuffling and renumbering many of the rest, and setting all of them in more readable type on thinner paper.

The revised hymnal retreated somewhat from its musical ideals. It omitted some venerable Protestant hymns, such as "Angels from the Realms of Glory," "Good Christian Men, Rejoice," and "We Gather Together," while adding primarily gospel songs in their place. This revision was formally introduced at churchwide hymn-singing festivals, beginning in January 1951 with a well-publicized event in the Tabernacle, at which the Tabernacle Choir sang and J. Reuben Clark chronicled some of the changes in the work and explained how best to use it. Reflecting on the revised hymnal, Tracy Cannon ambiguously described it as "the most utilitarian and unusual of any other yet published."[46]

It became increasingly clear that the committee would have to yield to the executive committee in matters of taste. In 1948 the committee formally acknowledged that it was not a governing board but an advisory group that could improve church music only by education, not by mandate.[47] Yet, despite the subduing effects of apostolic correlation, the Church Music Committee worked zealously for their ideals. They succeeded in perpetuating the professionally taught, itinerant music training programs that were begun in the 1930s and by 1956 had enrolled more than twenty-three thousand students altogether.[48] In connection with these music classes they published two textbooks as well as a comprehensive statement of church music policy, with the gentle title *Some General Recommendations Concerning Music in the Church.* Moreover, the committee sponsored choral festivals throughout the church, surveyed and recommended hundreds of non-Mormon choral works for use in church, continued to battle the installation of electric organs, and in 1943 founded "ward music guilds," local alliances of musicians to oversee the selection and performance of music in their own congregations.

In striving to educate the tastes of the Saints, the Church Music Committee sought to suppress any church music it thought irreverent or undignified, including virtually all solo singing and instrumental music other than that of the pipe organ.[49] Despite the free and conscious borrowings of the hymnal, the committee refused to adopt the liturgical music of other churches, particularly the Catholic church. But a *Deseret News* editorial in 1948 suggests that the music of local congregations continued to fall short of the professional music committee's ideals: "At times some have injected discordant notes into our sacred services by providing love songs and other things quite as inappropriate. Some have rendered operatic arias that have nothing sacred about them, and secular music of other kinds which really has no place in a religious meeting. At times, others have rendered in our services selections which form an integral part of the rituals and forms of worship of other churches. These, too, are entirely out of place in our meetings."[50] Over the next four years the committee further specified the four things required of appropriate Mormon music: words free of sectarian doctrines, music free of secular or Roman Catholic implications, numbers that would not detract from the spirit of meetings, and, ironically, caution in revising words or music created by others.[51]

The First Presidency likewise feared the taintings of denominationalism, particularly when it came to liturgical customs and ritualism. In May 1946 it prohibited the playing of music during the passing of the bread and water in church.[52] Wishing to avoid the loss of Mormonism's basically populistic spirit and lay-oriented worship, it repeatedly spoke and wrote against such Oxford-style innovations as wearing choir robes, giving choral benedictions, and meditating during musical postludes. Even the practice of standing to sing hymns, for which there was considerable tradition in the church, was discontinued.[53] J. Reuben Clark, in fact, argued that if the Tabernacle Choir could sing to millions over the radio while sitting, congregations should be able to sing well enough without standing up.[54]

Clark also warned the church's bishops in 1950 against letting musicians usurp control of the music in their congregations. Of a local Sunday evening service he had attended, he remarked disdainfully that not one Latter-day Saint hymn had appeared on the program. "There was Bach and some others I do not know about," he noted, adding that he remembered Bach "because I do not like him."[55] Clark's apparent parochialism offended committee member Spencer Cornwall, who demanded to know just how indeed, in the light of the church's eclectic musical history, the Presidency intended to define "our own music."[56]

In the 1960s the Church Music Committee continued to be dominated by professional musicians. By now these consisted primarily of university professors, such as Leroy Robertson of the University of Utah, who took over as committee chairman after Cannon's death in 1961. Robertson and his colleagues dedicated themselves to supporting the high standards of the past. One member of the committee, Brigham Young University Music Department Chairman Crawford Gates, even proposed that his department offer a degree in "LDS Church Music" to qualify recipients for employment by the Church Music Committee.[57]

But the struggle between populism and aestheticism continued as it had for decades. Indeed, one of the committee's members regarded the church as now being in a musical state of "emergency."[58] When asked in 1960 for a list of songs that should not be sung in church, the committee simply replied that "the list would be far too long."[59] As inquiries persisted and its leadership changed, the music committee gradually grew more specific, sending out letters opposing the singing of black spirituals in church—although they could not get the First Presidency to rule on this matter[60]—and religious popular songs such as "I Believe," "I'll Walk with God," and "How Great Thou Art."[61] They also spoke against the mingling of sacred and secular styles, as had occurred in a mildly notorious case where the story of Joseph Smith's first vision was set to the tune of "Tumblin' Tumbleweed."[62] Robertson wrote in 1964 that the committee "feels that songs which emphasize intimate association with our Father in Heaven on a cheap commercial basis are not worthy of our great and kind Creator." The following year he called for the abolition of such songs from Mormon meetings because "they are an abomination."[63] Furthermore, most committee members sought to suppress the Evan Stephens style, even though Alexander Schreiner thought it should be fostered. In 1966 the committee came to the consensus that Stephens's music was "good for some purposes" but unintelligent and less than challenging for good musicians.[64]

The debate over organs reached its zenith in the 1960s.[65] The First Presidency had made it clear that the expense of pipe organs should preclude their further use, but the committee remained unanimous in its opposition to installing anything but pipe organs in Mormon chapels. They argued that not only were pipe organs superior for worship by the richness of their tone, but that they were, in the long run, cheaper to maintain than the electronic organs that would demand occasional replacement. And they were disturbed that the poor quality of many of the electronic organs being bought by the church seemed to be driving more and more church musicians to use the piano.[66] In 1965 Spencer Kimball announced to the committee that the church would no longer be able to afford organs at all in many of its mission-field chapels; pianos would have to suffice.[67] In addition to the expense of the instruments, some apostles feared that church members would not be able to play pipe organs anyway, apparently believing that pipe organs were more difficult to play than their electronic counterparts.

Alexander Schreiner, the church's best-known organist, assessed the situation pointedly. Church members, he said, "being as children, musically speaking, have a strong preference for what I call a sweet organ—may I call it an ice cream sundae organ—which gives out the quality of sweetness of a gum drop or an all-day-succor [*sic*]. This is the specialty of electronic organs which are produced mainly for non-musicians and tired businessmen who wish a little something to play when they come home tired from work. . . . In a like manner children tend to choose sweetness in their food and sometimes mistreat their stomachs . . . [but] a good musician will prefer nobility to cloying sweetness."[68] Leroy Robertson urged the committee to be "aggressive" on the matter of organs, and at Harold Lee's suggestion the committee in 1966 drafted a letter to be read by the First Presidency. It voiced "alarm" at the continuing trend toward electronic instruments, which, the committee asserted, failed to meet the standards demanded by sacred music.[69] But money pressures in a decade of vast church growth put the matter more or less beyond discussion: the church would pay up to a certain amount for all organs—any more would have to be raised by local congregations.[70]

In the late 1960s the committee came under the churchwide "Correlation" program, of which Lee had been a prime mover. The executive committee to the Church Music Committee secured approval in early 1969 to have Robertson and his professionally oriented colleagues released and to have the Tabernacle Choir broadcast personnel (under apostle Mark Petersen) become the new Church Music Committee, with the former committee acting as advisers.[71] These advisers, however, continued with candor and good humor to advocate musical education in the church. When it was suggested that the church produce a simplified hymnbook for novice keyboard players, for example, Alexander Schreiner wrote that "it would be simpler for our pianists and organists to undertake some additional practice and lessons so that they shall be better able to play the hymns as they are now written."[72]

In 1972, however, Harold Lee became president of the church, and before the close of his foreshortened tenure—he died eighteen months after succession—he formed a large "Church Music Department," to be headed by one of the new general authorities of the church, O. Leslie Stone. As part of the Music Department (which included the Tabernacle Choir and organists, and the Mormon Youth Symphony and Chorus), a new music committee was formed with the BYU Music Department chairman at its head. This committee of the 1970s eventually consisted of five times the number of personnel in the committee of the 1960s.[73] And there were subcommittees for nine "specialized areas," including one whose charge was to prepare a new hymnbook.

The 1960s had been a fruitful decade for Christian ecumenism, an ideology that continued to reveal itself in hymnals: even Luther's Reformation standard, "A Mighty Fortress," began to be used in Catholic worship. Interfaith choirs sprang up, and the Gregorian Institute published its *Hymnal of Christian Unity* in 1964. Its preface was reminiscent of J. Reuben Clark in 1940, when it noted that "whatever differences may exist among the various Christian confession, there is always the great possibility of ever-increasing unity through sacred singing."[74]

But throughout this decade Mormon prestige faded. In the 1950s the church and its members had been admired widely for their respectability. In the 1960s this admiration waned with public criticism of church policy toward blacks, of church wealth, and of church secretiveness. It was not the sectarian persecution of the past so much as a new, secularist critique. Utah and Mormonism entered the headlines at almost regular intervals, and this enhanced Americans' latent curiosity about the church, whose members found themselves in a thicket of gentile acceptance and mistrust, reconciliation and fear.[75] In the midst of this the hymnbook committee set itself the task of creating a definitively Mormon hymnal, one that would underscore the divine aloofness of the true faith.

The hymnbook committee began meeting on 18 December 1973 with auspicious hopes to produce a book of about five hundred hymns drawn, its chairman suggested, from a pool of ten thousand.[76] In its quest for new material the committee intended to research as many Mormon and non-Mormon hymnbooks as they could find and also to comb the Mormon populace for newly written hymns, particularly those treating Mormon history and doctrine. Within two years, they postulated, the work would be printed, bound, and distributed. But eight days after this meeting,

President Lee died, leaving another former adviser to the music committee, Spencer Kimball, at the church's helm.

Immediately upon Kimball's succession, the committee proposed the project to the new First Presidency, noting that changing times required a new hymnbook, with songs that would "proclaim the revealed truth in this day and time and . . . that are most meaningful to the present-day worldwide church." This would mean, adviser Leslie Stone added, "less 'Protestant-type' hymns."[77] Although they seemed unsure as to what Lee had intended the revision to entail, Kimball and the apostles approved the work. By that spring church magazines were soliciting new words and music from the membership at large. As the soliciting proceeded, however, the committee privately resolved to guard the collection against being overrun by popular tastes and to ensure that it contain enough sophisticated music to make it appeal to trained musicians.[78]

The committee continued to scrutinize hymns steadily over the next two years, expanding the project's scope and pushing back its deadlines. All the while, some committee members worried that their revision was not being understood by church leaders, that the committee's authority was unclear and its expertise unappreciated. At least one apostle recommended they include among the new hymns the sentimental gospel song "How Great Thou Art." Another suggested the committee do away with the extra verses for hymns that were once required by the First Presidency. Other church leaders proposed changing established texts, retaining hymns the committee hoped to delete, and rejecting hymns, such as "Break Forth, O Beauteous Heavenly Light," a work that the committee was determined to keep. Complicating the revision process, the church Correlation Committee now had to scrutinize the propriety of all hymn texts.[79]

After more than three years of review and discussion, in March 1977 the hymnbook committee sent to the First Presidency a complete evaluation of all hymns in the old hymnbook, a list of possible new hymns, and a single-page brief on the rationale of the new book. The brief summarized the hymnbook compilers' point of view, arguing both that the Protestant (especially gospel song) tinges of the earlier generation should be eradicated in favor of more indigenous work, and that the new book should transcend the American and regional flavor of its predecessors, broaden its cultural boundaries.

Most favorite hymns would be retained, especially those favored by general church leaders.[80] But the evaluation proposed dropping songs such as Heber Grant's beloved "Beautiful Zion for Me," Phelps's "Adam-ondi-Ahman" (which church president David O. McKay had ordered restored to the hymnbook in 1959),[81] "Who's on the Lord's Side?" (which the Church Music Committee had tried unsuccessfully to delete in 1948), and the lilting gospel song "Each Cooing Dove," (which one hymnbook committee member privately called "a blot on the church"[82]). This official evaluation of the old hymns was, on the whole, more charitable than some of the committee's discussions had been. But even so, after reviewing the document, the First Presidency decided that the course the revision was taking was incorrect, and that the project would be shelved indefinitely. That same year the Music Department was dissolved and replaced by a smaller "Music Division" headed by Michael F. Moody.[83]

In 1983, after the church had produced new editions of their scriptures, the First Presidency directed the Music Division to proceed with a new hymnbook. But the presidency asked the committee members to put aside their musical training when it came to matters of taste. Instead the committee was to try to discern what the masses in the church—now over five million strong—needed and wanted. Church leaders hoped that the work would appeal equally to the schooled and the unschooled alike. Indeed, one of the committee's advisers said that the committee had "only one disability: they knew too much about music."[84] Fueled by a sense of duty and conciliation, the Music Division accommodated its leaders' request. It built upon the selection of the previous hymn committee, but systematically "field-tested" hymns to be used in the book, submitting them to congregations and fireside groups for evaluation. The completed hymnbook appeared in August 1985. (This was the sesquicentennial of the church's first hymnbook's imprint date, a coincidence some members of the committee thought serendipitous.)[85] The book had the most authoritative imprimatur of any Mormon hymnal yet: a "First Presidency Preface."

The new hymnbook aimed at serviceability and met its mark. It stripped the collection of most seldom-sung hymns, smoothed out many peculiarities of diction, simplified the keys, and eliminated the distinction between choir and congregational hymns—suggesting the primacy of the common Saint by removing the hierarchy of schooled and unschooled singers. Certain text changes also reflected a broadening of social vision, consonant with the times: a verse from one Evan Stephens song in the collection was dropped for its emphasis on the pioneers finding Zion in the Rocky Mountains; and, to rid its implied gender bias, "O Sons of Zion" became "O Saints of Zion." Yet, in a curious reversal of early Mormon hymn adaptation, the point of view in one new hymn was changed from the communal "we" to the personal "I."[86]

As for its musical content, the work echoed and amplified the eclecticism of earlier Mormon hymnals, though it was less musically discriminating than its immediate predecessor. Almost one-fourth of its 341 hymns were appearing for the first time in a Mormon hymnbook.

The additions ranged from new Mormon hymns to evangelical songs such as "How Great Thou Art," from Anglican arrangements by Ralph Vaughan Williams to children's songs, most of them taken from the 1969 Primary songbook, *Sing with Me*.[87]

A criterion for the 1985 hymnbook committee, said Moody, was "to select music that people would want to hum as they walk down the street and go about their daily work."[88] This criterion reflected the modern retrenchment from the aestheticism of previous Church Music Committees, who had proposed to use the hymnbook more to elevate than reflect prevailing tastes. Many scholars have observed that from the turn of the twentieth century Christian hymnals generally have raised their editorial standards at the same time they have downplayed denominationalism, blending aestheticism with ecumenism.[89] If anything, the most recent Mormon hymnal seems to have manifested the reverse: a trend toward populism and parochialism.

For Christians at large, one scholar has asserted, the exhortation of all hymnody may be summed up in a single word: "win."[90] For Mormons the word has come to mean two things: appeal to the masses the church hopes to save, yet maintain the church's distinct cultural identity. How to do this in music remains a dilemma that haunts not only the church's worship music, but also its most esteemed musical organization, the Mormon Tabernacle Choir.

NOTES

1. From the preface to the work. On sacrament emphasis in this period see *Instructor* 84 (December 1949): 269–72.

2. See Evangeline T. Beesley, Oral History (interviewed by Ronald W. Walker, 17 September 1981), typescript in James Henry Moyle Oral History Program, HDC, pp. 1–6; J. Spencer Cornwall, Oral Histories, Moyle Program, HDC, II, pp. 63–64; "Efficacy of Music Discussed by Speakers," *DN,* 22 August 1921; Heber J. Grant, "Sing Only What We Believe," *IE* 15 (July 1912): 784–87, and "The Power of Song," *IE* 22 (May 1919): 634–36.

3. Careless was not a first choice, but replaced the deceased Horace G. Whitney on 20 October 1920. See the open letter of the CMC, 14 December 1920, announcing its formation, CMD Subject and Correspondence Files, HDC.

4. See Alexander, *Mormonism in Transition,* pp. 307–10.

5. CMC Minutes, typescript in HDC, 1 December 1920. Access to these minutes by scholars is generally restricted. However, an excellent abstract of the minutes for 1920–1962 appears in Jay Leon Slaughter, "The Role of Music in the Mormon Church, School, and Life" (Ph.D. diss., Indiana University, 1964), pp. 319–403.

6. CMC Minutes, 22 November 1923, 10 January 1924.

7. CMC Minutes, 5 January 1921.

8. CMC Minutes, 19 October 1925.

9. Tracy Y. Cannon (1879–1961) was the literal son of Salt Lake City bandleader and virtuoso trumpeter Mark Croxall, who was a son-in-law of Brigham Young; he was the adopted son of First Presidency member George Q. Cannon. He began playing as a Tabernacle organist in April 1909.

10. CMC Minutes, 30 April 1925.

11. Other than Stephens and Whitney, the predominant new lyricists were Theodore Curtis and Bertha Kleinman, who, between them, contributed twenty comparatively simple hymn texts, including "Why Should I Falter?," "Give Me a Home in the Heart of the Mountains," and "O Sheep of Israel."

12. Evan Stephens, "Songs and Music of the Latter-day Saints," *IE* 17 (June 1914): 760, 765, 767. Tracy Cannon echoed Stephens when, upon visiting a cathedral in 1921, he lamented the "mournful" atmosphere and said he "hoped never to see such conditions at our Church" (CMC Minutes, 8 December 1921). Another observer at this time, however, noted that "an outstanding feature of the 'Mormon' hymns is their sadness" (Joseph A. Smith, "Mormon Hymnal Literature," *DN*, 23 June 1923).

In 1930 B. H. Roberts explained to non-Mormons that LDS hymnody had not only transcended the "solemn grandeur of Vatican . . . music" but also the "hysterical thinness" of revivalism. See Roberts, *Comprehensive History*, 6:245.

13. For notes on some of these changes see George D. Pyper, *Stories of Latter-day Saint Hymns* (Salt Lake City: Deseret Book, 1939), pp. 17–19, 91. See also Fae Decker Dix, "Never Change a Song," *Utah Historical Quarterly* 44 (Summer 1976): 261–66.

14. For a study of the school see Donald George Schaefer, "Contributions of the McCune School of Music and Art to Music Education in Utah, 1917–1957" (Master's thesis, BYU, 1962). On other educational efforts of the church see Harold R. Laycock, "A History of Music in the Academies of the Latter-day Saint Church, 1876–1926" (D.M.A. thesis, University of Southern California, 1961); and Grant Lester Anderson, "Some Educational Aspects of the Music Training Program of the Church of Jesus Christ of Latter-day Saints, 1935–1969" (Master's thesis, Brigham Young University, 1976).

15. One of these records was made by a popular Protestant group bearing the distinctly non-Mormon name the "Trinity Mixed Quartet." See the copy of this recording in HDC.

16. For a full account of the self-study see CMC Minutes, 15 and 22 November 1934.

17. See "Developments and Considerations in Our Church Music Today" [1937], typescript in CMC Files 1939–49, HDC, and "The Stand of the General Music Committee on the Use of the Piano in Connection with the Organ in Accompanying Sacred Music," typescript in CMD Subject and Correspondence Files. See also CMC Minutes, 3 June, 1 July, 5 August, 2 September, and 2 December 1936; 1 December 1937.

18. See "Developments and Considerations" and First Presidency to CMC, 17 April 1936, CMC Files 1939–49.

19. Tracy Cannon, "Church Music Steps Up," *IE* 43 (January 1940): 45.

20. The 1937 *Missionary Handbook* called the Sunday school hymnal, "the book in common use in the stakes of Zion [because the] music of these songs is generally lighter and simpler than that of 'L.D.S. Hymns' ''; the green book was to be used primarily for "choir and part singing."

21. See CMC Minutes, 3 June 1936 and 15 January 1940.

22. See his letter to the committee in CMC Minutes, 26 January 1940.

23. Tracy Cannon, "Church-Wide Hymn Singing Fostered," *IE* 43 (April 1940): 203.

24. See CMC Minutes, 1 May 1942, and Alexander Schreiner, "Worship in Song," *IE* 47 (July 1944): 454.

25. J. Reuben Clark, Introduction to "Your Hymns and Mine," manuscript in J. Reuben Clark, Papers, HBLL. Compare Clark's observations to the very similar papal injunctions of 6 April 1940, Harry C. Koenig, *Principles for Peace: Selections from Papal Documents, Leo XIII to Pius XII* (Washington, D.C.: National Catholic Welfare Conference, 1943), pp. 661–62.

26. In 1930 church apologist B. H. Roberts explained the use of borrowed hymns in Mormonism thus: "as [the church] recognizes among revolutionists and religious reformers . . . the vanguard . . . of that on-coming New Dispensation which when it comes, may consistently appropriate that which it recognizes as of its own nature. There are earlier lights in the morning than the outburst of the rising sun" (*Comprehensive History*, 6:251–52).

27. Ph.D. diss., University of Maryland, 1943.

28. CMC Minutes, 5 February, 12 March, 2 April, and 3 September 1943.

29. On this appointment see Tracy Cannon to Leroy Robertson, 13 May 1944, CMC Files 1939–49.

30. Harold B. Lee et al. to First Presidency, 25 October 1944, CMC Files 1939–49.

31. CMC Minutes, 7 and 20 July 1944.

32. See especially CMC Minutes, 16 January 1948, and Grant, "The Power of Song," p. 634.

33. Cf. the comments of Adam Bennion, CMC Minutes, 12 April 1944.

34. Despite the strength of this hymn its third verse was disapproved (see CMC Minutes, 6 April 1945). For a brief biography of Kooyman see J. Spencer Cornwall, *Stories of Our Mormon Hymns,* 2nd ed. rev. (Salt Lake City: Deseret Book, 1963), pp. 112–13.

35. CMC Minutes, 15 December 1944, 2 February 1945.

36. See CMC to "Dear Friend," 1 August 1945, CMD Circular Letters, HDC. One well-known Mormon composer, George Durham, refused to submit a hymn because the CMC had changed one note of his setting to "God Our Father, Hear Us Pray" in the 1927 hymnal. See G. Homer Durham, "George Henry Durham (1883–1974): A Memoir," typescript in HDC.

37. CMC Minutes, 7 December 1944. The resolutions on the format of the hymnal may be found in the minutes for 13 March 1946. At least some contributors to the new hymnbook were paid ten dollars per hymn. See CMC to Harry Dean, 29 August 1947, Harry Dean Papers, HBLL.

38. Cannon to G. W. Richards, 19 October 1945, CMD General Files, HDC.

39. These recordings were prepared by Spencer Cornwall (see Tracy Cannon to Leroy Robertson, 12 March 1945, CMC Files 1939–49).

40. CMC Minutes, 13 September and 22 November 1946; 17 March and 21 April 1947. See also Tracy Cannon to Leroy Robertson, 24 October 1946, Leroy Robertson Papers, UU.

41. CMC Minutes, 16 April 1948. To help get the new hymnals out, the old ones would be taken in by the church in trade.

42. CMC Minutes, 6 September 1946, and 16 July and 23 December 1948.

43. CMC Minutes, 11 January 1949.

44. CMC Minutes, 12 January 1949.

45. Tracy Cannon to Frances G. Bennett, 19 October 1948, CMC Files 1939–49; cf. Cannon to J. Talmage Jones, 22 August 1950, CMD Subject and Correspondence Files, and CMC Minutes, 12 January 1949.

46. On some of the revision discussion, see Minutes of GMC Executive Meeting, 22 December 1949, CMD Subject and Correspondence Files; CMC Minutes, 30 November and 14 December 1949. On introducing the revised hymnbook see CMC Minutes, 29 November 1950. For Cannon's comment see Tracy Cannon, "The Music Committee," *IE* 59 (November 1956): 854.

47. These objectives are filed among the CMC Minutes for February 1948.

48. See Cannon, "Music Committee," p. 855; cf. CMC Minutes, 22 August and 13 September 1946.

49. See GMC to Eloise Cluff, 8 March 1951; GMC to Thelma S. Hansen, 28 July 1953; and Council of the Twelve to Stake and Mission Presidents and Bishops, 1 November 1948, all in Subject and Correspondence Files. The policy of discouraging solo piano playing in sacrament meetings dates at least to 1 June 1922 (CMC Minutes).

50. "Appropriate Music," *DN* (Church Section), 6 June 1948. Specific mention of the Ave Maria and the Rosary as being inappropriate was made in the first edition of *Some General Recommendations Concerning Music;* this was dropped in the second edition (1965). But debate on the question of using Catholic music, especially "Ave Maria" settings with different (non-Marian) texts, persisted into the 1970s. See, for instance, CMC Minutes, 10 November 1963; Leroy Robertson to Martha M. Harris, 11 August 1966; and GMC to Ann Marie von Blankenstein, 27 April 1972, both in CMD General Files.

51. CMC Minutes, 29 January 1952.

52. First Presidency to Stake Presidents, 2 May 1946, CMD Subject and Correspondence Files. See also the discussion by David O. McKay on the subject, *CR*, April 1946, p. 115.

53. See CMC Minutes, 3 November 1939, 16 July 1948, and 29 January 1952, as well as the letter filed in the minutes, First Presidency to GMC, 10 May 1944; GMC to W. D. Warner, 2 July 1953, both in Subject and Correspondence Files. Cf. First Presidency to GMC, 8 January 1952 in CMC Minutes, 15 January 1952; Tracy Cannon to Karleton Driggs, 12 September 1948, CMD General Files. An early discussion of the practice of standing to sing during sacrament meetings took place on 7 September 1926 (CMC Minutes). In 1961, after Clark's death, the First Presidency approved a short term "experiment" to have congregations

stand for opening and closing songs. The Presiding Bishopric of the church also approved a return to the practice of having the first line of a hymn text read before singing (see CMC Minutes, 31 October 1952, and Presiding Bishopric to CMC, 25 March 1953, CMD Subject and Correspondence Files).

54. Clark to Tracy Cannon, 28 February 1950, Clark Papers.

55. Address to Bishops, 7 April 1950, typescript in Clark Papers. For a humorous perspective on Bach's reception among church members see Robert Cundick to Nancy Wood, 21 March 1973, CMD General Files.

56. CMC Minutes, 14 February and 28 March 1950.

57. CMC Minutes, 6 October 1961. For the committee's continuing concern on the lack of music-theory training in the church, see Harold Lundstrom, "About Those Rejection Slips," *Church News*, 7 December 1966, and the cover letter with which Lundstrom sent it to Robertson (Robertson Papers).

58. Crawford Gates in CMC Minutes, 17 March 1962. One independent attempt to address this "emergency" in Mormon worship in the 1960s rankled some church leaders. See M. Ephraim Hatch to Harold Lundstrom, 7 October 1968, Robertson Papers, and Lorin F. Wheelwright to Michael Moody, 27 January 1969, University Archives, HBLL.

59. GMC to Marcia Going, 4 January 1960, CMD General Files.

60. See the correspondence on the typescript article "Questions Most Frequently Asked by Choir Directors" in CMD Subject and Correspondence Files.

61. See GMC letters to: Vivian Pace, 31 January 1966; Karen Siddoway, 29 August 1966; and Eduardo Wynveldt, 29 February 1968. See also Leroy Robertson to Clayton Hurst, 17 October 1967, and Roy Darley to Bernice Munk, 16 May 1966. All of the above letters are in CMD Subject and Correspondence Files. See also CMC Minutes, 10 November 1965; and Edward L. Kimball, ed., *Teachings of Spencer W. Kimball: Twelfth President of the Church of Jesus Christ of Latter-day Saints* (Salt Lake City: Bookcraft, 1982), pp. 518–19.

62. Darley to Munk, 16 May 1966.

63. GMC to Barbara Johns, 15 September 1964 (cf. Leroy Robertson to Carol Barnard, 18 December 1963), and Leroy Robertson to Bengt Lilja, 17 February 1965, all in CMD General Files.

64. CMC Minutes, 8 February 1960 and 27 April 1966, and Alexander Schreiner to Donald P. Ries, 11 August 1964, CMD Subject and Correspondence Files. Compare Tracy Cannon's earlier lukewarm assessment of Stephens in Cannon to David W. Swenson, 20 July 1950, Subject and Correspondence Files.

65. For interim discussions on organs see CMC Minutes, 16 July, 30 November, and 13 December 1948, 30 November 1949, 6 November 1951, 22 March 1954, 7 December 1959, 8 February 1960, 13 and 20 October 1961, 8 October and 5 November 1963.

66. CMC Minutes, 23 July 1963.

67. CMC Minutes, 5 January 1965.

68. Schreiner to Charles Ursenbach, 7 February 1964, Robertson Papers; cf. Schreiner's memo on the subject "Organs in the Church," CMC Minutes, 16 May 1966.

69. CMC Minutes, 30 June and 10 November 1964, and GMC to Harold B. Lee et al., 24 October 1966, CMD Subject and Correspondence Files.

70. CMC Minutes, 24 November 1964. On the later discouraging of all pipe organs see "The Organ and Mormon Church Music," *Dialogue* 10 (Spring 1975–1976 [*sic*]): 34–39.

71. First Presidency to Leroy J. Robertson, 3 March 1969, Robertson Papers.

72. Schreiner to Mrs. Spencer Hamilton, 3 November 1970, CMD General Files. The simplified hymnbook was eventually produced.

73. On the formation of the Music Department see Mark E. Petersen et al. to First Presidency, 16 November 1972, photocopy in my possession. See also "Changes Made in Music Area," *Church News,* 8 December 1973. On the committee's size, see Michael Moody, interviewed by Michael Hicks, 27 May 1987, transcript in author's possession.

74. For this preface and a treatment of musical ecumenism in this period see Hiley Ward, *Documents of Dialogue* (Englewood Cliffs, N.J.: Prentice-Hall, 1966), pp. 381–86.

75. See Dennis L. Lythgoe, "The Changing Image of Mormonism," *Dialogue* 3 (Winter 1968): 45–58, and Stephen W. Stathis and Dennis L. Lythgoe, "Mormonism in the Nineteen-Seventies: The Popular Perception," *Dialogue* 10 (Spring 1977): 95–113.

76. Hymnbook Committee Minutes, 18 December 1973. These and all hymnbook committee minutes from the 1970s are in private possession.

77. O. Leslie Stone to First Presidency, 4 January 1974, CMD Correspondence, 1967–77.

78. Hymnbook Committee Minutes, 28 May 1974.

79. See Merrill Bradshaw, interviewed by Michael Hicks, 11 August 1986, transcript in author's possession, p. 13; Michael Moody to Howard W. Hunter, 25 November 1974, CMD Office Files, HDC; Sterling Sill to O. Leslie Stone, 20 September 1974, and Daniel Ludlow to Ralph Woodward, 7 October 1974, both in CMD Correspondence 1967–77; Hymnbook Committee Minutes, 21 August and 12 September 1976. On the committee's determination to "fight" for certain hymns, see especially Hymnbook Committee Minutes, 19 October 1976.

80. Hymnbook Committee Minutes, 25 February 1975; Moody Interview.

81. CMC Minutes, 22 January 1959.

82. Bradshaw Interview and Hymnbook Committee "Interim Report," submitted to Dean Larsen, 24 March 1977, and various drafts of the same in private possession.

83. See Michael Moody to Merrill Bradshaw, 26 April 1977, in private possession; Bradshaw Interview, p. 12; Moody Interview. Moody had been the executive secretary of the CMD since fall 1972, just after he completed his "Contemporary Hymnody in the Church of Jesus Christ of Latter-day Saints" (D.M.A. diss., University of Southern California, 1972).

84. Hugh W. Pinnock, quoted in Kathleen Lubeck, "The New Hymnbook: The Saints Are Singing," *Ensign* 15 (September 1985): 9. I am grateful to Marshall Smith, M. D., for his detailed analyses of the new hymnal, photocopies of typescript in my possession.

85. Moody Interview.

86. The hymn thus changed was "With Humble Heart" (hymn no. 171).

87. For a survey of all the material in the 1985 hymnbook see Karen Lynn Davidson, *Our Latter-day Hymns: The Stories and the Messages* (Salt Lake City: Deseret Book, 1988).

88. Quoted in Lubeck, "New Hymnbook," p. 9.

89. See, for example, Edward Dickinson, *Music in the History of the Western Church* (New York: Scribner's, 1902), pp. 384–89, and Foote, *Three Centuries of American Hymnody,* pp. 307–8.

90. Stevenson, *Protestant Church Music in America,* p. 132.

9

The Mormon Tabernacle Choir

At the close of the nineteenth century Mormon musicians were searching for their place in American culture. Fortuitously, America's own search for cultural identity would open the way for Mormons to show the world what musical beauty could be produced by a religion which many citizens still regarded as a blot on the nation. In 1892, the four-hundredth anniversary of Columbus's landing in the West Indies, Chicagoans organized a "World's Columbian Exposition" to celebrate American enterprise and art. As part of the exhibition, which took place in 1893, they planned a massive choral competition (Eisteddfod) to be run by Welsh entrepreneurs. Evan Stephens's Welsh heritage helped secure him an invitation to the competition, an event which would provide the first great public success of a new American musical institution: the Mormon Tabernacle Choir.

By the time the choir left for the competition, on 29 August 1893, the sixteenth anniversary of Brigham Young's death, Stephens had been drilling them for months, with many extra rehearsals, working the group "hard but intelligently industriously interestingly and successfully," according to a longtime choir member.[1] Despite an average of 45 percent absenteeism at rehearsals the choir was extremely active under Stephens.[2] They had rehearsed their repertoire at no less than thirty-one dedicatory services for the Salt Lake Temple and had also performed in dozens of concerts throughout the territory—some of them even held on Sunday, which struck certain Mormons as sinful.[3]

In Chicago the choir impressed the festival crowd and placed second among the four choirs competing. But Stephens and his entourage (which included the Mormon First Presidency) viewed their success with some dissatisfaction. Many of them insisted for years thereafter that the Tabernacle Choir should have been awarded first prize. Wilford Woodruff even claimed that the contest was fixed by the Welsh organizers, a claim that swept through the church, despite Stephens's attempts to discredit it.[4] Woodruff's associate, Joseph F. Smith (namesake and nephew of the church's founder), wrote sardonically to his wife that the Mormon choir merited the first prize "fairly and honestly" but that "this was too much honor to confer upon Utah and the Mormons." However, he conceded, the "seed sown will be a good fruit in a day to come. . . . I consider it has done more good than five thousand Sermons would have done in an ordinary or even in an extraordinary way."[5]

The choir, of course, was scarcely faultless. Like all large choirs, it tended to go flat. And the peculiar nervousness of the choir amid the splendor of a gargantuan national fete seems also to have afflicted their powers of expression: the judges felt the performance lacked "soul." The Chicago journal *Music* complained that the singing was forced and lacked delicacy, yet praised Stephens's ability, even though he showed disdain for stage protocol and conducted awkwardly: all of his beats were upbeats.[6] Whatever the choir's flaws, the judges and crowd admired what the St. Louis *Globe Democrat* described as the choir's "spirit of enthusiasm," a vigorous amateurism which "more properly rendered the chosen selections than could have been done by professional skill alone."[7]

Once back in Utah, Stephens grew increasingly discontented with the provincialism of musical tastes and abilities there. In October 1894, just thirteen months after his Chicago success, Stephens hinted to the choir that he would not remain their conductor much longer and would return to directing children's singing schools. By January 1895, he flatly told the choir that it was "non-progressive and decaying" and threatened to resign if the singers did not increase their zeal and if church leaders did not show him more appreciation.[8] Not anxious to lose a man of Stephens's abilities after his triumph in Chicago, the First Presidency doubled his salary to $2,000 on the condition he would devote his full energies to the choir.[9] Joseph F. Smith came to a rehearsal and announced that all choir members were now to regard their musical work as "a mission," for they were "doing much to remove the prejudice that have [*sic*] existed against us."[10] The First Presidency then issued a card to each member of the choir explaining that choir work was missionary work, that all public duties should be subordinated to it, and that singers should meticulously follow their director. This card also expressed the hope that the choir would become the finest in the nation and "a great auxiliary to the cause of Zion. By means of its perfection in the glorious realm of song, it may unstop the ears of thousands now deaf to the truth, soften their stony hearts, and inspire precious souls with a love for that which is divine. Thus removing prejudice, dispelling ignorance and shedding forth the precious light of heaven to tens of thousands who have been, and are still, misled concerning us."[11] Regarding these actions, Thomas Griggs noted in his diary for 24 January 1895 that, with Smith's announcement, "music has received a recognition from the authorities not heretofore accorded it." But it seemed a recognition borne of utilitarianism rather than aesthetics, for above all the choir had proven itself indispensable to reconstructing the church's image.

In the fall of 1895 the church's magazine *The Contributor* published an auspicious tribute to Stephens. Lavishing praise on the professor, the article also quoted Stephens's views on himself. Stephens explained that he had no love for "public work" and only persisted in it at times because of his affection for some of the singers. Had he time, he would devote all his energy to composing and other musical ambitions—which to list, he said, would overflow a book. However, Stephens added, so long as he was conducting, "my authority must be absolute. I would permit no one to interfere in my work."[12]

With their national reputation well established by the Eisteddfod, the choir was able to entertain invitations to perform with many celebrities. More important to Zion's musical growth, renowned visiting artists such as Sousa, Paderewski, and Melba could be attracted to perform at the Tabernacle. The choir members often basked in the praise of such visitors at the same time that they were privately questioning the character of the artists. Nellie Melba provoked the most scandal, for the patriarchal Saints were peculiarly unaccustomed to a woman speaking in vulgarisms and with "proffessional haughtiness."[13] Stephens too, while praising her high notes, castigated her manner. But he proved himself equal to her repartee. When she asked how many wives he had, the bachelor quipped "not so many . . . but what I could take one more." Delighted at his spunk, she consented to hear the choir sing one of Stephens's pieces, "Let the Mountains Shout for Joy"—but only because it was his, she insisted, "not because it's Mormon." Stephens obliged, but nonetheless refused to put on a swallow-tailed coat for her concert.[14]

Six months after Melba's visit the choir faced a challenge to its own moral standing from no less than a Mormon apostle, the namesake son of John Taylor. At the general church conference in October 1898, with the assembled choir behind him on the Tabernacle stand, John W. Taylor repeated a story, whose source he said he could not doubt, to the effect that members of the choir were having lewd encounters in a local rooming house after choir practices.[15] This public accusation outraged not only the choir members but also the First Presidency, who thought Taylor's hearsay indictment of the church's missionary arm a breach of protocol. Taylor complained to the press that his remarks had been misconstrued, and before the conference ended he tried to make a public apology. The Presidency refused to allow him time, apparently fearing that the apostle would only do more damage by reviving the controversy. Taylor did, however, make satisfaction to the choir in a short post-conference address that included the sheepish admission: "Why, I would just as soon think that an angel was impure as the great body of the Salt Lake

Tabernacle Choir.''[16] The incident suggested how crucial to the social salvation of the church the Tabernacle Choir's reputation had become.

In January 1901 Stephens stunned the choir by announcing that he would retire in three years, upon reaching his fiftieth birthday, at which time, he said, a younger man should take over. According to Thomas Griggs, Stephens then added that ''the choir had not come up to what he desired it to attain. He wanted rest.''[17] He apparently had grown weary of lecturing the choir on their public manners and of arguing over who and how many of the choir should be allowed on their tours. He was likewise upset at how the Tabernacle organ was being remodeled. In April 1901 he announced to the choir that the First Presidency's rebuilding of the organ had ruined its tone and when he repeated his judgment to the then anti-Mormon *Salt Lake Tribune,* the *Deseret News* roundly rebuked him for promoting discord and even accused him of impugning the president of the church (who had contracted for the remodeling). As to Stephens's criticism that the new brilliance of the pipes might drown out the choir, the *News* testily asked, ''Is that a fault in the organ?''[18]

The organ controversy was only one of those in which Stephens found himself entrenched in the century's early years. He attempted to retire the senior members of the choir and tried to put an age limit of forty on those who could tour. He scolded the choir for not attracting larger audiences to their concerts. He openly refused to sing John Taylor's ''The Seer'' and publicly regretted having sung Eliza Snow's ''O My Father'' to the James McGranahan tune that had since become a favorite among church leaders.[19] He increasingly slanted his programs toward his own arrangements and compositions. His manner became so overbearing in the eyes of some that one apostle began scornfully calling the group simply ''Stephens's Tabernacle Choir,'' while some members protested the director's ''czarlike autocracy.'' One in particular complained that all Stephens wanted was a group of ''automatons in a great big chorus.'' Years later, another recalled Stephens as ''a musical Mussolini.'' Stephens characterized himself in 1902 as ''the sole head, eyes, brains, body, arms, and legs of the choir.''[20] Yet, when coupled with his evident skill and undeniable charisma, Stephens's strong will unified the choir. As often as members complained at his manner they celebrated his insights and capacity to blend intelligence and emotion in their performances.

Stephens offered a tentative resignation in 1904, as he had promised. But as the part-time Tabernacle organist Edna Dyer recorded in her diary, 1 August 1904, Stephens ''merely told the 1st Pres. he was willing to resign if they desired—but of course they didn't desire, and hence everything will go on as heretofore.'' At this time the church was embroiled in fresh trials. Reed Smoot, a Mormon apostle, had been elected to the U.S. Senate in 1903 and petitions from anti-Mormons provoked a series of legislative hearings on Smoot's fitness to serve. The hearings lasted through 1907 and the disclosures that Mormon polygamy had not fully abated among high church leaders enflamed the general anti-Mormon sentiment in the eastern states. In the next few years caustic critiques of Mormonism appeared in magazines and motion pictures.[21]

But during the 1910s the Tabernacle Choir's celebrity expanded, partly through the medium of the phonograph. Although the first cylinder recording of the group appears to have been made as early as 1900, in 1910 the choir recorded twelve numbers for Columbia—the Mormon hymns "We Thank Thee O God for a Prophet" and "O My Father"; Stephens's "Let the Mountains Shout for Joy" and "Hosannah Anthem" (an elaboration of the old "Spirit of God Like a Fire Is Burning"); "America," "The Star-Spangled Banner," and the Welsh song "Light and Truth"; Gounod's "Unfold Ye Portals" and the Soldiers' Chorus from *Faust;* Rossini's "Inflammatus" and Verdi's "Pilgrims' Chorus"; Victor Herbert's "Gypsy Sweetheart"; and of course, Handel's "Hallelujah." The recordings testify to the choir's grandiloquence and to Stephens's penchant for ponderous tempi and colossal ritardandi at phrase endings. Some "scooping" from pitch to pitch, a nasal tone in the tenors, and an enthusiasm that sometimes overwhelmed precision suggested the group's frontier origins. But Stephens's anthem in particular manifested an ambition to create a Mormon choral style rooted in the oratorio and grand opera style of which the conductor was so fond.

In 1910 Stephens and the choir planned a trip to Wales for the huge Eisteddfod there, if they could obtain the funding from local businessmen. John Philip Sousa had told the group they would be a "sensation" in New York, and Stephens hoped to prove out his prophecy with a tour of the East Coast on the way to Wales.[22] This trip to Wales eventually was scuttled, but the Eastern tour took place nevertheless, for the express purpose of building good relations for the church after the anti-Mormon media crusades of the post-Smoot hearings years. In April 1911 the choir agreed to sing a series of eighteen concerts at the American Land and Irrigation Exposition in New York that fall. Hoping to turn the engagement into a public-relations tour for the church, choir leaders began trying to secure halls in cities throughout the East, providing that the group, according to one apostle's remarks, not be exploited "as if it were a common troupe of minstrels."[23]

In some of the twenty-three cities where the choir eventually appeared protests erupted, with religious groups claiming that the choir's tour was simply a Mormon ploy to "propitiate favor for Mormonism with the uninformed and thoughtless." The Union Theological Seminary asked people to "give up fine music rather than lead your fellowman toward [the] standards of Joseph Smith."[24] Such sentiments, coupled with a newspaper boycott of events connected with the controversial Exposition itself, led to poor showings for the choir and a tour deficit of $20,000. But the choir's invitation to sing for President Taft and a small group of senators and ambassadors at the White House struck the tour manager as "worth all our losses."[25] The choir's sound also left favorable impressions of their religion among many of their hearers. Of their singing on this tour a St. Louis critic wrote this vivid assessment: "They sing in entirely different fashion from any other chorus. In the Mormons' song there is a magnificent note of religious frenzy, a diapason of devotion, an echo of deeds of fanaticism and of grappling with the desert, to make it blossom like a rose. . . . Their song has the note of triumph over difficulties, and dangers overcome. It is the note of the pioneer, the roadbreaker into the wilderness; and, indeed, they do not in looks belie their ancestry. There is fire in their eyes, and thunder in their throats."[26]

Upon returning from the Eastern tour, Stephens continued to enflame church leaders and choristers with his forceful opinions and the constant programming of his own music.[27] He also endeavored to sway the First Presidency into taking measures to enlarge the choir and quell disaffection, measures which apparently included mandatory recruitment of the best singers from local Mormon congregations.[28] After refusing the conductor's proposals several times, church president Joseph F. Smith wrote to Stephens in 1916 that the two of them had reached an impasse, that Stephens could not be placated, that some church leaders had long since urged his release, and that his successor had now been chosen: Tony Lund, son of one of Smith's counselors in the First Presidency and chairman of the music department at the church's principal academy, Brigham Young University. Citing Stephens's vague resignation of 1904, Smith gave the conductor the option of resigning or requesting an honorable release. Stephens chose the latter of these in a bittersweet letter that was published on the front page of the *Deseret News*.[29]

Except for his fiery temperament and devotion to church music, forty-five-year-old Anthony C. Lund differed from Stephens in many particulars. Stephens, a lifelong bachelor, was Welsh-born and American-trained, while the divorced Lund was American-born and a graduate of the Royal Conservatory in Leipzig. Where Stephens had been wildly emotional in his conducting, Lund was methodical and precise. And whereas Stephens had been essentially orthodox, despite his controversies over church music, Lund was not: he had a weakness for gambling and an occasional beer, and he belonged to a heterodox clique of Danish Mormons, many of whom were centered at Utah universities. In the first decades of the twentieth century Brigham Young University had been more or less unable to accommodate the spirited intellectualism of many of its increasingly secularized professors and students. Nevertheless there remained a cohesive bohemian subculture and Lund was one of its chief citizens. Notorious for his lecture-hall absenteeism, Lund nevertheless achieved fame for his vocal training and retained a coterie of disciples who delighted in his passion for European classical music and for jokes. One former student said that Lund was "one of the most wholesome and outstanding personalities the west has ever known."[30] Another put it more tersely: "I thought he was some sort of a God."[31]

Tony Lund revamped the choir in 1916, releasing all of its approximately 250 members and inviting only 162 of them to return to the group. (The 1927 Victor recordings of the reconstructed choir manifest substantial improvement in tone and phrasing, although some raggedness remains, especially in the choir's rendering of Handel's "Worthy Is the Lamb," one of the pieces with which they had won the 1893 Eisteddfod prize.) Lund's European training not only made him more rigorous with his singers than Stephens had been, it strongly shaped his views on church music and the Tabernacle Choir's proper aspirations. He called for a musical organization in the church that would "strike a well aimed blow at the frivolous unorthodox trash" that permeated Mormondom. He argued for more singing of works "ringing true to doctrine, and in universal noble appeal," and warned against music that was less than profound, even though it might be "momentarily pleasing, from the melody standpoint." And he proposed that the church officially discourage any social or liturgical activities that might conflict with Tabernacle Choir rehearsals, since the choir's singing was to be an example to the whole church.[32]

When Lund took over the choir the Mormon image in America was still faltering. The Smoot hearings had technically vindicated the senator's standing, but the public was scandalized by disclosures during the hearings that Joseph F. Smith had continued to live with his plural wives after the 1890 manifesto and that some church apostles had married polygamously as recently as 1901. "Yellow journalism" had already found Mormonism an apt topic, and now a number of motion pictures transferred lurid anti-Mormon tales into vivid, irresistable images, including the pseudo-documentary *A Mormon Maid*, produced under Cecil B. DeMille in 1917.[33] The virulent anti-German propaganda that accompanied the United States' entry into the Great War diverted some of the anti-Mormonism of the media long enough for the Saints to recoup. When radio came to prominence in the 1920s, Heber J. Grant saw how the choir could use it to give a healthy image of Mormonism to a new generation.

Although Lund was fond of the phonograph and even appeared in advertisements endorsing the Steger brand as "unquestionably the finest," he strongly resisted involving the choir in broadcasting, fearing that the radio could never capture the subtleties of the group.[34] Nevertheless, at Grant's urging, a trimmed version of the Tabernacle Choir began occasional local broadcasts from the tin shack above the Hotel Utah about 1927. The results vindicated Lund's objections: the broadcasts ill-represented the choir's massive sound and (more important) the Tabernacle's warm acoustics. Mormon apostles apparently complained that the music in these 1927 broadcasts was "inappropriate" and often "poorly and inadequately rendered," and they ordered the broadcasts to be taken over by quartets and double quartets under the direction of B. Cecil Gates, the choir's assistant conductor.[35] Nevertheless, in 1929, one year short of the church's centenary, the Tabernacle Choir accepted an offer to begin what the Newark, New Jersey, *Call* quickly labeled "one of the most pretentious series of vocal programs ever undertaken on the air": a weekly broadcast for the National Broadcasting Company, direct from the Tabernacle every Monday afternoon at four o'clock.[36]

The choral portion of the first NBC broadcast, 15 July 1929, reflected Lund's tastes for sacred and "highbrow" secular music: a chorus from Wagner's *Die Meistersinger* and the Finale of Mendelssohn's *Elijah* billed alongside Parley Pratt and George Careless's "The Morning Breaks, The Shadows Flee."[37] The organ portion was lighter in character. As the national economy plummeted, the organists increasingly began to pad the Tabernacle broadcasts with popular music that would appeal to the stricken American masses. The Jersey City *Journal* advised readers who had been put off by the choir's classical and sacred repertoire that folk songs and popular ballads, including Stephen Foster songs, were being performed: "Those who imagine because this feature comes from a house of worship that sacred music is the rule and therefore fail to tune it in, are making a mistake."[38]

Although the network pressure to include popular music in Tabernacle broadcasts undoubtedly troubled some church leaders and musicians, the Saints' intense need to maintain their airtime persuaded them to mingle sacred, secular, popular, and classical. Lund, however, refused to compromise what he considered the choir's essential dignity, provoking pleas from listeners such as this: "Sing old familiar, immortal hymns, including 'negro spirituals.' Radio listeners become over-tired with operatic and classic music, and long for soul stirring singing."[39] But a review in the Albany *Times* in 1930 apparently expressed the general public response to Lund's work: "if you can listen to that magnificent Choir and not get a thrill, something is decidedly wrong."[40] And in 1932 the Welsh–American newspaper, the *Druid*, named the choir the best in the country, showering them with profuse and colorful praise.[41]

Lund was constantly dogged by illness in the early 1930s. He recovered from a seven-month bout with kidney disease in 1931 to lead the choir (at Henry Ford's behest) in a tour to the Chicago Century of Progress exhibition in autumn 1934. Having prepared an astonishing sixteen concerts with no duplication of pieces, the group attracted the largest crowds of any of the exhibitors' guest artists. They also received invitations to sing at the Chicago Daily News Plaza, where they jammed traffic for blocks, and at the University of Chicago chapel, where after the singing Heber Grant gave a weighty speech on the political loyalty of Mormons. Although the choir's solo violinist was prohibited by the Chicago musician's union from playing, and thunderstorms interrupted several outdoor concerts, the choir conductor and the church president pronounced the tour a total success. But in late spring 1935 Lund suffered a massive heart attack and, despite a brief recovery, died at the age of sixty-four.

Some weeks before his death, Lund was taking a walk when he encountered J. Spencer Cornwall, the Northwestern University–trained superintendent of music for Salt Lake Schools. Lund told Cornwall that he would not be able to direct the choir much longer and that Cornwall had better "get [his] plate right side up." When Lund died Cornwall told his family he would succeed Lund, even though he conceded that he knew almost nothing about the Tabernacle Choir. Church leaders assured Cornwall's father that Spencer was not being considered, even though Lund's former assistant director, Cecil Gates, had become incapacitated. But on 23 August 1935 Grant called the forty-seven-year-old Cornwall to his office and announced that the church presidency had elected him to the position the night before. Some choir members protested at not being consulted on the decision. Cornwall, in turn, subjected all of the singers to auditions and dropped ninety of them from the rolls, later remarking that many of them "couldn't sing at all, just nil, nothing."[42]

Having little use for popular music and opposing its use in Tabernacle broadcasts, Cornwall also understood that the radio shows depended on light fare to attract listeners. Grant's counselor, J. Reuben Clark, warned the new director not to "get this choir away from the people" by performing esoteric works.[43] Afraid of confrontation on the matter, Cornwall asked Grant to appoint a committee to choose music for the broadcasts. But Grant retorted, "That's your job. You put your ear to the ground and find out what you ought to sing from what people say." Then, after relating to Cornwall his personal distaste for certain devotional pieces, including Weatherly and Adams's phenomenally popular "The Holy City," Grant ingenuously asked, "Who am I to say what music should be sung to other people?"[44]

Throughout his tenure as director, Cornwall persistently slanted the broadcasts toward hymns, anthems, and opera and oratorio choruses. Many choir members and listeners complained that the choir had "gone highbrow." Others rejoiced; one fan letter to Cornwall read simply, "More Bach, less bunk."[45] The conductor explained in 1951 that he would always favor serious works for the choir in order to "bring these people up to our standard." He also spoke strongly to choir members who resented performing so much Bach, calling on them to "get rid of this resentment," that it betrayed the singers' "lack of training or capacity." But like his champion, J. Reuben Clark, Cornwall disliked all "modernistic" music. After hearing a Leonard Bernstein program on "Modern Music," Cornwall rhetorically asked the choir, "has beauty been lost? . . . There may be ears who can hear this music, but will there be hearts that will be moved?"[46]

Despite his antagonism to most popular or serious contemporary music, Cornwall also leaned away from performing Stephens's pseudo-operatic anthems, which he found to be composed in "an idiom not for sacred music."[47] He also shunned Stephens's hymn arrangements, preferring those of his own and of several non-Mormons. His slighting of Stephens irritated some observers. Leading Mormon brethren called for more of "our own music" and criticized the abundance of "outsiders' music" in the choir's repertoire. Cornwall countered by asking them to define what they meant by such terms—well aware from his studies of Mormon hymnody that his church's musical origins were highly eclectic.[48] Cornwall further risked offending church authorities by frequently programming black spirituals, which, as he explained to the choir in 1944, "have been knocking at the concert door for sometime now."[49] But the First Presidency under Grant refused to usurp Cornwall's prerogative, taking the general attitude that "while all of us love music with more or less appreciation . . . we can hardly qualify as competent critics."[50]

The choir Cornwall inherited was more or less an anachronism: a high-spirited nineteenth-century festival chorus in the midst of a colossal twentieth-century depression. But broadcasting enabled the group to speak vicariously for the masses. Public devotion to radio, a cheap but captivating fireside escape from the troubles of the marketplace, enabled the choir to enter the consciousness of a highly susceptible audience. By the final days of World War II the choir had assumed the image of a huge blended voice carried by the power of the air—a group representing, as one Mormon apostle asserted, something to live and fight for.[51]

In 1944 the choir sang for the Army Corps propaganda film "The Battle of San Pietro," despite J. Reuben Clark's feelings that the choir should promote peace and brotherhood by shunning such work.[52] That same year they received the Peabody Award for distinguished broadcasting, prompting Cornwall to exclaim: "When this type of program can receive one of radio's highest awards, there is renewed hope for the sanity and spirituality of the nation."[53] At the death of Roosevelt in April 1945 the choir was called upon to prepare a commemorative program for CBS, which they did in a matter of hours. Carried by 143 stations, the program deeply impressed a generation with the idea that Utah's Mormon choir sang with the voice of the whole nation and, ironically indeed, with the voice of the White House itself.

Conscious of Clark's dictum to spread the "good Christian music so vital to the world in this post-war era," Cornwall intensified the choir's discipline in 1946, even producing a brochure with a pseudodecalogue of "Dos and Don'ts for Choir Members," to be read by all singers twice weekly until memorized.[54] Within two years the choir had recorded its first long-playing record, one of the first by any group. At the same time the choir approached twenty years on the network airwaves and had just reached its one thousandth broadcast. After that broadcast aired (17 October 1948), Cornwall publicly outlined his objectives for the choir. He wanted first to create a group that would be praised by trained musicians. Second—and he conceded that most would put this first—he wanted to enhance the church's image. Third, he wanted to eradicate vibrato in the choir. Fourth, he wanted to build up a huge repertoire for the singers. This last, he said, was perhaps the most treacherous, for while he wanted to keep the music close to the people, according to Clark's mandate, his first aspiration for the choir demanded that they perform sophisticated music. The problem was how to find "good Christian music" that would build a repertoire that would satisfy both competent musicians and untutored listeners.[55]

Buoyed up by victory in Europe and Asia, many Americans renewed their faith in a God who, it seemed, presided over their nation in the postwar period. As devotion to traditional religion and morality spread through the states Mormonism reaped the benefits of its ever-brightening image. The Tabernacle Choir became the preeminent choir in the nation; Mormon businessmen and politicians rose in prominence; and a new church president, David O. McKay, presented an appealing alternative to the archaic image of the wizened Grant (who had died five days after VE Day) and Grant's short-termed successor, George Albert Smith. Whereas all earlier twentieth-century Mormon church presidents, with their rough, bearded appearance and frontier mannerisms, reinforced the public's suspicions about Mormon provincialism and radicalism, McKay was tall, clean-shaven, soft-spoken, and charming to the press. In the wake of changing perceptions of Mormonism, the church's postwar conversion rate, not to mention its birth rate, soared.

Confident of the Tabernacle Choir's usefulness in perpetuating the church's new growth, McKay undertook a strategy of frequent touring and recording, to be inaugurated by a 1955 European tour, the group's first foray outside the United States. With its tour repertoire personally reviewed and approved by McKay—fifty-seven memorized pieces—the choir embarked on an ambassadorship to the Old World, singing an all-sacred assortment of Mormon hymn arrangements, Bach chorales, sacred anthems, and oratorio choruses. The curious turned out to see the group billed as America's "most famous" or even "most beloved" choir. Indeed, many observers considered the choir more a kind of United States delegation amid the Cold War than a religious body struggling to proselyte the world. The choir sold out many houses, including the eight-thousand-seat Albert Hall, although the London *Times* noted that the program "came as a reminder that the singers were here as much in the role of evangelists as musicians."[56] The demand for tickets in Paris grew so intense that the national radio network opted to broadcast the entire two-hour Palais de Chaillot concert, where the audience was double the size of the one that turned out the following night to hear the New York Philharmonic. A cascade of praise issued forth from the European press, and at the tour's conclusion McKay said, "the money spent is the best investment we have ever made in spreading goodwill for Utah, the United States, and the Church."[57]

McKay, however, had fully intended the tour to be Cornwall's final moment in the sun before the church president retired him.[58] After the choir returned from Europe, McKay decided to let Cornwall stand as director for two more years, allowing him to mark the choir's twenty-fifth anniversary with CBS. On the day of that anniversary, 8 September 1957, Cornwall told the choir that he still felt the need to choose broadcast music with "fear and trembling," knowing that whatever he chose anymore was likely to offend someone. He then cryptically announced: "Where the sword of Damocles will fall next no one knows."[59] One week later McKay came to the choir rehearsal and announced Cornwall's retirement. "Leaders may come, leaders may go," McKay explained, "but the choir continues constantly." Within days Cornwall graciously echoed McKay, barely concealing his bitterness at what he considered a premature release: "There is one thing that must persist. The choir must go on. Its welfare is more important than any of the individuals in it."[60]

Cornwall's assistant conductor, Richard P. Condie, took over the choir. He released dozens of choir members, demanded absolute loyalty from those that remained, and in return promised them a stunning future of touring and recording, quipping that "the past may be glorious but the future may be more interesting."[61] He quickly and assiduously courted Eugene Ormandy and the Philadelphia Orchestra for a series of joint recordings. Listening to the choir's recordings Ormandy criticized the choir's tendency to go flat, its imprecise attacks, and its bland, colorless sound. To remedy the last of these Condie insisted the choir abandon Cornwall's straight-tone singing and inject vibrato. When Ormandy recorded with the group in September 1958 he had changed his mind and openly declared the choir the world's finest.[62] Thereafter the choir drew the attention of scores of magazines, and attracted television offers of various sorts—from network Christmas specials to a spot on "Sing with Bing." By October 1959 the group had sold 60,000 copies of its latest album with Ormandy, *The Lord's Prayer, Vol. 1,* and an astonishing 300,000 copies of its single release, "The Battle Hymn of the Republic," which had reached number one on the single release charts (and which the group performed at the church's general conference that month). The following month the group won a Grammy Award in a new category seemingly created just for them: "Best Performance by a Chorus." Their manager for the Grammy tour that followed the award put all of this into perspective: "Our only reason for going out like this and spending several hundred thousand dollars is to break down prejudice so that our missionaries can get entrance into more homes."[63]

Throughout the 1960s and early 1970s the group launched a series of grandiose projects: recording as many as five albums in one six-month period, adding television cameras to their weekly broadcasts, performing at the inaugurals of presidents Johnson and Nixon, and singing in such public spectacles as their 1962 performance from Mt. Rushmore, transmitted by satellite throughout the world. With monies flowing to the group from its recording successes, the First Presidency urged the Tabernacle Choir to expand its touring schedule. Hence, from 1962 to 1974 the choir toured three times in Canada, twice in Mexico, once in Europe, and also performed at five different World's Fairs. But this extensive touring irritated some church leaders. Church apostle Joseph Fielding Smith, namesake son of Joseph F. Smith, declared on public television that the choir was touring "too much for their own good. The choir . . . was not organized to travel around the world. . . . I think they are overdoing it."[64] And the choir's popularity aggravated the already sharp divisions over their repertoire.

Executives of the church's broadcasting division, Bonneville International (founded 1964), urged the choir to program more music accessible to a mass audience, while Columbia Records pressured the group to produce more potential hits, beginning in 1960 with a two-album package of Civil War songs. Late in the 1960s, popular, folk, and patriotic songs came to pervade the broadcasts. Although such music lay at the heart of Mormon music-making in the nineteenth century, and Condie enjoyed most of it, some church leaders and choir members balked at the new repertoire. When a Broadway show-tune album was contemplated, Joseph Fielding Smith tersely observed, "I don't think the Tabernacle Choir belongs on Broadway."[65] Perhaps more troublesome, Condie programmed a number of the "modernistic" works shunned by Cornwall—in one case inciting some choir members to circulate a petition against singing a piece they thought too dissonant. Condie warned his singers that they were not to question his programming, but privately complained that he was losing the freedom to choose the groups's own music amid the demands for hymns (and what he called "syrupy" religious music from some church leaders and their simultaneous urgings to expand the Tabernacle Choir's audience.[66]

An exhausting 1973 tour of Europe, with the choir singing as much as nine hours a day, depleted the singers' energies and set Condie on edge. After briskly retiring a number of choir members who he thouht were undermining his programming, Condie sought an audience with longtime friend and new church president Harold B. Lee, apparently to resolve matters of repertoire. That same month, December 1973, two prominent church musicians wrote to Church Music Committee chairman O. Leslie Stone about the evident sinking morale among choir members, the increasing secularization of their repertoire, and the fading reputation of the group among non-Mormon professional musicians.[67] On 21 December 1973, the Church Music Committee and two apostles drafted a letter to Lee reiterating these concerns, and calling attention to lyrics sung by the choir, texts apparently thought to be offensive by the committee, including "Sleep thou not when affection seeks thine ear. . . . When passion cries, oh my darling, open thine eyes," and these lines from "Oh, Shenandoah": "For seven years I courted Sally. For seven more he [*sic*] longed to hold her." The letter urged that the Presidency of the Church not allow the choir to become a mere "polished and competent entertainment group."[68] Whether Lee contemplated any action is unclear. He was a devoted fan of the choir, assiduously followed their career, and often quietly sat in on their rehersals, entranced. But he died five days after the music committee drafted its letter.

Spencer Kimball, Lee's successor, quickly moved to resolve the situation. In June 1974 he announced that Condie would be retired at the end of the choir's World's Fair tour that summer. Kimball lauded Condie not anly as a great musician but as "one of the foremost missionaries of the day."[69] But the conductor remained bitter over the retirement, blaming choir members who he believed had subverted his reputation.[70]

Condie's replacement was the popular University of Utah professor Jay Welch, who had been a patient, meticulous assistant director since Cornwall's release, and whose musicianship was universally regarded as superior to Condie's. Welch substantially elevated the sophistication of the choir's brodcast music, giving unprecedented emphasis to serious contemporary music. But, to everyone's shock, Welch tearfully resigned during rehearsal a few days before Christmas 1974, citing only "personal reasons." Rumors circulated, and the choir president pleaded with the singers not to pursue the matter, insisting that the resignation had been God's will; to question it would be to question the prophet.[71] The tender feelings of the Christmas season helped the choir to welcome Welch's relatively unproven assistant, Jerold Ottley, as the new conductor. Since that time Ottley has proven his competence and has led the choir in many respectable recorded performances, including works by Brahms, Bruckner, and Copland, and an entire album of contemporary choral music. These have been interspersed with far more lucrative recordings of popular music.

In 1986, with broadcast markets dwindling, the choir reached a crossroads on the matter of repertoire. Several church leaders proposed that radio and television audiences, a field for potential conversions, might be put off by the gravity of the choir's music—perhaps they needed to veer from their cultivated austerity. But when the live audiences for six broadcasts were surveyed that summer, they made it clear that they wanted, if anything, more hymns, and that the longtime format of the broadcasts was a tradition they cherished. The audiences were older than the eighteen to thirty-six-year-olds from whom the church usually proselyted, well-educated, and interested in serious music.[72] While the choir members were not likely to prevail as broadcast evangelists, they were fulfilling their historic mission as image-makers for the church, helping to "remove the prejudice."

The surveys confirmed that the onetime emblem of the Mormon menace had become an American institution. Even a cursory examination of the country's mass culture suggests how thoroughly it has embraced and absorbed the Mormon Tabernacle Choir. The choir has been the object of presidential commendations, the focus of a *Reader's Digest* record anthology—endorsed by Billy Graham—the topic of a widely distributed commemorative volume, and even the subject of a U.S. postal stamp. It has produced the longest-running radio show in history and at the same time has become the butt of thousands of media jokes and parodies and has been regularly referred to in situation comedies and comic monologues.

The choir has come to symbolize what seem to many non-Mormons the church's most admirable and even most "American" traits: cooperation, conservatism, ceremoniousness, and the pursuit of recognition. In attracting audiences it seems to have steered successfully between populism and aestheticism. And as an enduring vestige of America's past, the choir presents an image of stability amid changing times.

For Mormons, moreover, the choir is a symbol of the perennial quest for Zion, a kingdom and culture destined to surpass that of the gentile world. And nowhere has that quest manifested itself more blatantly than among the grandiose choral and orchestral works of Mormonism's native composers.

NOTES

1. Griggs Journal, 9 July 1893.
2. "The Tabernacle Choir," *Deseret Weekly* 45 (22 October 1892): 561–62. At this time 550 members were enrolled, with slightly more than 300 attending on the average.
3. See Griggs Journal, 27 August 1893.
4. Woodruff took his First Presidency counselors with him on the choir tour to Chicago. When severe colds afflicted many of the singers en route, he blessed them in the name of God to recover. Many reported a miraculous recovery when they stepped on stage. See Edna Coray Dyer, "Music in Church Service," typescript in HBLL, p. 3. See also *WWJ* 9:261 (8 September 1893), and Evan Stephens, "The Famous Singing Contest," *Deseret Weekly* 47 (30 September 1893): 467–68. See also Abraham Cannon Journal, 13 September 1893, and Heber J. Grant's remarks in "Evan Stephens Lauded as Genius at Funeral," *DN,* 1 November 1930.
5. Joseph F. Smith to Sarah Ellen Richards Smith, quoted in Charles Jeffrey Calman and William I. Kaufman, *The Mormon Tabernacle Choir* (New York: Harper and Row, 1979), p. 70.
6. "The Welsh Eisteddfod," *Music* 6 (September 1893): 545–48; "The Tabernacle Choir," *Deseret Weekly* 49 (1 September 1894): 340–41. On Stephens's conducting see *Alexander Schreiner Reminisces* (Salt Lake City: Publishers Press, 1984), p. 104. Schreiner also noted that under Stephens, "It seemed impossible to sing flat; the singers were hypnotized." For a lengthy assessment of Stephens by a Welsh contemporary see Phillips G. Davies, "William D. Davies Visits the Welsh in Utah in 1891," *Utah Historical Quarterly* 49 (Fall 1981): 374–87.
7. Quoted in J. Spencer Cornwall, *A Century of Singing: The Salt Lake Mormon Tabernacle Choir* (Salt Lake City: Deseret Book, 1958), pp. 66–67. For an earlier treatment of the choir see Mary Musser Barnes, "An Historical Survey of the Salt Lake Tabernacle Choir of the Church of Jesus Christ of Latter-day Saints" (Master's thesis, University of Iowa, 1936).
8. Griggs Journal, 1 February, 15 March, 26 April, 6 May, 25 October, 22 November, and 9 December 1894; 3 January 1895. See also Abraham Cannon Journal, 17 January 1895.
9. Abraham Cannon Journal, 24 January 1895.
10. Griggs Journal, 24 January 1895.
11. Clark, *Messages of the First Presidency,* 3:266–68.
12. *Contributor* 16 (September 1895): 661–62.

13. Griggs Journal, 15 April 1898. See also Edna Coray Dyer, Journal, holograph and typescript in HBLL, 17 April 1898: "Mme. Melba seemed to have the ability to sing just as clearly and accurately as a flute could be played but she didn't put quite so much soul into her work as did Mme. Nordica—perhaps she had no soul to express, for her language and actions behind scenes showed her to be anything but a pure woman—greatly to the chagrin of choir people who heard her."

14. Mary Jack, Oral History (interviewed by Mabel Jones Gabbott and Lucille Reading), typescript in Music Department Oral History Collection, HDC, pp. 5–6; "The Great Musician," transcript of address by Evan Stephens to the Daughters of the Utah Pioneers, 5 February 1930, *OPH* 10:89.

15. The text of his remarks on the choir, perhaps with some emendations, was published in *Deseret Weekly* 18 (15 October 1898): 545. See also the front page stories in *Salt Lake Tribune*, 8 and 9 October 1898; the latter of these reported the story that Taylor had long disliked the choir, thinking it "entirely too bulky and unwieldy."

16. *Salt Lake Tribune*, 10 October 1898. As reflected in Taylor's remarks, the choir was then generally known within the church as the "Salt Lake Tabernacle Choir." While non-Mormons have tended to refer to the choir as the "Mormon Tabernacle Choir," the official title for most of the choir's history has been "The Salt Lake Mormon Tabernacle Choir."

17. Griggs Journal, 24 January 1901.

18. *DN*, 20 April 1901. Cf. *Salt Lake Tribune*, 19 and 20 April 1901. For a detailed study of the organ see Donald Gordon McDonald, "The Mormon Tabernacle Organ" (Master's thesis, Union Theological Seminary, 1952).

19. Griggs Journal, 24 November, 19 and 21 December 1901. Cf. 16 February 1899. See also Dyer, "Music in Church Service," pp. 5–6, on Stephens's meticulous planning of service music.

20. All the citations in this passage are from Griggs Journal, 29 January 1902, except for the "Mussolini" statement, which appears in George D. Pyper, "Evan Stephens," *IE* 36 (July 1933): 573.

21. On the Smoot hearings and the subsequent anti-Mormon magazine crusade see Roberts, *Comprehensive History*, 6:390–417.

22. The church, then as now, demanded the group fund its own enterprises without relying on church monies. See "Shall The Choir Go to Wales in 1911?" in E. H. Pierce, comp., *Mormon Tabernacle Choir: Being A Collection of Newspaper Criticisms and Cullings from Metropolitan Magazines and Musical Journals* (Salt Lake City: n. p., 1910).

23. Anthon Lund Journal, microfilm of holograph in HDC, 17 April 1911.

24. The quotations are from "Presbyterians Oppose Mormon Choir's Appearance in City," *Richmond News Leader*, 15 November 1911.

25. George D. Pyper to Benjamin Goddard (telegram), 15 November 1911. This and much other material connected with this tour are in the Pyper Papers.

26. Cited in Cornwall, *Century of Singing*, p. 81.

27. See Tracy Y. Cannon to David W. Swenson, 20 July 1950, CMD Subject and Correspondence Files.

28. See the discussions recorded in Anthon Lund Journal, 13, 20, 21, and 25 July 1916. See also Cornwall, *A Century of Singing,* pp. 11–12. During Stephens's tenure, Tabernacle Choir singers apparently were not auditioned and choir membership came with the incentive of free passes to all musical events in the Tabernacle. See Harry Dean Journal, holograph in HBLL, 4 October 1912.

29. First Presidency Letterbooks, 19 July 1916, copies in private possession, and *DN,* 27 July 1916. See also Stephens's farewell poem to the choir, published in Cornwall, *Century of Singing,* pp. 82–83.

30. Leroy Robertson, Autobiographical Sketch, typescript in Robertson Papers.

31. William King Driggs, "L.D.S. Church Academies Music Departments—1904 to 1921," holograph in HBLL. Much of the information and characterization of Lund in this paragraph is taken from this source. Compare *The Banyan* (Provo: Brigham Young University, 1911), p. 25. On Lund's joketelling see also the editorial on his death in *DN,* 12 June 1935. According to one reminiscence, Lund was almost released from his conductorship after an alcohol-related accident; see Mary Jack Oral History, p. 8.

On the day Lund's appointment was publicly announced, Brigham Young University administrators drew up a letter of protest to Joseph F. Smith, explaining that "it will be almost impossible for us to keep up the standard if he severs his connection with us." University President George Brimhall then wrote to Lund that the music professor's departure would be more devastating to the school than the loss of any of Lund's colleagues—including Brimhall himself. Lund, however, had already committed to the position and quickly left the music department. See the letters concerning Lund quoted by Ernest L. Wilkinson, ed., *Brigham Young University: The First Hundred Years,* 4 vols. (Provo, Utah: Brigham Young University Press, 1975), 1:513–14. A more extensive excerpt of the Brimhall letter appears in Benjamin Mark Roberts, "Anthony C. Lund, Musician, With Special Reference to His Teaching and Choral Directing" (Master's thesis, Brigham Young University, 1952), pp. 32–33.

32. "What Shall We Do for Our Singers?," manuscript in Cornelia Lund Papers, HBLL. Cf. Lund's comments in *DN,* 19 March 1932.

33. See Richard Alan Nelson, "From Antagonism to Acceptance: Mormonism and the Silver Screen," *Dialogue* 10 (Spring 1977): 59–69.

34. See the Steger Phonograph brochure in Cornelia Lund Papers, Scrapbook II. On his resistance to radio, see the remarks by Earl Glade, the choir's engineer during the early period, in TC Minutes, 17 October 1948, 5 December 1963. Coincidentally, on 5 February 1930, Evan Stephens announced that he had banished the radio from his house and threatened not to pay his housekeeper if she brought one in ("The Great Musician," *OPH* 10:91). For a general treatment of early Mormon broadcasting see Pearl F. Jacobson, "Utah's First Radio Station," *Utah Historical Quarterly* 32 (Spring 1964): 130–44.

35. CMC Minutes, 12 January 1927.

36. The *Call* quotation appears in Cornwall, *Century of Singing,* p. 226.

37. Tracy Cannon observed that Mendelssohn appeared to be Lund's favorite composer. See Roberts, "Anthony C. Lund," p. 52.

38. 5 November 1929, quoted in Cornwall, *Century of Singing,* p. 228.

39. W. C. Holt to Lund, 27 January 1930, quoted by Roberts, "Anthony C. Lund," pp. 38–39.

40. Quoted in Cornwall, *Century of Singing,* p. 229.

41. See *Druid,* 15 December 1932.

42. For Cornwall's account of these events see his *Century of Singing,* pp. 362–64, and Cornwall Oral History I, pp. 14–17.

43. As recalled by Cornwall in TC Minutes, 17 January and 21 July 1957.

44. Cornwall Oral History I, p. 17, and Cornwall, *Century of Singing,* p. 153.

45. TC Minutes, 5 February 1953.

46. The quotations are all from TC Minutes: 22 February 1951, 27 March 1955, and 17 January 1957. See also Cornwall Oral History II, p. 70. On Clark's musical views see D. Michael Quinn, *J. Reuben Clark: The Church Years* (Provo: Brigham Young University Press, 1983), pp. 244–48.

47. TC Minutes, 28 February 1957.

48. CMC Minutes, 14 February 1950.

49. TC Minutes, 19 October 1944.

50. First Presidency to Tracy Y. Cannon, 18 December 1944, CMC Files 1939–49. The comment was made with specific reference to Leroy Robertson's music.

51. Joseph Fielding Smith, TC Minutes, 22 November 1942.

52. See Clark's Office Diary, 29 November 1944, Clark Papers.

53. J. Spencer Cornwall, "New Honor Comes to Tabernacle Choir," *Relief Society Magazine* 31 (July 1944): 390.

54. For Clark's statement see TC Minutes, 21 April 1946. The pamphlet is filed in the minutes under the date of 12 December 1946 and is reprinted in Cornwall, *Century of Singing,* pp. 39–42.

55. See clippings filed with TC Minutes, 17 October 1948.

56. Review of 29 August 1955.

57. Cornwall, *Century of Singing,* p. 153. For a personal account of the 1955 tour see Earl H. Ottley, "Passport through Europe," photocopy of typescript in HDC.

58. TC Minutes, 15 September 1957.

59. TC Minutes, 8 September 1957.

60. See TC Minutes, 15 September 1957, and *DN,* 20 September 1957. McKay explained that Cornwall, knowing he would be released soon, chose to take an immediate retirement. However, Cornwall's successor, Richard P. Condie, said that Cornwall told him he asked McKay for a little more time, but McKay insisted Cornwall retire at once. See Richard P. Condie, Oral History (interviewed by Jerold Ottley, 1978–82), typescript in Moyle Program, HDC, pp. 24, 35. See also Lowell M. Durham, Oral History (interviewed by Michael F. Moody, 1977), typescript in Moyle Program, p. 33, and the poignant letter of Allen S. Cornwall to Mark E. Petersen, 13 April 1955, TC Tour Files, HDC.

61. TC Minutes, 16 November 1958.

62. See his initial comments, TC Minutes, 25 March 1958; cf. "Ormandy Hails Choir as World's Finest," *DN,* 6 September 1958. For an interesting reminiscence of Ormandy's recording of the *Messiah* with the choir, see C. Alexander Schreiner,

Oral History, interviewed by Nancy Furner Renn (1973–75), pp. 40–43 of typescript, Moyle Program, HDC.

63. Lester Hewlett to George Romney, 17 February 1958, TC Tour Files.

64. A partial transcript of this KUED-TV (Salt Lake City) interview (date unavailable) appears in Lowell Durham to Jessie Evans Smith, 30 March 1970, photocopy in Robertson Papers.

65. Ibid.

66. Condie Oral History, pp. 28–29, 32–33. See also TC Minutes, 11 August 1960 and 10 November 1963. For a comparison of Cornwall's and Condie's programming, 1947–67 (i.e., before most of Condie's difficulties), see Fern Denise Gregory, "J. Spencer Cornwall: The Salt Lake Mormon Tabernacle Years, 1935–1957" (D.M.A. diss., University of Missouri-Kansas City, 1984), pp. 54–97. For a study of the church's expanding interests in radio broadcasting, see Fred C. Esplin, "The Church as Broadcaster," *Dialogue* 10 (Spring 1977): 25–45.

67. See Michael F. Moody to Stone, 14 December 1973, and A. Harold Goodman to Stone, 19 December 1973. Both of these documents are in Music Department Office Files, HDC. Lowell Durham, chairman of the University of Utah Department of Music, had earlier written to longtime Tabernacle Choir soloist Jessie Evans Smith, hoping that she might influence her husband, then church president Joseph Fielding Smith, to revamp the choir. (See Durham to Smith, 30 March 1970, Robertson Papers.)

68. CMC to First Presidency, 21 December 1973, in CMC Office Files.

69. "Richard Condie Praised as Release Comes," *Church News,* 29 June 1974.

70. Condie Oral History, pp. 32–33.

71. For a detailed contemporary account of this episode see the letter dated 28 December 1974 in Orvilla Stevens Oral History (interviewed by Charles Ursenbach, 1975), typescript in Oral History Program, HDC, pp. 356–59.

72. Notes from a public meeting on the Tabernacle Choir at the Salt Lake City Assembly Hall, 29 January 1987, photocopy in my possession.

10

Mormon Classics

Perhaps no American religion has clung to the belief in progress as has Mormonism. Brigham Young championed the virtues of newness, even in doctrine, on the grounds that every innovation manifested advancement. Young preached that God inspired scientific and artistic progress among the gentiles as much as he revealed new theology to the Saints. Each was ultimately to prepare mankind for Christ's return: "All the great discoveries and appliances in the arts and sciences are expressly designed by the Lord for the benefit of Zion in the last days."[1] In Young's conception of Zion, modernity became an article of faith.

A few months before his death in 1877, when he learned two of his sons wished to study music, Brigham Young encouraged them to go to the New England Conservatory. Arranging lessons for them with Dudley Buck, Young urged his sons to study music seriously, and be "thorough in all things. . . . Lay a good foundation. It has been wisely said that he is the best builder who builds well from the foundation up."[2] In the decades after Young's death many Mormon musicians, as if constrained by Young's advice to his sons, traveled by railroad car to the gentile East to acquire mastery sufficient to build his musical Zion.

While in the latter decades of the century Salt Lake City music was dominated by British immigrants, the Great Basin had attracted many German immigrant musicians as well. At least two such music masters lived in Paris, Idaho, and tutored young Arthur Shepherd. Arthur's father hoped his son would become "a great musician, whom not only the world would honor, but one whom God and his people would delight to honor also—one who would reflect credit to the church which, in a sense, gave him birth."[3] Arthur's German teachers taught the young man piano and gave him his first taste of classical music. When he was twelve, his teachers urged Arthur's parents to send the boy either to the Leipzig Conservatory or to the New England Conservatory. Choosing the latter, the Shepherd family put Arthur on the train to Boston, a city that was then, as Arthur later recalled, "an outpost of German musical culture."[4]

In Boston, Shepherd heard symphonies for the first time and encountered passionate debates over the relative merits of Wagner and Brahms. "With an omnivorous appetite," he later said of these days, "I devoured everything I could lay hands on." Shepherd took for a mentor not the conservatory's effervescent George Chadwick, but rather the austere German teacher Percy Goetschius, who indoctrinated Shepherd in theory and, to some extent, antimodernism. Receiving his diploma in 1897, Shepherd hoped to remain in "Papa" Goetschius's tutelage even after graduating. But Salt Lake Theatre manager George Pyper lured the young man away from the glories of Boston to direct the theater orchestra.

Shepherd impressed and intimidated the musicians in Salt Lake City with his conducting, piano teaching, and composing.[5] In Shepherd's first year in the city Evan Stephens pronounced him a "genius," though in later years faulted Shepherd for neglecting "home topics" in his music.[6] (Shepherd, in turn, found some of the high praise that had been heaped upon Stephens's music rather dubious.)[7] Shepherd composed as much as his schedule would permit, sending his manuscripts to Goetschius for his scrutiny and comment. Nine years after leaving the conservatory Shepherd won the Paderewski Prize for his "Overture Joyeuse," which was performed both by the Russian Symphony and the New York Symphony (under Walter Damrosch). The award dismayed some Eastern critics who pronounced the work "laborious and inconsequential," "muddy," "meager," and "a sad reflection on the musical productivity of the country."[8] Nonetheless, in 1909 the New England Conservatory hired Shepherd away from Utah, partly on the strength of his prize-winning work. Shepherd's departure disappointed some Salt Lake musicians, but others expected he would become a beacon of Mormon culture to Eastern gentiles.

After only one year back in Boston, Shepherd quit the church. In a letter to his father Shepherd explained that his time in Utah had felt like "bondage" to him and that he had experienced in Boston a "spiritual awakening," a "death" and "re-birth" of his faith in God. While studying literature—especially Darwin—Shepherd claimed to have achieved a "cosmic consciousness" that transcended Mormon beliefs.[9] He resolved henceforth to attend no more LDS meetings. Nevertheless, he wrote to his brother in 1921, "in spite of all the shattered ideals of my life there must be, deep down, some pretty fundamental foundations of faith."[10] Trying to build on these foundations, Shepherd later offered to prepare hymn settings for the 1927 hymnal (though he declined to write an anthem for the "home anthem" book the Church Music Committee was preparing).[11] Although one of his hymns, a setting of a text by Milton, appeared in *Latter-day Saint Hymns,* it was clear that

Shepherd would remain estranged from the church as his fame among the gentiles increased.

One musician who was apt to succeed Shepherd as the Mormon composer laureate was the Tabernacle Choir's assistant conductor, Brigham Cecil Gates. An offspring of Brigham Young's esteemed daughter Susa, Gates had studied piano and theory with Shepherd in 1904, at the New England Conservatory in 1905, and at the Schwarenka Conservatory in Berlin, 1910–13. In 1916, while employed at the Latter-day Saints' University in Salt Lake City, Gates wrote an oratorio entitled *The Restoration* for his students to perform. The work set texts written by the composer's mother; it also attempted to transpose his grandfather's notions of divine progress into musical terms.

The oratorio's first part, which treated the "gloom and warring confusion of the religious world a century ago," was set by Gates in what he called "the profound old contrapuntal forms illustrative of the dogmatism of that time." To portray the coming of Mormonism—the restoration of the true gospel—Gates used what he considered "modern highly-colored harmonies" and "modern classical forms."[12] (These latter were Wagnerian—leitmotives, enharmonic chord relationships, chromatic mediant progressions, and so forth.) Some non-Mormon critics who examined the score considered parts of the work "worthy of Chopin," and felt that Gates had a good sense of motivic transformation and counterpoint. A staff member of *Musical America* even claimed the work had "the best counterpoint and fugal work I have seen in any contemporary composers."[13] In 1922 the First Presidency commissioned a performance by the Tabernacle Choir and the concert evoked praise enough to encourage Gates to produce another Mormon oratorio, *Salvation for the Dead.*

The score to this 1923 work has been lost, but its program and reviews suggest its content. It was predominantly minor in mode—too much so according to some listeners—and overtly Wagnerian in harmony and leitmotivic structure. Indeed, its overture introduced the leitmotives and, in Wagnerian fashion, interwove them, symbolically summarizing the dramatic course of the four-part work to come. The *Salt Lake Tribune* critic felt the work had passages of great beauty, though the whole was "too dramatic; the musical atmosphere savors, at frequent intervals, of the crudely earthly rather than the inspirationally divine." The *Deseret News* was even more specific in its criticism: Gates had quoted Sunday school melodies in his oratorio, and while "they are pretty little jingles . . . to some [they] would seem to detract to an extent from serious consideration of the subject."[14] But church president Heber Grant pronounced Gates's music "the best of anything of the kind we have had from any of our local musicians."[15]

Evan Stephens produced two "dramatic cantatas" in 1920–21. To commemorate the centennial of Joseph Smith's first vision, President Grant and Mormon presiding bishop Charles Nibley asked Stephens to write a large work for choir and orchestra. He did so, libretto and all, in twenty days, calling the work simply *The Vision*. The 185-line text was a lyrical account of the vision, with opening lines that read:

> Morning gently wakes the songsters of the grove,
> With its gentle touch of living light and love;
> And, with whisp'ring breezes stirring at their wings,
> Bids the choirs give voice to all they feel, and sing,
> Join in harmony the rustling of the leaves,
> As they wave their welcome to the rising sun,
> While in the eastern skies a victor bright he cleaves
> Through the mists of night, his resurrection won.

Compared to Gates's music, Stephens's twelve-part work was lean and direct, echoing both the drama and the sentimentality that had characterized much of Dudley Buck's music, some of which Stephens had studied. Partly owing to the vast text, the choir sang continually, and during the vocal passages the four parts almost always intoned the words syllabically to quarter-, half-, and dotted-eighth-cum-sixteenth-note rhythms. The harmony was decidedly more adventurous than Stephens's typical anthems had been: *The Vision*'s first twenty-nine measures alone moved harmonically from C to A minor to B-flat to G-flat. And its bravura close, "Shout Ye Hosanna," contained some crowd-pleasing fugal writing.

While it was less ambitious and learned than Gates's *Restoration*, *The Vision* conveyed an earnestness that overwhelmed its first audience of ten thousand hearers. The *Deseret News* claimed the work was "destined to take its place among the Mormon classics" and even the non-Mormon *Salt Lake Tribune* praised the work's reverence and sincerity. Its harmonies, the newspaper added, "in some places . . . are strong and suggestive of the lofty thoughts they purport to interpret."[16]

Inspired by the acclaim, Stephens wrote a companion piece, *The Martyrs*, during the following year. Virtually identical in style to *The Vision*, *The Martyrs* was more varied in its interplay of solo melodies, chordal and contrapuntal writing. Like Gates's *Salvation for the Dead*, *The Martyrs* used quotations of hymns for dramatic effect. With its dark subject (the assassination of Joseph and Hyrum Smith) and its particularly poignant ending, *The Martyrs* turned out to be a more powerful work than Stephens's earlier cantata. Nevertheless, it drew an audience only one-fifth the size of its predecessor because, unlike *The Vision*, it was not performed at the church's general conference. Its subsequent influence was slight, as the fate of its one thousand published copies suggests: in December 1921 the work went on sale at Deseret Book; by May 1923 only seventy copies had been sold; forty years after its premiere, the remaining eight hundred copies were discounted to twenty-five cents apiece.[17]

In 1930 church leader and man of letters B. H. Roberts lamented that "the great Oratorio of the New Dispensation remains to be written."[18] Oddly enough, the centennial of the church's founding that year seems not to have inspired a large original work. Stephens was elderly and unproductive; he would die in October. Gates, meanwhile, had been stricken with a progressive paralytic disease that disrupted his compositional impulses, which by now were leading him toward popular music anyway.[19] The church's centenary pageant, titled *The Message of the Ages,* ended up being a conglomeration of borrowed classical works and Mormon hymns: excerpts from Mendelssohn's *St. Paul,* Haydn's *Creation,* and, of course, the *Messiah,* appeared alongside sacred songs by Careless, Daynes, Stephens, and even an excerpt from Gates's *Restoration.* The only new music in the pageant apparently was the instrumental interlude composed for it by the thirty-three-year-old BYU professor Leroy Robertson.

Robertson had come from origins as humble as Shepherd's. He was raised in Fountain Green, Utah, and was trained in violin and self-taught on the reed organ, on which he improvised and learned by ear "all the trashy tunes of the day."[20] After painstakingly notating some of his keyboard improvisations, Robertson showed some manuscripts to an itinerant musician who warned the boy against attempting to compose without training in harmony. This warning lingered with him and prompted him at age seventeen to study with Tony Lund at BYU. Thereafter, like so many forebears, he enrolled at the New England Conservatory.

At Boston, Robertson made George Chadwick his mentor. Chadwick reciprocated by trying to groom his student for the Prix de Rome. But the rigors of the conservatory and the pressure Chadwick placed on him led Robertson to a nervous breakdown within a year of enrollment. His mental state grew so poor that he could hardly compose at all for a time. When he regained some stability he relegated himself primarily to writing short piano works, songs, and hymns. Despite the breakdown, Robertson maintained the quality of his composing in both sacred and secular genres. In 1922 he surprised the Church Music Committee by winning both first and third prizes in that year's hymn contest. (Stephens, of course, won second and fourth.)[21] And the next year he won the Endicott Prize for his only orchestral work, the Overture in E Minor. Upon securing his diploma he returned to Utah, grateful for his training but doubtful he would ever recoup his health.

Robertson joined the BYU faculty in 1925, but continued to seek training elsewhere. Over the next twenty years he left from time to time for advanced study with Ernest Bloch, Hugo Leichentritt and, briefly, Arnold Schoenberg. Of the three, Bloch affected Robertson the most: "I can truthfully say he has had more influence upon my artistic career than anyone else."[22] With his creative powers refined and disciplined by his studies with Bloch, Robertson produced in the 1930s a series of growingly modernistic—or, as he put it, "not very polite"—works, including his award-winning Piano Quintet and his second symphony, subtitled "Trilogy," which would soon give him international fame.

Tracy Cannon saw in Robertson an emerging world-class composer who could write well-crafted modernistic music that could exemplify the progressive tendencies of Mormonism to the world. When Robertson received the 1944 New York Critics Circle Award for his String Quartet, Cannon persuaded the First Presidency to reduce Robertson's teaching load at BYU to give him more time to compose.[23] In September 1946 the presidency further lightened his load and informally commissioned him to write an oratorio on the Book of Mormon. Robertson had been contemplating such a work since the late 1930s, when Melvin Ballard suggested to him that some passages in the book would lend themselves well to choral-orchestral treatment. J. Reuben Clark pursued the idea with Robertson, hoping the oratorio could be performed as the climax of celebrations at the 1947 pioneer centennial. Robertson wrote that this commission made him feel a growing sense of "great responsibility"; "I sincerely hope that with the help of the Lord and all your faith and prayers I may do this work justice."[24]

His extant sketches for the oratorio show his constant grappling with the problem of modern harmony, how to make chords progress convincingly without benefit of keys. The sketches, like the final work, also manifest Robertson's eclecticism: they fluctuate between formal neo-Baroque counterpoint—the legacy of his studies with Bloch—and mannered modal chorales and pseudo-Middle Eastern synthetic scales.[25] Robertson always described the work not in harmonic but in formal and leitmotivic terms: the whole was an arch, centered on C, with recurrent melodic figures that symbolized various characters and ideas. But, even though a preliminary version of the work apparently could have been ready for performance, the oratorio was not played at the pioneer centennial. Instead, a reprise of *Message of the Ages* was mounted. The substitution came in part because Robertson intended his work to be performed by the combined forces of the Tabernacle Choir and the controversial Utah Symphony.

The state-run symphony had descended from the Salt Lake Symphony that Arthur Shepherd had organized upon his 1897 return from Boston.

The orchestra became a WPA project during the Depression and survived the World War II years. But its promoters recognized that it could not continue without official church backing.[26] A collaboration between the symphony and the Tabernacle Choir in summer 1945 (on Haydn's *Creation*) forecast an era of good relations between the church and the symphony. The following year the First Presidency committed five thousand dollars of church money to the orchestra, along with free use of the Tabernacle for rehearsals and concerts. The only conditions of the gift were that the symphony employ as many Utahns as it could and that it "put into its work a spirituality that comes in no small part only from voluntary service"—a concession to the lingering Mormon belief that money polluted musical service.[27]

Two months after this pledge of support, J. Reuben Clark learned that thirty-seven musicians were being hired from out of the state. This struck him as a clear breach of the church's wishes. He concluded, along with some of his fellow church leaders, that "somebody is taking all of us nitwits for a ride."[28] Misgivings multiplied when, in the centennial year of 1947, the symphony hired the fine young conductor Maurice Abravanel, who according to rumor was anti-Mormon.[29]

The rumor was prevalent, though unfounded, and a rift was inevitable. Upon Abravanel's arrival, Spencer Cornwall refused to allow the Tabernacle Choir to sing any more with the orchestra.[30] Many Mormon leaders and the Church Music Committee wanted the church to keep backing the orchestra, and many Tabernacle Choir members hoped to sing with the orchestra. But Cornwall held firm to his policy of not mingling the state and church musical organizations throughout his tenure as director. Abravanel nonetheless devoted himself to advancing Utah music, especially Robertson's works, one of which, two months into Abravanel's first season, won an award as the best work composed in the Western Hemisphere.[31]

Many American patrons of the arts in the postwar era advocated music training and appreciation as a remedy to the savage impulses that had brought on the war. Nowhere was this advocacy exemplified more than in Henry Reichhold's offer to award $25,000 and a premiere by the Detroit Symphony to a major work composed in the Americas. One of about 400 composers from 17 countries, Robertson entered his *Trilogy,* an imposing 123-page score for large orchestra. The judging of scores lasted more than a year beyond the original award date, but in the end Robertson claimed the prize, even above prominent United States composers such as Samuel Barber, William Schuman, and Aaron Copland. Reviews of *Trilogy* echoed the Reichhold committee's praise: the symphony was "constant[ly] blooming, forever bursting with surprise . . . fresh and free and altogether American," and "as moving as the snowy peaks of the West that gave it birth."[32]

Some church leaders viewed the award as a success for Mormonism. BYU mounted an evening tribute to Robertson at which university and church dignitaries, including J. Reuben Clark, spoke. Clark remarked that Robertson's achievement was "proof" that famous composers need not be profligate, that "the loftiest expression can come from the heavenly uplifting influence of a beautiful home where the highest standards of morality and right living are observed."[33] But Clark was disappointed when, the following year, Robertson left the church university to join the faculty of the state-run University of Utah.[34]

Robertson's reasons were clear. Although BYU then had the better music department, a move from Provo to Salt Lake City would allow Robertson proximity to the Church Music Committee, to policy makers in public music education, and, most important, to the Utah Symphony. Despite these reasons, Robertson's decision to resign from BYU at the zenith of his fame grieved some church leaders. The composer remained devout but felt keenly that he was being considered a betrayer of his people and that the Oratorio from the Book of Mormon might be rejected because of this.[35] Robertson continued to tinker with it, and used it for his dissertation composition at the University of Southern California, convinced it would never be produced with the forces he envisioned. Finally, in 1953, at Abravanel's insistence, the Utah Symphony and University of Utah Chorale produced the work three times, twice at the Tabernacle and once at BYU, against the objections of at least some church university officials.[36] Robertson's "betrayal" of BYU notwithstanding, church administrators and musicians who attended lauded the work as a new summit of Mormon artistic achievement, the standard for masterworks to come.[37]

The following year one of Robertson's former students, Crawford Gates, began writing a programmatic symphony depicting events from the Book of Mormon. While studying at the Eastman School of Music, Gates was asked by the director of Palmyra's Hill Cumorah Pageant to consider writing original music for the event.[38] Since its inception the pageant had used music borrowed from various nineteenth- and early-twentieth-century composers, from Tchaikovsky to Victor Herbert. (The prophet Abinadi, for example, was burned at the stake to Wagner's "Ride of the Valkyries.") Partly because Gates had composed the pioneer centennial hit musical *Promised Valley*, both the pageant managers and the First Presidency considered him well-suited to create a distinctively Mormon score for Cumorah.

As did many of his forebears, Gates thought in Wagnerian terms, and tried to create, in his words, "a structure of solidly conceived thematic materials, symbolic of the personalities of the main characters and situations." At the center of his leitmotivic web was the "Christ theme," a fanfare-like diatonic motive built principally of fourths. Gates thought the musical emblemization of the Savior so crucial to the work that he wrote eighteen different versions of the motive over two and a half years. He settled on the final version only after Harold B. Lee gave him a priesthood blessing on the matter.

When he completed the work in 1957 Gates recorded it in the Tabernacle with the Utah Symphony and the A Capella Chorus from BYU. The work, subtitled "Scenes from the Book of Mormon," was essentially a romantically styled, cyclic symphony with Hebraic affectations. It displayed Gates's vivid sense of orchestral color and conservative use of modern harmony. It also manifested a range of moods much broader than Robertson had evoked in his more ascetic work. What was perhaps most important about the work was that in it Gates obtained an enormous audience for a sophisticated Mormon composition: tens of thousands attended the pageant each year, and a souvenir phonograph recording made in 1960 was stocked in church bookstores. "Scenes from the Book of Mormon" allowed serious Mormon music to extend beyond the concert hall.[39]

Gates's former pupil Merrill Bradshaw began in the early 1960s to try to reshape compositional thinking in the church. As he wrote in 1961, Mormon music heretofore had sought to embody the grandeur of Mormon experience at the expense of the intimate sensations at the religion's center: "There are emotions in Mormon experience that belong in the heart rather than on the mouthpiece of a trumpet, emotions beclouded by tears in the eyes and fire in the breast until words become sacrilege and actions fumble awkwardly through their embarrassment at their own inadequacy."[40] Among the first fruits of his attempt to write music along these lines was his a capella choral setting of Joseph Smith's "Articles of Faith." This piece continued the well-established Mormon tendency toward leitmotivic composition, associating certain motives with the Father, the Son, and the Holy Ghost. Other symbolic associations and numerological proportions were also plotted into the meditative piece. Although it was difficult to perform, relatively abstract, and somewhat limited in its performance appeal—it was a liturgical work in concert garb—the "Articles of Faith" effectively complemented its large-scale ancestors.

Throughout the next two decades Bradshaw, Gates, and others tried to unite their "brother composers" in the quest for a definitive Mormon art music and aesthetics. As early as 1962 the two men compiled a list of thirty-four Mormon composers and solicited scores from them, with hopes to promote performances at the church university, to establish a Mormon archives, and, most ambitiously, to foster a "unity of purpose that would produce works that could be considered in general to be in similar styles.''⁴¹ The list revealed a Mormon academic genealogy: virtually all of the composers bore some kind of student-teacher relationship to one another. But the composers varied widely in their skill and devotion to Bradshaw's aspirations and only a few sent in scores (the least skilled composers were often the most eager). The planned alliance failed.

Few "official" responses to Mormon art music were voiced during the 1960s. The Church Music Committee favored elegant Mormon sacred music and seemed content to let modernism have its day. BYU president Ernest Wilkinson declared in 1965 that art music should be composed at the church university "in an atmosphere where [our young people] will not be poisoned with agnostic or atheistic or 'Jack Mormon' philosophy."⁴² The following year apostle Boyd K. Packer mildly criticized those who "feel the necessity, feel responsible, to 'up-grade' and introduce 'culture' into our worship services," though the targets of his critique were unclear.⁴³ The most passionate official voice in favor of Mormon high culture was that of apostle Spencer Kimball.

In 1967 Kimball addressed the faculty and staff of BYU at great length on the theme of "Education for Eternity." Kimball surmised that "there must be many Wagners . . . in the BYU . . . [and] men greater . . . but less eccentric, more spiritual." He suggested that young Mormon composers could even surpass Handel's *Messiah* because "they can use the coming of Christ to the Nephites [in the Book of Mormon] as the material for a greater masterpiece."⁴⁴ The university's Fine Arts College dean, Lorin Wheelwright, considered Kimball's address a manifesto endorsing the pursuit of serious, deliberately "Mormon" composition. While only some of Wheelwright's colleagues echoed his views, most of them supported his proposal that BYU begin a yearly "Mormon Arts Festival" that would embrace modern, even experimental work in all the arts.⁴⁵

But Kimball had failed to address the problem of musical modernism. More than a century earlier, Brigham Young had noted with some sadness that composers of his day "introduce as much discord as possible into their compositions, without actually destroying the rules of music."⁴⁶ To Young, as to perhaps most listeners, complex harmonies seemed to symbolize contention, spiritual conflict. To emancipate the dissonance in twentieth-century Mormon music might seem to loose a disharmonious spirit in the church. Moreover, many sorts of modernistic art seemed to derive from secularist, even atheistic philosophies that challenged the very idea of the sacred. As young Mormon composers continued to be schooled away from Mormondom's parochial centers, they were compelled to reconcile the inherent conservatism of sacred music traditions with their religion's yearning for progress. Some Mormon composers attempted to synthesize the two in sessions with their students and in writings such as Bradshaw's "Reflections on the Nature of Mormon Art."[47] Here Bradshaw described Mormonism as a parallel to modernism and called for a "cross-fertilization" of the two. While rejecting willful avant-gardism, with its implicit rejection of the past, he called for Mormon artists to exploit "the unique advantages of Mormonism's view of history and its synthesizing nature of thought." Perhaps the most important aspect of the article, however, was its title, which quietly proclaimed that Mormon art had a distinctive "nature."

In 1969 Bradshaw and others founded the "LDS Composers Association," a national affiliation that promoted no particular "Mormon style," but sought to promote fellowship among composers in the church. The association published an occasional mimeographed newsletter, *Notes.* Each issue contained polemical articles on the state of Mormon music and its future, ruminations on what a Mormon style should be, and news on recent performances by member composers, with pieces ranging from the most commercial sorts of music to the most experimental.

The following decade seemed ripe for grand undertakings. Mormon missionaries were baptizing tens of thousands each year, especially in the Third World. Brigham Young University was prospering as never before, expanding its course offerings and reaching a peak of enrollment. Exponents of high culture in Mormondom strengthened their rhetoric. During the years 1972–76 several books were published, including the handsome coffee-table volume *Mormon Arts, Volume One,* and Bradshaw's didactic *Spirit and Music: Letters to a Young Mormon Composer.* A spate of articles devoted to Mormon art also appeared, some of them in a refined, typeset version of the LDS composers' *Notes,* and others in the unofficial Mormon journals *Dialogue* and *Sunstone.* In Provo a new publishing house devoted to contemporary art music by and for Mormons was opened.[48]

In 1974 BYU produced Bradshaw's new oratorio, *The Restoration.* What had been occasional stylistic incongruities in Robertson's Book of Mormon oratorio became in Bradshaw's work a studied eclecticism. The composer hoped the juxtaposition of styles would suggest the Mormon dispensation's consummation of all previous ages. While it borrowed from many styles, including jazz, most of Bradshaw's piece used relatively accessible modern harmonies, partly in the hope that the music would neither alienate nor intimidate the concert audience. Not unlike *The Restoration*'s 1916 namesake, with its Sunday school song quotations, Bradshaw's work inserted whole well-known hymns to be sung by the audience. The work's formal opening (for "angelic choir") stated its purpose in frank terms:

Brothers and sisters!
Tonight we have assembled together
To sing to each other,
With each other
And to God our Father.

The work was widely praised in the church and deemed by some a kind of Mormon *Messiah*.[49]

In February 1976 apostle Boyd K. Packer renewed and extended his critique of Mormon high culture in a severe address rebuking the elitism and worldliness he saw creeping into Mormon artistic and musical circles. He faulted church musicians for neglecting the hymns and showing "contempt for the homespun" in Mormon arts. He insisted that one could find more of the Spirit of God in "quiet, homey moments as contrasted to classic moments of exultation" and warned against the pursuit of newness for its own sake. The comfort of the familiar, he said, should be paramount in Mormon worship. When asked for an idea of a work that would meet his criteria, Packer immediately named Bradshaw's *Restoration*.[50]

Packer's address provoked much soul-searching and debate. Some BYU students openly confronted their mentors about the dissonance and complexity of the older generation's work. Some of these teachers countered by expressing their belief that they simply were continuing a longstanding tradition of progressivism in Mormon art. Many professors at the church university feared that the address would erode Mormonism's aesthetic foundations. (Even Bradshaw remarked that the talk had "chopped the philosophic feet out from under my work.")[51] Others felt secure that Packer's voice was not a representative one and that Mormonism's progressive heritage would survive such critiques. In any case, the quest for a progressive Mormon music continued.

In the same year that Bradshaw's *Restoration* premiered, one of Bradshaw's former students, David Sargent, composed his dissertation piece, an oratorio entitled *Apostasy and Restoration*. It was a ferocious work that juxtaposed passages of freely chromatic lyricism with masses of orchestral sound, echoing the difficult sacred music of Penderecki. The score contained much unusual notation that, if realized, would produce shifting, indeterminate bands of sonority that presumably suggested the grandeur of the work's subject. Through its instrumental demands, its dense harmonies, and its extreme contrasts, the work bewildered the BYU music directors who had championed more traditional Mormon oratorios and, as yet, it remains unperformed.

As the techniques and aesthetics of avant-garde and experimental music began to be taught more vigorously at BYU, a number of younger

Mormon composers forged new musical ideals for their sacred works. Helge Skjeveland has composed in relative isolation a body of complex sacred choral work—again, almost none of it yet performed—in the style of contemporary East European composers. Working from different models—including Harry Partch and John Coltrane—Will Salmon has written a number of cathartic religious works for improvisatory chamber groups. Some of these have been performed at BYU, others by the Open Gate Theatre in the Pacific southwest. Murray Boren has composed sacred works for large ensembles, including his opera entitled *Emma,* a study of Mormonism's first arbiter of music, Emma Smith. Played during the regular opera season at BYU in 1984, the work delighted some listeners for its freshness, dismayed others for its relentless chromaticism, but mostly perplexed audiences accustomed to more genteel treatments of Mormon themes.[52]

In 1984 Mormon magnate Milton Barlow established an endowment at Brigham Young University primarily to promote the creation of large-scale works by Mormon composers. Directly inspired by Kimball's "Education for Eternity" address, Barlow hoped that the endowment would help develop "a body of music that defines and extends the culture inherent in the Mormon environment, doctrine, and history."[53] The music so far produced under the endowment's auspices has ranged from secular concertos and chamber pieces to sacred choral-orchestral works, with the quality of the compositions themselves being decidedly mixed. Moreover, most of the endowment's monies flow out to non-Mormon composers through competitions and commissions. How far the Barlow project will go in fostering Mormon art music remains to be seen, though it cannot help but hearten the aspiring heirs to Stephens, Shepherd, Robertson, and their musical brethren.

Mormons, like their Christian counterparts, have often ascribed spiritual properties to their tastes. They sometimes liken the comfort of the familiar to the warmth of the Spirit, and their mistrust of high musical culture to scorn for the devil. While in earlier days leading Saints shunned the anti-aestheticism of Protestantism, some recent Mormon leaders implicitly have called the Saints to retreat from high culture in an attempt to consolidate and preserve Mormon identity, to make all Mormons feel comfortable in their "home" culture. Ironically, the current tendencies toward anti-aestheticism have reinforced many church members' inclinations toward popular music. And while twentieth-century Mormon leaders have vacillated in promoting art music, at one time or another they have censured virtually all popular music.

NOTES

1. *JD* 10:225.

2. Dean C. Jessee, ed., *Letters of Brigham Young to His Sons* (Salt Lake City: Deseret Book, 1974), pp. 276–77.

3. William Shepherd to Arthur Shepherd, 1 May 1910, Arthur Shepherd Papers, UU.

4. Arthur Shepherd, " 'Papa' Goetschius in Retrospect," *Musical Quarterly* 30 (July 1944): 308. On Shepherd's early biography see Richard Loucks, *Arthur Shepherd: American Composer* (Provo: Brigham Young University Press, 1980), pp. 3–13.

5. He was severe as a teacher, following his German models. Edna Dyer wrote in her diary that Shepherd "is prescribing for my very bad piano playing, but as he keeps discovering new ailments that need heroic treatment, I'm beginning to fear that I am incurable. I always knew that I wasn't good for much, but he finds me *shockingly* bad" (29 August 1905).

6. Griggs Journal, 14 February 1898 and 18 December 1902.

7. See Arthur Shepherd to William Shepherd, 13 May 1896, Shepherd Papers.

8. These quotes are selected from the excerpted reviews in "Shepherd's Prize Work Does Not Please New York Critics," *DN*, 24 March 1906, reprinted in Basil Hansen, "An Historic Account of Music Criticism and Music Critics in Utah" (Master's thesis, Brigham Young University, 1933), pp. 44–46.

9. William Shepherd to Arthur Shepherd, 1 May 1910. This thirty-six-page response to Arthur's letter quotes that letter; the quotes here are taken from those found in the response.

10. Arthur to Harry Shepherd, 8 November 1921, Shepherd Papers.

11. See CMC Minutes, 5 April 1923 and 7 September 1926. His only piece on a Mormon scriptural text, the Doctrine and Covenants anthem "The Lord Hath Brought Again Zion," was published by Oliver Ditson in 1907 and eventually sung over the radio by the Tabernacle Choir, though Shepherd missed the broadcast (see J. Spencer Cornwall to Arthur Shepherd, 16 February 1945, Shepherd Papers).

12. See the two differing versions of the work's "Musical Argument," one in the program to the work, in Emma Lucy Gates Bowen Papers, HBLL (reprinted in Lyneer Charles Smith, "Brigham Cecil Gates: Composer, Director, Teacher of Music" [Master's thesis, Brigham Young University, 1952], pp. 12–13), and in the score published by the church in 1917.

13. Cited in Smith, "Brigham Cecil Gates," pp. 13–15.

14. "New Oratorio Well Received," *Salt Lake Tribune*, 7 October 1923, and "Doctrinal Theme Superbly Treated in Oratorio Form," *DN*, 8 October 1923. See also the program notes to the work reprinted in Smith, "Brigham Cecil Gates," pp. 25–26.

15. Heber J. Grant to Emma Lucy Gates, 31 March 1916, Bowen Papers.

16. *DN*, 6 April 1920, and " 'Vision' Charms Great Audience," *Salt Lake Tribune*, 6 April 1920.

17. See CMC Minutes, 1 December 1921, 10 May 1923, 1 March 1927, and 6 April 1961.

18. Roberts, *Comprehensive History,* 6:245.

19. Gates's biggest success came in his set of minstrel-style spirituals, *Cornfield Melodies,* one of which the publisher E. C. Schirmer would anthologize as one of its "most successful" of male choruses. On pageants in the church see Davis Bitton, "The Ritualization of Mormon History," *Utah Historical Quarterly* 43 (Winter 1975): 67–85.

20. The quotations and most of the information in this and the following paragraphs are from Leroy Robertson, "A Confession" (holograph) and Autobiographical Sketch, both in Robertson Papers.

21. The committee almost immediately asked him for a home anthem to add to their collection. When he sent a group of anthems the committee picked one and had Stephens write new words to it. See CMC Minutes, 7 September 1922 and 25 October 1923.

22. Handwritten note in Autobiographical Sketch, Robertson Papers.

23. Tracy Cannon to First Presidency, 15 December 1944, and First Presidency to Tracy Cannon, 18 December 1944, CMC Files 1939–49.

24. Leroy Robertson to Tracy Cannon, 6 October 1946, CMC Files 1939–49.

25. See the various analyses in the Robertson Papers, including a one-page typescript, a typeset note for his dissertation at the University of Southern California, and Leroy Robertson to J. M. George, 21 April 1955.

26. For a full history of the symphony see Conrad B. Harrison, *Five Thousand Concerts: A Commemorative History of the Utah Symphony* (Salt Lake City: Utah Symphony Society, 1986).

27. First Presidency to Adam Bennion, 9 September 1946, Clark Papers.

28. J. Reuben Clark to Adam Bennion, 4 November 1946, Clark Papers.

29. Maurice Abravanel interviewed by Jay Hammond, 14 October 1981, UHS Oral History Program, typescript, p. 13.

30. Part of his concern appears to have been that Abravanel would not treat the singers' voices with respect and delicacy. According to Abravanel, Cornwall also dismissed his offers of collaboration with the terse observation, "We are the church, you are the state, the two don't mix." Abravanel had told this story often; for a full version see Abravanel–Haymond Interview, 24 September 1981, typescript, pp. 19–20.

31. See the survey in Lowell M. Durham, "The Abravanel Years," *Proceedings of the Utah Academy of Sciences, Arts, and Letters* 43 (1966): 1–12.

32. Reviews from the *Detroit News* and *Detroit Free Press,* both 12 December 1947. For a history of the Reichhold Award see "Winners Named for Reichhold Award," *Musical Digest* (1947), photocopy in Robertson Papers.

33. "Program of Tribute in Honor of Leroy Robertson" (25 November 1947), bound typescript in Robertson Papers, p. 35.

34. There were many machinations toward this end. See, for example, Lowell Durham to Leroy Robertson, 22 January 1947, and Lorin F. Wheelwright to Ray Olpin, 11 March 1948, both in Robertson Papers. The Church Music Committee may have also supported the move (see CMC Minutes, 19 March 1948).

35. Durham Oral History, p. 21, and Abravanel–Haymond Interview, 14 October 1981, pp. 8–9.

36. Abravanel–Haymond Interview, 14 October 1981, pp. 15–16. The work was performed again in 1955 as a fund-raiser for the Tabernacle Choir's European tour.

37. See especially Tracy Cannon's comments in CMC Minutes, 24 February 1953. A packet of reviews of the 1962 Vanguard recording of the work is in Robertson Papers. For a treatment of Robertson's oratorio in the light of other twentieth-century oratorios, see Stevenson, *Protestant Church Music in America*, pp. 113–25. See also Lowell M. Durham, "A Mormon Record," *Dialogue* 2 (Autumn 1967): 149–51.

38. Held annually since 1937, the pageant dramatically commemorated Joseph Smith's obtaining of the golden plates. The information and quotations in this and the following two paragraphs are from Crawford Gates, "A Sacred Choral Pageant," *Music Journal* 19 (February 1961): 68–70, and "Spiritual Experiences in Preparing Hill Cumorah Pageant Music," BYU *Selected Speeches*, 17 June 1959.

39. In 1987, Gates was commissioned by the First Presidency to write a new score as part of a revision of the whole pageant. According to Gates, the presidency wanted the new score to appeal to the eighteen- through thirty-four-year-old age group, from which the church apparently has the most successful conversion rate, yet not to be pop-oriented. To a large extent, the rewritten pageant music emulates Hollywood fantasy-movie music and Broadway show music as well. For Gates's remarks on his new score see " 'Double honor' for composer," *Church News*, 30 July 1988, p. 10; also his address given on the "Why I Believe" fireside series, Edgemont Utah Stake, 7 August 1988, notes in my possession.

40. Merrill Bradshaw, "The Articles of Faith—Composer's Commentary," *Brigham Young University Studies* 3 (Spring-Summer 1961): 73.

41. Merrill Bradshaw to Crawford Gates, 26 December 1961 and 21 March 1962, University Archives, HBLL. A folder of papers related to this endeavor is also in this collection.

42. Quoted in "Quality Teaching Number 1 Goal for BYU Faculty," *DN*, 14 September 1965.

43. Packer, "Shall the Youth of Zion Falter?," BYU *Speeches of the Year*, 12 April 1966.

44. Spencer W. Kimball, "Education for Eternity," BYU *Speeches of the Year*, 12 September 1967, pp. 13–15.

45. For Wheelwright's enthusiastic responses to Kimball's address, see his letters to Ernest L. Wilkinson, 13 September 1967, and to Spencer W. Kimball, 6 October 1967, University Archives, HBLL.

46. Brigham Young Office Journal, 3 June 1860, typescript extracts in the possession of David Whittaker, HBLL archivist.

47. *Brigham Young University Studies* 9 (Autumn 1968): 25–32.

48. For other treatments of Mormon art in this period see the articles in *Dialogue* 2 (Spring 1967): 48–54; also Lowell M. Durham, "On Mormon Music and Musicians," *Dialogue* 3 (Summer 1968): 19–40.

49. Bradshaw Interview, pp. 3–4.

50. The quotes in this paragraph are taken from Packer's introduction to the address, in his *"That All May Be Edified": Talks, Sermons & Commentary,* Salt Lake City: Bookcraft, 1982), p. 251. The address itself has been reprinted several times, including in Steven P. Sondrup, ed., *Arts and Inspiration: Mormon Perspectives* (Provo: Brigham Young University Press, 1980), pp. 3–21, which also contains the follow-up interview cited here.

51. Bradshaw Interview, p. 16.

52. For a review of the opera see Dorothy Stowe, " 'Emma': Forget Preconceptions," *DN,* 29 January 1984.

53. From Barlow Endowment brochure (1985), copy in author's possession.

11

From Rags to Rock

In 1922 British moralists produced a silent feature film entitled *Trapped by the Mormons*. It depicted the exploits of Isoldi Keane, a fictional Mormon elder who coaxed young women away from their families to his harem in Utah. Toward the climax of the film, Keane escorted his latest victim, as the film narrative placard explained, to "a restaurant where one would hardly expect a Saint to dine." The camera then revealed that the dance floor of the restaurant was filled with couples dancing to the wild beat of a black quartet. Mormons, the film suggested, were infected with the latest cultural disease: jazz.

The truth was that Mormons had joined these moralists in the worldwide crusade against the new music and dancing. The same year that *Trapped by the Mormons* was produced, a speaker at the Salt Lake City convention of the American National Association of Masters of Dancing triumphantly announced, "Jazz has passed." Having just returned from a tour of New York, Fred Christensen explained that the syncopated melodies and jerking movements that had spread from Southern dance halls throughout the states were now abating in favor of the gentle strains and graceful steps of high society. "We do hear these 'blues' tunes," he conceded, "but withal, one finds the dance music more harmonious, soft and pleasing than for any season yet."[1] But the idea that jazz had passed was as groundless as the idea that Mormons were secretly fostering it. For years thereafter, Mormons, like most religious Americans, joined in a national campaign of invective against unconventional music and fad dances.

In the 1910s the syncopated "coon songs" and clogging that had pervaded minstrelsy in Utah turned to full-fledged "ragging" in the music and dance of the restaurants, cafés, and resorts. Despite the chaperoning of Mormon elders, "belly-rubbing" dances such as the tango, the turkey trot, the bunny hug, and the grizzly bear entered Latter-day Saint social gatherings. These dances appeared frequently at the flamboyant Saltair resort on the Great Salt Lake, where the massive dance pavilion had been unabashedly designed by church architects to resemble the Salt Lake Tabernacle. As early as 1913 the "ragging beast" was said to have "ravaged the community" in Utah County and a dance that did not feature moves such as the "goose glide," the "worm wiggle," or the "coon flop" was said to be "conspicuous."[2]

Although Mormon leaders disliked such dancing, they feared that to suppress it too harshly might drive young people away from the church. President Joseph F. Smith circumvented the issue of proper dancing by urging Saints to downplay dancing as a form of recreation altogether.[3] If it were indulged in, the regulations adopted at the turn of the century were to be abided. But the church's MIA (Mutual Improvement Association) General Board insisted that "we cannot expect to do away with the undignified dances unless we supply something better in their place." The "something better" they supplied were the once-forbidden round dances, four of which the MIA officially sanctioned in the years 1910–13.[4]

Church leaders charged Brigham Young University's Physical Education Department to educate Mormon congregations in proper round dancing during the mid-1910s. Saltair (by now under non-Mormon ownership) countered with free lessons in several disapproved modern dances, including the tango, the hesitation waltz, and the maxixe. The Saltair dance master boasted in 1914 that "before the summer is over, more people in Salt Lake will be dancing the new and modern steps than in any western city."[5] To keep this prophecy from coming true, in 1915 the church's 800-student Latter-day Saint's University officially banned "hugging dances" and the MIA sponsored a convention on dancing for schools throughout the state. At this convention BYU's Eugene Roberts laid out strategies for driving "rowdy" dances from social affairs. Ironically, he urged abandoning the old Virginia Reel—a favorite of pioneer Mormons—which he deemed "a little too boisterous."[6]

Rag music had already crept into virtually all areas of public recreation. In 1909 the *Intermountain Republican* complained that "ragtime and hash" could be heard in every café and restaurant in the community.[7] Four years later, when a University of Utah professor critiqued the musical culture of Salt Lake City, the *Deseret News* protested that much of what now passed for music in the city was not music at all. Unquestionably referring to ragtime, the paper complained: "Most of the compositions that flood the market have no more claim to be classed as music than have the discordant noises in a sawmill. They have no meaning, no soul, no inspiration. They are notes laboriously strung together on a still-born theme, printed to sell, and selling by virtue of advertisements. . . . We often hear even in public, a piano manipulated with great technical skill, and yet the effect is about the same as would be produced by the vigorous beating upon a tin pan. . . . Salt Lake is too musical for that."[8]

Members of the church hierarchy hesitated to indict specific bands or pieces, perhaps uncertain about what to indict and how to describe it. But church leaders did attempt to legislate proper rhythm, tempo, and volume in the instrumental music of Mormon socials. In 1914 the MIA cautiously insisted that dance musicians play "in strict time [to] assist in eliminating ragging, and other objectionable forms of dancing." At the 1915 dancing convention the MIA urged that dance music always be "quiet and refined" and that floor managers continually scrutinize the music's "fitness." The following year the church published a list of thirty-one approved dance pieces (all waltzes and two-steps) and forbade any dance music with "broken rhythm"—a euphemism for ragtime.[9]

At about this time the term "jazz" emerged in American slang. (The term denoted "pep" or "sex," depending on whom one asked.) By the time America entered World War I "jazz" came generally to denote the high-spirited improvisatory band style that accompanied the objectionable dances. The first extended attack on "jazz" in Mormonism seems to have come in Joseph Tanner's series of articles in 1918 entitled "Problems of the Age," which devoted several pages to what it called "sinful intonations" in music. Likening jazz to the orgies of Rome, the seductions of the Middle East, and the savagery of Africa, Tanner explained: "There is perhaps no more sinful temptation among our young people today than the insinuating sounds that come from the siren voice of a license-loving age. The thoughtful world is just beginning to realize how far the Jazz and kindred music is carrying us from the moorings of our moral safety. . . . Applied to the dance, it brings to its aid the baser imaginations which give thoughts and feelings of the most degenerate character. It is a powerful truth, and yet we have scarcely begun to sense it, that there is an evil music to be shunned, just as there is an evil companionship."[10]

Jazz's incursions into Mormondom could best be seen in Provo, Utah, during the years following World War I. Having perhaps the thickest concentration of Mormon membership anywhere, this conservative farming community was also the setting for Brigham Young University, educational home to a diverse group of Mormon youth, from the most orthodox to the most heterodox. In the mid-1910s some students had boasted of the university's relative freedom from modern dances, while others had used the school newspaper openly to challenge church proscriptions against the dances.[11] In 1917 the student body passed a resolution to abandon all forms of "vulgar" dancing and to shun local cafés and dance halls. But with the close of World War I the popular dances of the gentiles made their way with the "freshies" to Provo.

Jazz dances appear to have become a rite of passage for postwar students at BYU, some of whom arrived from communities that were still divided over the propriety of round dancing. Class dances and public dances at the resort on nearby Utah Lake attracted students eager to try the new fads. By fall 1919 the university had its own "Freshman Jazz Orchestra" who played "every kind of jazz imaginable" and at whose first concert "some could hardly keep from shaking the wicked 'shimmie,' [although] they abstained remarkably well." Professor Eugene Roberts voiced his hope that such dances would fade "within a week or two" of the jazz orchestra's debut. They did not, and near the end of that fall semester Edward Kimball, former BYU basketball coach turned Tabernacle organist, addressed the student body with a critique of jazz that would become the model for a decade of official Mormon denunciations.[12]

Kimball explained that there were no such things as jazz instruments, only "jazz contraptions," i.e., mischievous ways of playing standard instruments. Nevertheless, he condemned the use of certain instruments in dance bands, notably the banjo, which he denounced as "a hybrid, a hyphenated instrument, a drum with only one side and therefore without resonance." Kimball then attempted to define jazz and what made it objectionable: it was not the rhythm or harmony, as such, but the *improvisation* that debased it as music. "Jazz," Kimball asserted, "is a digression from the correct; it is a getting away from the intent of the author." Playing recordings of several examples of well-known melodies "jazzed up," he accused jazz musicians of being no better than "grave robbers" of old music, then asked the students, "Are you going to stand for that sort of thing?" The campus newspaper reviewed Kimball's address with a curious article that was either slavishly admiring or dryly sardonic, depending on how one read it.[13]

Over the next few years, however, jazz dominated the dance music around the university. By the summer of 1921, the county school board had bought the two largest dance halls in the area, the county commissioners had outlawed modern dances, and local mothers were calling for the prohibition of jazz in the community, claiming that visitors from New York, Chicago, and Los Angeles had all found the dance hall scene in Provo more vulgar than in any of the big cities. That fall, raids of the Geneva Resort on Utah Lake revealed that jazz music and dancing prevailed. "There was no liquor floating around," the deputy sheriff explained, "but liquor wasn't needed to intoxicate the girls and boys. The jazz music did that."[14]

Dance records had thoroughly revived a sagging phonograph industry in the mid-1910s. By the end of the decade recordings identified as "jazz" were coming to dominate the market. While Edward Kimball used recordings to illustrate his 1919 denunciation of jazz, that school year's yearbook ironically carried a phonograph advertisement from Taylor Brothers inviting its readers to "dance to the merry strains of a Jazz Orchestra" in "the comfort of your own home." A writer for the church's *Young Woman's Journal* expressed his hope in 1921 that Mormon fraternity boys would tire of "jazz music on their Victrola" and start listening to Caruso or Mischa Elman. Later that year, in an official *Improvement Era* paean to the phonograph, the anonymous author suggested that bringing better recordings into Mormon homes would "make jazz music, which is a departure from the correct, unwelcome."[15]

Jazz's hold on Mormon youth provoked debate among the auxiliary committees of the church, who were acquiring more and more responsibility over the church's rapidly growing membership. A coalition of auxiliary leaders, the "Social Advisory Committee," had been formed in 1916, partly to cope with the new dance crazes. In the fall of 1919 the committee resolved to take a public stand against jazz and especially against the "shimmie," the dance movement of throwing the shoulders back and shaking the breast. Apostle Stephen L Richards called the shimmie "the most fearful thing ever introduced."[16] By 1922 he was chiding the five-month-old Church Music Committee for having done so little to regulate social and recreational music in the church.[17]

Overwhelmed with work on a new hymnbook and anthem collection, the music committee apparently delegated Edward Kimball to prepare a statement on jazz for the Executive Handbook of the MIA. In 1923, the year that jazz dance marathons swept through the nation, the MIA handbook introduced a section on jazz. It appealed to the Saints' aspirations toward high culture, defined jazz as "departure from the correct," and condemned the playing of anything not found in the musical score, "making the instruments perform that which is not written, and in a way contrary to their accepted, proper use. This type of playing is rank 'faking' and should not be tolerated by intelligent people. Very few of the so-called 'Jazz' effects are, or can be written, and if performers on musical instruments will confine their performance to the written music of their parts there will be very little 'jazz.' . . . The practice which often prevails of supplying music only to the violin or piano while the other players lazily 'fake' their parts, should positively be discontinued. Dance players . . . should be influenced to always play 'by note.' " Continuing its attack, the handbook claimed that to improvise in jazz style was to "abuse" an instrument, making it "do something for which it was never intended." The handbook discouraged playing the banjo, as well as cowbells, rattles, frying pans, and other musical "instruments of torture."[18]

From the rhetoric of the *Ladies Home Journal* (where one learned that jazz made the brain incapable of distinguishing right from wrong) to the regulations of the American National Association of Masters of Dancing (which claimed that the music "almost forces dancers to use jerky half steps and invites immoral variations") Mormons adapted gentile anti-jazz polemics to their own use in the early 1920s.[19] But the music flourished through the proliferation of dance halls and Victrolas. A sign of the times was the 1925 breakup of the venerable Provo Band. Its members, because they refused—or perhaps were unable—to "jazz up" their dance music, could find no work. While Mormon youth generally refused to patronize the group, the *Improvement Era* praised the Provo Band's integrity: "All honor to these musicians! They have set an example of which all real lovers of music should be proud."[20]

As the decade progressed, moderating voices began to be heard. The 1928 MIA handbook called for "tactful supervision" of music generally, asking that rhythms not be "augmented beyond the written score." But unlike its predecessors, the handbook specifically called for "good, modern dance music" and refused to mention the word "jazz." Even the banjo, if played "as an instrument of harmonic percussion," was deemed "not objectionable." The handbook noted: "These recommendations are not intended to convey an impression that orchestras should not play music that is lively and in snappy rhythm. . . . They should create a joyful atmosphere and carry the crowd along with them in this wholesome spirit."[21] That same year Tracy Cannon of the Church Music Committee used a KSL radio broadcast to attack modern "musical charlatans" who had "taken advantage of the natural love of rhythm." Yet he insisted that the cure was not condemnation but better music education.[22] A writer for the *Relief Society Magazine* even listed jazz as an "invoker of joy," while Tabernacle Choir director Tony Lund mildly noted that the growing dominance of jazz in American life was simply an aspect of the evolution of music "in keeping with the spirit of the times."[23]

Inevitably, elements of jazz entered Mormon church services. In 1928 the *Instructor* editorialized on the subject of jazz in church, concluding that it was not much of a problem in Mormondom and that "our standard Sunday School Songs, universally used, overcome that danger."[24] But by 1932 the Church Music Committee in general—and Edward Kimball in particular—was outraged by the young people's tendency to "croon" the hymns in church, imitating the inflections of dance band singers. The committee appointed Kimball to prepare an article on the problem. Under the rubric "A Reprehensible Practice," the article called the singing style a "prostitution of art" and a "hideous error," for "its birth was not of the mind or the spirit, but of the flesh."[25]

During the Great Depression, radio overtook the phonograph as the lord of America's musical life. By 1932 record sales had dropped to about 6 percent of what they had been in 1927, chiefly because radio provided the latest music live for free (as a 1930 article proclaimed it, "Something for nothing at last!"[26]). The omnipresence of the medium troubled some Mormon youth leaders, who feared it would continue to spread jazz. In 1932, the church's youth magazine the *Instructor* complained that broadcast jazz was starting to overwhelm even the saying of blessings on food in Mormon homes. And in 1938 the Relief Society urged its members to begin complaining about jazz on the airwaves and calling for more programs like the Ford Sunday Evening Hour.[27]

But radio jazz spread, record prices fell dramatically, phonograph companies began frantic promotion campaigns, and the juke box—a gaudy machine that played the latest "swing" music for a nickel—began to appear in hotels and cafés throughout the country. Perhaps more than anything else the juke box resuscitated the phonograph industry and, indeed, brought explosive big-band jazz onto dance floors where it never would have been heard live. In 1936, the year the juke box was introduced, some Oklahoma politicians confidently announced that "the age of jazz is over." But the *Salt Lake Tribune* cautiously replied that only time would tell.[28]

After the attack on Pearl Harbor, Mormons turned their attention with the rest of the nation to the war effort and more or less abandoned the formal repression of youthful passions. A long-running series of articles by sociologist Mark Allen in the *Relief Society Magazine* urged that parents not censure their young people too much amidst a "war-torn world" lest they alienate the children altogether.[29] Fortuitously, dance floors fell prey to a special tax and the ban on shellac use forced American phonograph companies to curtail the making of records from 1942 to 1944, leaving the popular music industry virtually stranded. When record-buying resurged in the mid-1940s, the dominant music seemed more relaxed than before the war, more seductive than exciting. The return of the American troops brought on a wave of romantic recreation accompanied by smaller bands and smoother music.

The year after the Yanks returned the MIA again preached against the evils of the new dancing and music. At the 1946 conference of the MIA, its general superintendent, George Morris, declared that the only systematic traits he could find in modern dancing were "vulgarity and cheapness." His counselor John Giles announced that the church had reached a "crisis" in its practice of recreation by subscribing to worldly fashions of music, dancing, and dress. And he attacked the longstanding idea that a little worldliness must be tolerated to avoid alienating young people: "If we think our young people will leave us because we insist on conducting our recreation on a higher plane than that of the world we must change our thinking."[30] The strongest rhetoric emanated from First Presidency counselor J. Reuben Clark: "Never in my lifetime has there been such a whining, shameless, sometimes perverted sensuality in our music as there is today. Popular songs are filled with expressions of the lowest immorality that some of us older ones do not understand, but I am sure that some of the youth do."[31] A year later the *Deseret News* warned that "foul, suggestive" songs were slipping into Salt Lake City juke boxes, and called for their banning—either by proprietors or by the local government.[32] It is difficult to say what songs the *News* referred to, although one of them was probably Tex Williams's chart-topping hit of that year, "Smoke, Smoke, Smoke That Cigarette." But warnings against hidden messages in pop lyrics were consonant with the national postwar fear of secret subversion.

In order to combat the suggestive music and dancing, church leaders inaugurated a new program of eschewing dance bands and playing only approved recordings and, curiously, motion pictures for church dances. The 1947 MIA executive manual labeled much of the current dance music "atrocious" and announced that the Bell and Howell "Filmosound" machine was being sent out to local congregations, not only to provide proper musical accompaniment to dancing but to provide filmed floor shows for dance intermissions. The MIA officers were quick to admit that "one of our big problems thus far has been to find films where the standards are our standards." Even where the "Filmosound" was not used, local church leaders eagerly substituted records for orchestras at dances, not only because records allowed the leaders to screen the music to be played, but also because, as one leader ingenuously told John Giles, "they could use the records over and over again."[33]

Meanwhile, at BYU, a proposed 1948 concert by "bop" bandleader Dizzy Gillespie was scuttled by the faculty. The following year the school president himself rejected student pleas to hire the Duke Ellington band because, he later said, he feared repercussions from church leaders.[34]

Long known for his liberal views toward church-sponsored recreation, David O. McKay succeeded in 1951 to the highest office in Mormonism. Whereas McKay's close associate J. Reuben Clark took a rather dim view of human nature, McKay seemed radiantly certain that human nature would ultimately lead people to seek the highest and most ennobling forms of culture.[35] To no one's surprise, cautions about popular music and dance during McKay's eighteen-year administration were relatively mild and unspecific. McKay seemed more concerned about proper exchanging of dance partners, avoiding "pairing off" and assuring that even "wallflowers" had their turn, than he did about the sort of music performed there. He occasionally allowed that dancing could turn to a vice when carried "beyond propriety and decency," but said the same about eating.[36] The strongest statements continued to come from J. Reuben Clark, who wondered out loud "how far above the tom-tom of the jungle [and] the voodoo huts" modern dance music was.[37]

Rock and roll emerged in the mid-1950s from a blend of styles, including jazz and the blues. It had in abundance all the traits that should have launched fresh attacks from Mormon leadership: it was emphatic in its pulse and full of syncopation, it was transmitted by ear (not by note), its lyrics hovered between the ludicrous and the perverse, and it was loud. Moreover, it attracted audiences that were rather evenly mixed racially, leading some observers, especially in the south, to fear that the music would reduce whites to "the level" of blacks. Not only could this music be heard through juke boxes and radios, but the improvisatory dances that it accompanied could be seen in teen movies and television, notably on the Philadelphia-based *American Bandstand* show, which was broadcast nationally on weekday afternoons from 1957 to 1963.

Reflecting the spirit of McKay's leadership, Mormon church and community leaders rebuked rock and roll mildly. When the *Deseret News* cited a Hollywood disc jockey in 1955 that the lyrics of rhythm and blues were " 'filthy' " and perhaps " 'as bad for kids as dope,' " it added, "whether or not the music itself leads teenagers astray is a more debatable question."[38] Responding to early rock-and-roll concert riots the paper urged not that rock be suppressed, but that better music be cultivated: "These delinquents of today do not know it, but what they need is some training in good music. The amazing long-lived popularity of jive shows that kids need some kind of releases from nervous tension. . . . Hopped up on their diet of 'r & r' [they] need to have their musical beat refined and slowed to an andante. Best way we know is to have them struggle through the scales, or better still, let Bach and his vaunted three-part inventions slow them down."[39]

The Mormon auxiliaries began to regulate the music of church recreations in only the most general (and occasionally anachronistic) terms. The 1957 MIA handbook, for example, asked youth leaders to "be sure [dance bands] play good danceable music without too much 'jive' " and to forbid "any of the crouching styles, or the wild, acrobatic antics of 'jitterbug' or 'bop.' " In their place the handbook encouraged the once frowned-upon "swing" dancing. Meanwhile, the closest McKay appears to have come to the subject of the emerging rock-and-roll craze was in his remark in 1959 that "there is in music that which appeals also to the baser emotions of man." But he singled out no particular type of music and assured his readers that people who were enamored of music in any case "are not a bad people."[40]

After Chubby Checker's version of "The Twist" soared to the top of the record sales charts in January 1962, the MIA singled out the new dance for censure, partly because it promoted self-expression above societal grace: "This dance is not up to the standards of good taste. Since it is a self-expression dance, it is felt that even if it were taught in a dignified and modest manner, the participants through their self-expression could make it undignified and immodest. We feel therefore, that it should not be done at our dances and should be discouraged at all times among our young."[41] But as quickly as the "twist" was quelled it was replaced by other fad dances, whose names were popularized through hit songs: the watusi, the jerk, the monkey, and even the long-dreaded shimmie.

Beginning in 1964 several network prime-time television shows appeared, featuring the latest (chiefly British) bands and the newest "self-expression" dances, executed by female "go-go" girls behind and around the musicians. By this time president McKay had surpassed ninety years of age and was severely ailing. Even had he been inclined to speak against the new dances, he was now delegating many of his affairs to counselors. Dismayed at the church authorities' failure to condemn the new dances, BYU's president, Ernest Wilkinson, took measures of his own.

Wilkinson had tried to ban rock-and-roll dances from the campus of the church university without success. In a student assembly in fall 1965 he spoke out against the frug, the monkey, and the swim, reproving any "shimmering contortionist" who might dance them at BYU. He also recommended to the students a new pamphlet recently produced by church auxiliaries, "For the Strength of Youth." This pamphlet argued for good posture in dancing and against "crouching, slumping over, trying to do a back bend, or having too close a body contact."[42] Attendance at school dances dropped as off-campus dancing spots apparently experienced a boom not unlike that of the 1920s. Wilkinson persuaded the University Board of Trustees (all high church officials) to watch a demonstration of some of the new dances, hoping they would prohibit them. But to Wilkinson's chagrin the Board turned the matter over to McKay and his counselors—an "obvious stall," in the university president's words.[43]

Wilkinson subsequently persuaded McKay's secretary to issue with the church president's signature a statement on dance that Wilkinson had drafted. The statement, which later was cited in church recreation handbooks, announced that approved dances for Mormons included the waltz, the fox trot, the rhumba, and the tango, all of which had been forbidden at one time or another in Mormondom's past. Wilkinson's statement also provided a twofold rationale for discouraging amplified rock and roll. First, the music of "electronic bands" was simply too loud to be healthful. Second, it put far too much emphasis on the beat. Following the public release of the document, rock-and-roll dances were briefly banned on the BYU campus.[44]

Meanwhile, the *Deseret News* discussed rock and roll, especially the Beatles, with sarcasm. It noted with glee in the summer of 1965 that the group had no records in the top twenty, and later that year labeled their music "music to kill weeds with."[45] The following spring the paper observed that the fad dances were fading, citing bandleader Sammy Kaye as its source for this news. Subsequent editorials in the newspaper focused on the high amplification levels of rock concerts, observing that "rock 'n' roll [has] all the charm of riveting, drop forging, or boiler making."[46]

But throughout most of the 1960s church authorities said little against fad dancing or popular music, which was growing in its sophistication (and volume) and was coming to be known simply as "rock." In 1969 the MIA published a statement on music and dance, a statement which urged its readers not to condemn dances by name (although it mentioned no fewer than six problematic dances by name). "We should listen to combos with appreciation for the rhythm and enthusiasm they have. Much of today's music and dance is acceptable and should be encouraged, but there are a few elements that need definite discouragement. In regard to music, these are: MUSIC THAT IS TOO LOUD, BAD LYRICS, AND TEMPO THAT IS TOO SLOW."[47]

During the last years of the decade pressure built amid Mormonism to act officially against the rise of a whole "counterculture." One of the first Mormon responses to this counterculture came when a professor at the church's Ricks College issued a detailed attack on modern rock lyrics, aimed at Mormon parents. The pamphlet argued that all rock lyrics boiled down to four more or less "hidden" themes: drugs, sex, revolution, and atheism. Some Mormons amplified the professor's remarks and argued that MIA leaders could not be trusted to monitor song lyrics, since they would not understand their encoded messages.[48] When David O. McKay died in January 1970 at the age of ninety-six, the mounting dismay over rock culture found an official voice in conservative apostle Ezra Taft Benson.

Benson lashed out against rock in his October 1970 church conference talk, echoing and expanding upon J. Reuben Clark's rhetoric of a quarter century earlier. Benson claimed that much rock was "purposely designed to push immorality, narcotics, revolution, atheism, and nihilism, through language that often has a double meaning and with which many parents are not familiar." He urged Mormon parents to warn their children of "the demoralizing loud, raucous beat of rock" and suggested that even Mormon dances had sometimes come to resemble "a modern Sodom with short skirts, loud beat, strobe lights, and darkness."[49] Benson continued his campaign in the following year, joined by his apostolic colleague Mark E. Petersen (an advisor to the Church Music Committee). Petersen blamed the Beatles for popularizing "the 'hot' music" with its "sensual, suggestive, vile" lyrics, which young people, like "sheep," had "blindly followed."[50] In 1971 Benson invoked the harshest language yet used in the church to attack the growing rock culture. He decried the legacy of the Woodstock festival, a saturnalia of rock, drugs, and political invective: "Its music, crushing the sensibilities in a din of primitive idolatry, is in glorification of the physical to the debasement of the spirit. In the long panorama of man's history, these youthful rock music festivals are among Satan's greatest successes. The legendary orgies of Greece and Rome cannot compare to the monumental obscenities found in these cesspools of drugs, immorality, rebellion, and pornophonic sound. The famed Woodstock festival was a gigantic manifestation of a sick nation. Yet the lurid movie and rock recordings of its unprecedented filth were big business in our own mountain home."[51]

More than a third of Benson's 1971 address was taken verbatim from the writings of Richard Nibley, a Snow College (Utah) music professor who regularly attacked rock and the MIA's apparent tolerance of it. Indeed, Benson used Nibley's language to censure the MIA and "liberal Mormons" generally, even quoting Nibley's rhetorical question, "What could be more misguided than fear that 'if rock music were not endorsed by our leaders, we may lose many young people'?"[52] Whether Benson had been encouraging Nibley to make his attacks, or had simply been persuaded by them, is unclear. In either case, the Mormon apostle continued to champion Nibley's views during the next several years.

Ten days after Benson's October 1971 conference talk, the church's First Presidency (now headed by Joseph Fielding Smith) addressed a more disturbing problem: the rock opera *Jesus Christ Superstar*. This popular work took a humanistic view of Christ that irritated clergymen throughout the nation and the world. When asked for a statement on the work in April 1971, Church Music Committee member and Tabernacle organist Robert Cundick took a cautious view of the work. While some of the work was "trite and somewhat blasphemous," Cundick said, if it were to strike "a responsive chord in a youth who would otherwise not be drawn to Christ, it may have some merit." Even so, he added, the work could only be a "starting point," only "a pale imitation of the sublimity and grandeur of the Gospel Plan."[53] The official church position, however, came clear in a notice published in the August 1971 *Priesthood Bulletin*, and again in the First Presidency's declaration issued that October, which bluntly labeled the opera "a profane and sacrilegious attack upon true Christianity." It and "other productions of a similar nature" were forbidden to be played in any church-sponsored gatherings.[54]

During his brief tenure as church president (1972–73), Harold B. Lee reconstituted both the MIA and the Church Music Committee, placing both squarely under priesthood control. As part of his expansion of the music committee, Lee appointed a Youth Music Task Committee, a group of leading church musicians who were charged to recommend some church policies toward popular music. One of the Music Department's advisers, apostle Boyd K. Packer, took a guarded position toward popular music. At an early meeting of the task committee, he called for a balanced approach to youth music: "Our youth must be able to adapt themselves to the climate by which they are surrounded. They are in the world, and yet not fully a part of it. Their clothing, hair styles, and their music may resemble in moderation those of the world, but extremes must be avoided.''[55]

At the next church conference, 5 October 1973, Packer addressed the Tabernacle congregation on the subject. Music itself had become corrupted by its constant agitation, he said, and much of it had become ''repellent to the Spirit of God.'' But some, he added, was ''soft enough to be innocent.'' He urged all church members to go through their collections and discard all the inferior, ''hard'' music. The task committee adopted Packer's talk as a credo, echoing it in their writings and adapting it into a filmstrip to be shown to church youth groups.[56]

Packer's address reverberated in affairs at BYU. Immediately after the church conference, the university cancelled the appearance of the rock group Three Dog Night and undertook a thorough reevaluation of rock music and dancing on campus. Ernest Wilkinson's recently installed successor, Dallin Oaks, had rejected the charge that any music sponsored by BYU could be categorized as ''hard rock.''[57] But he had privately expressed concern that the school's jazz ensemble had changed its name to the ''jazz-rock ensemble.'' Oaks's concern prompted the group's director to revise its name to ''Synthesis.''[58] Ironically, while BYU labored over the question of what groups to invite to campus, the Mormon youth seminaries in Salt Lake City sponsored a concert by the soft-rock group The Association, whose first hit, ''Along Comes Mary,'' was widely rumored to be about marijuana.[59]

In 1974 the *Priesthood Bulletin* urged church leaders to oversee the dress, amplification, lyrics, and ''unusual lighting effects'' of church dances.[60] As some local congregations began calling for a list of music disapproved for church dances, the Youth Music Task Committee began the arduous screening of popular music.[61] The committee decided to construct a list of approved rather than disapproved music, giving their work a more positive tone. But they found themselves stymied by the proposition. Early in November 1973 they tallied the results of a song survey sent out to nine musicians outside the committee. The songs that were overwhelmingly disapproved included Marvin Gaye's hit ''Let's Get It On'' and the Electric Light Orchestra's ''Evil Woman.'' The survey respondents were split, however, on Stevie Wonder's ''Higher Ground.'' Despite its upbeat, almost preachy lyric (which included the lines, ''God is gonna show you higher ground / He's the only friend you have around''), several respondents suspected it of carrying a hidden drug message. Among the overwhelmingly favored songs were the Rolling Stones' ''Angie,'' Paul Simon's ''Loves Me Like a Rock,'' and, predictably, Marie Osmond's ''Paper Roses.''[62]

The Osmonds, the all-Mormon family singing group, had become celebrities in America through their frequent television and Las Vegas appearances in the 1960s. They were also well known in Sweden and especially Japan, where the youngest of the family, Jimmy, had been named Best New Male Vocalist for 1969. In 1971, the group had produced one of the biggest-selling soft-rock records of the year, 'One Bad Apple,'' the first of a string of more than twenty best-selling records by the Osmond Brothers, Donny Osmond and Marie Osmond solo, and Donny and Marie together. The following year ABC television created a Saturday morning cartoon show on the brothers, a white parallel to its "Jackson Five" cartoon series. Rock aficionados treated the Osmonds coolly for their bland pop style.[63] But the brothers—especially Donny—entranced millions of pubescent fans throughout the world.

Mormon responses to the group ranged from the ecstatic to the scornful. The Osmonds had vowed to keep themselves untainted by rock culture and to keep their music as inoffensive as possible. Indeed, they promised to employ the "hypnotic" power of the rock beat to preach positive values.[64] Some church leaders touted the group as a positive alternative to typical rock images. In 1975 a Salt Lake City publishing house issued the Osmonds' "official story," as written by a high church authority. The Osmonds toured Mormon youth rallies throughout the country, speaking on the church's behalf and bringing thousands of new Mormons into the fold.[65] But some Mormons bristled at the apparent acceptance of even soft rock by the church. One member even complained that the church had "now sanctioned officially the Satan inspired products of the gutters of Liverpool." Mormon intellectuals also criticized the Osmonds in subtler but essentially likeminded terms.[66] Although such views seemed to be in the minority, a small controversy did begin to sprout around their 1973 album *The Plan*, a rock treatment of the Mormon plan of salvation.

In the early 1970s evangelical protestantism spread among youth who had been disillusioned by the counterculture. A resurgence of frontier-style revivalism, the "Jesus movement" began to translate Christianity into familiar rock idioms. From Larry Norman's lavish Capitol "concept album" *Upon This Rock* to Stephen Schwartz's enormously successful rock musical *Godspell*, overtly Christian messages were set to rock music of all sorts. Even in many Protestant denominations rock musicals were undertaken in order to attract youth to church. As Mormon missionaries began to reap thousands of converts from the national Jesus movement, religious rock inevitably entered Mormondom.

The Osmonds' *The Plan* was an attempt both to proselyte through religious rock and to create a unified "concept" album. Its pop-apocalyptic song "The Last Days" provided a modern update of early Mormon millennialism:

Nations take up their battle stations
Patrons of Zodiac revelations
Lustations breaking family relations
Litigations allowing shoot up sensations . . .
It's gotta be the last days
Gotta be the last days.

The album sold well among Mormons. But some church leaders questioned its propriety, considering it, in the words of a Church Music Committee member, "celestial truths in terrestrial garb."[67]

Meanwhile, Mormon rock stage productions began to appear in southern California. *Open Any Door* attracted sizable crowds in 1973 with its soft rock and confessional lyrics, such as: "O, heaven's gift so long did I fight / O, heaven's gift, I know that it's right . . . The choice is mine and I believe / No greater joy could I receive . . . The Holy Spirit takes my hand / The narrow road is clearly planned." Investigating complaints about the musical, a Youth Music Task Committee member found some settings of the words "God" and "the Lord" irreverent. But apostle LeGrand Richards, reflecting on the constant turnover of musical style in his lifetime, judged the work—in principle, at least—a possible "starting point" for better efforts to come.[68]

Lex de Azevedo was at that time a successful film and television composer and arranger, and former producer of the rock group the Human Be-inz. He began planning a Mormon musical directly modeled on the Christian rock movement. After observing firsthand the revivalistic energy that attended Christian rock musicals in southern California, de Azevedo decided with playwright Doug Stewart to adapt the form to Mormonism, adding a choir to the soft-rock music (to obscure the beat), and using hard rock only to portray evil situations.[69] After a disappointing premiere at BYU, the show, *Saturday's Warrior,* surged in popularity. It toured among Mormon congregations, inspired conversions and invigorated backsliders. Its began to be quoted alongside scriptural canon in church meetings and to be credited with drawing young Mormons to greater faithfulness. The success of *Saturday's Warrior* spawned dozens of imitations and gradually convinced church leaders that elements of rock could be used for religious, if not liturgical, purposes. In their own way, the lyrics of Mormon musicals tended to echo the intimate language of revivalism, which had been absent from Mormonism's earliest hymnals, but which had increasingly pervaded twentieth-century Mormon hymnals. And in its popular appeal, Mormon soft-rock became the logical successor to nineteenth-century Mormon folksong; in the end it was eagerly adapted and employed by the church in "official" productions.[70]

After more than a century of polemics, the futility of proscribing popular dance and musical styles became clear: each generation found its own tastes superior to those of its young. Not unlike many denominational leaders, Mormon leaders almost always came to accept the music and dances once forbidden by their elders. Improvisation, syncopation, and other musical effects took their place in the common language of Mormon culture, just as other musical effects had done a century earlier. As musical contexts changed, musical meanings blurred. Only the profane messages of popular lyrics were consistently fought. But even lyrics proved to be problematic; one generally found adults revealing and interpreting the textual meanings supposedly discernible only to the young.[71]

Spencer Kimball's tenure as president of the church (1973–85) helped to soften anti-rock discussions in the church. Kimball, who as an Arizona teenager had played ragtime in gentile dance halls, in many ways emulated the progressive McKay style of leadership, particularly when it came to implanting Mormonism into cultures outside the United States. As the Mormon missionary force grew by more than ten thousand during Kimball's tenure, the church had to confront new problems of musical style. These problems arose not only in the music of Christianized Europe but in the instruments and scales of ethnic cultures—even in the authentic "tom-tom of the jungle."

NOTES

1. "Dancing Music on Higher Plane," *Salt Lake Tribune,* 6 September 1922.

2. "Get Acquainted Party Drew Crowd," *White and Blue* 17 (22 October 1913): 29, and "Events and Happenings," *White and Blue* 17 (17 December 1913): 189.

3. "The Dance Craze," *DN,* 9 May 1914.

4. *Young Men's Mutual Improvement Association Hand Book* (Salt Lake City: General Board of the MIA, 1914), p. 67. On the fear of alienating young people, cf. Alexander, *Mormonism in Transition,* pp. 150–51.

5. *Salt Lake Tribune,* 24 June 1914. See also Nancy D. McCormick and John S. McCormick, *Saltair* (Salt Lake City: Bonneville Books, 1985), pp. 41–43.

6. See "The Dance Craze"; "Hugging Dances Are Barred at L.D.S.U.," *Salt Lake Telegram,* 2 December 1915; "Dancing and Ball-Room Management" and "Social Dancing and Its Direction," *IE* 19 (January 1916): 255–58, 276–77. On dance training during this period see Georganne Ballif Arrington, "Mormonism: The Dancingest Denomination," *Century 2* 5 (Fall 1980): 50–53, and Gary James Bergera and Ronald Priddis, *Brigham Young University: A House of Faith* (Salt Lake City: Signature Press, 1985), pp. 327–28.

7. "Music in the Cafés," 8 May 1909.

8. "A Musical Center," *DN,* 4 September 1913.

9. YMMIA *Hand Book* (1914), p. 68; "Dancing and Ball-Room Management," p. 276; "Music for Dances," *IE* 19 (February 1916): 372; Lucy W. Smith,

"Social Work," *IE* 19 (August 1916): 929. See also Joseph Fielding Smith's remarks on the evils of the modern dances in *CR*, October 1916, pp. 70–71, and the scathing assessment of "public dancing" in "How to Lessen Contributions to Crime," *IE* 21 (October 1918): 1091–92. For an anecdote on ragging in church see Andrew Karl Larson, "Reminiscences of a Mormon Village in Transition," in Thomas E. Cheney, ed., *Lore of Faith and Folly* (Salt Lake City: University of Utah Press, 1971), p. 41.

10. *IE* 21 (August 1918): 871–72.

11. See, for example, "The Dance: A Peep," *White and Blue* 17 (18 February 1914): 305, and "A Physical and Moral Defense of the Tango," *White and Blue* 17 (13 May 1914): 464.

12. See "Class Reports: Freshmen" and "Sturdy Oaks and Clinging Vines," *White and Blue* 23 (1 October 1919): 36, 40; "Social Events," *White and Blue* 23 (19 November 1919): 178; and "Calendar" (for 29 November 1919) in *Banyan* (BYU yearbook) 1920.

13. See the reports of Kimball's speech in the *Provo Post*, 5 December 1919, and "Lest We Jazz," *White and Blue*, 10 December 1919.

14. See the front page articles in *Provo Herald*, 27 June and 21 September 1921, and 17 November 1925. I was led to these by Gary C. Kunz, "Provo in the Jazz Age," *Sunstone* 9 (January–February [1984]): 33–38. See also "Bunny Hug Must Go," *Provo Herald*, 24 June 1921.

15. See the Taylor Brothers' advertisement in *Banyan* 1920; Frank R. Arnold, "Our Cultural Life," *Young Woman's Journal* 32 (February 1921): 68; "Sources of Joy and Factors of Happiness," *IE* 25 (December 1921): 149. On dance recordings in this period see Roland Gelatt, *The Fabulous Phonograph: 1877–1977*, 2nd ed. rev. (New York: Collier Books, 1977), pp. 188–95.

16. See Thomas G. Alexander, "Between Revivalism and the Social Gospel: The Latter-day Saint Social Advisory Committee, 1916–1922," *BYU Studies* 23 (Winter 1983): 25, 31. See also "Music Is Topic at Dancing Convention," *DN*, 18 November 1919, and "Speaker Declares Too Much Time Is Spent in Dancing," *DN*, 20 November 1919.

17. CMC Minutes, 2 March 1921, 14 December 1922.

18. YLMIA Hand Book (Salt Lake City: MIA General Board, 1923), pp. 95–96.

19. See "'Jazz' and Immorality," *DN*, 22 August 1922; Mary Roberts Rinehart, "Freedom and the Changing Standards," *Relief Society Magazine* 9 (May 1922): 275, 277–78; *Social Achievement: The Young Man and His Social World*, YMMIA Senior Manual for 1923–24 (Salt Lake City: YMMIA General Board, 1923), pp. 61–62.

20. "Provo Band Breaks Rank," *Provo Herald*, 17 November 1925, and Fred L. W. Bennett, "Why Not Abolish Jazz?," *IE* 29 (January 1926): 272.

21. *Handbook of the Young Men's and Young Ladies' Mutual Improvement Associations: Official Guide for the Leisure-Time and Recreational Program of the Church . . .* (Salt Lake City: MIA General Boards, 1928), pp. 374–76.

22. Tracy Y. Cannon, KSL radio talk, 22 January 1928, typescript in McCune School of Music Papers, HBLL. Cf. apostle Orson F. Whitney's remarks in

"Music and Motherhood, Each in Its Sphere Given Exalted Rank in the Lives and Minds of True Latter-day Saints," *DN*, 9 May 1926.

23. Ida P. Beal, "Music—Its Message and Ministry," *Relief Society Magazine* 16 (June 1929): 318–19, and "Tabernacle Choir Leader Gives Singing Directions," *DN*, 19 March 1932, Church Section.

24. "Sunday School Music," *JI* 63 (August 1928): 432–33.

25. CMC Minutes, 8 March 1932, and *IE* 35 (June 1932): 490.

26. See Gellatt, *The Fabulous Phonograph*, p. 255, and George W. Gray, "Signing Off on the First Ten Years," *World's Work* (December 1930), reprinted in George E. Mowry, *The Twenties: Fords, Flappers & Fanatics* (Englewood Cliffs, N.J.: Prentice Hall, 1963), pp. 59–65.

27. "Control of the Dial," *Instructor* 67 (January 1932): 17, and Wade N. Stephens, "A More Cultural Radio," *Relief Society Magazine* 25 (December 1938): 833.

28. "Origin and Effect of Jazz Music," *Salt Lake Tribune*, 4 October 1936.

29. See especially Allen's "Parents, What of Youth in a War-torn World?," *Relief Society Magazine* 29 (September 1942): 610–13.

30. "About-Face Demanded in Church Amusements," *DN*, 8 June 1946.

31. "Pres. Clark Appeals for Return to High Ideals," *DN*, 6 July 1946, Church Section.

32. "Shady Music for a Shiny Nickel," *DN*, 29 August 1947, and "Cleaning Up the Shady Music," *DN*, 9 September 1947.

33. *Mutual Improvement Association Manual for Executives and Recreation Committees* (Salt Lake City: MIA General Boards, 1947), pp. 152–53; *Executive Manual for Officers of the Young Men's and Young Women's Mutual Improvement Association* (Salt Lake City: MIA General Boards, 1948): 153–54; John Davis Giles to George Q. Morris, 6 September 1949, Giles Papers, HDC.

34. Bergera and Priddis, *Brigham Young University*, p. 321. Racism in Utah aggravated jazz's problems in Mormonism. See Jaren Jones, *Close Enough for Jazz: An Autobiography* (Salt Lake City: Published by the Author, [1982]), pp. 90–91.

35. See Quinn, *J. Reuben Clark*, pp. 116–18, and Marvin and Ann Rytting, "Exhortations for Chastity: A Content Analysis of Church Literature," *Sunstone* 7 (March–April 1982): 15–19.

36. "Pres. McKay Gives Key to Happiness in Home, Society," *DN*, 5 November 1955, Church Section.

37. Clark, "Home, and the Building of Home Life," *Relief Society Magazine* 39 (December 1952): 792.

38. "Music's Solid Beat," *DN*, 26 March 1955.

39. "Rock 'n' Roll 'n' Music," *DN*, 7 May 1958; cf. "Needed: A Better Export," *DN*, 31 October 1956.

40. See "Music . . . the Universal Language," *IE* 62 (January 1959): 14–15.

41. "MIA Bans the 'Twist,' " *Church News*, 3 February 1962.

42. Ernest L. Wilkinson, "Make Honor Your Standard," *BYU Speeches of the Year*, 23 September 1965, and "For the Strength of Youth," published as a pamphlet and also in *IE* 68 (September 1965): 832–35.

43. For a detailed account of this episode and that which follows see Bergera and Priddis, *Brigham Young University,* pp. 329–31.

44. *Daily Universe,* 3 December 1965.

45. "Sic Transit Gloria," *DN,* 19 July 1965, and "Music To Kill Weeds With," *DN,* 10 December 1965.

46. See "Swing and Sway Returning," 25 May 1966; "Agony or Ecstasy?," 13 January 1967; "This Is Music?," 6 September 1968.

47. *MIA Dance Supplement* (Salt Lake City: General Board of the MIAs, 1969), p. II-3 [*sic*], emphasis in original.

48. Darwin Wolford, *Four Messages of Rock* (Rexburg, Idaho: n.p., n.d. [ca. 1969]), and Blaine Elswood to Editor, *DN,* 22 July 1970.

49. "Strengthening the Family," *IE* 73 (December 1970): 49. Perhaps in response to these remarks, the First Presidency issued a moderate statement the same month as Benson's talk was published in the church magazine. It read, in part: "Music can be used to exalt and inspire or to carry messages of degradation and destruction. It is therefore important that as Latter-day Saints we at all times apply the principles of the gospel and seek the guidance of the Spirit in selecting the music with which we surround ourselves" (*Priesthood Bulletin,* December 1970, p. 10).

50. Mark E. Petersen, *Live It Up!* (Salt Lake City: Deseret Book, 1971), p. 65. Cf. Petersen's editorial "Get Really 'Turned On,' " *Church News,* 15 February 1969.

51. *CR,* October 1971, pp. 24–29.

52. Ibid.

53. Cundick to James M. Blaylock, 27 April 1971, CMD.

54. *Priesthood Bulletin* (August 1971), p. 2, and First Presidency letter in *Daily Universe,* 11 October 1971.

55. Youth Music Task Committee Minutes, in private possession, 18 September 1973. See also Music Correlation Committee Minutes, in private possession, 26 September 1973.

56. See Larry Bastian, "As a Parent or Youth Leader, What Should You Know about Today's Music?," *Ensign* 4 (April 1974): 37–38; Youth Music Task Committee Minutes, 20 January 1974; "Youth Music Filmstrip Proposal" [ca. March 1974], copy in my possession.

57. Dallin H. Oaks to O. Leslie Stone, 7 June 1973, CMD Correspondence 1967–77. On rock at BYU during this period, see Bergera and Priddis, *Brigham Young University,* pp. 322–26.

58. Newell Dayley, interviewed by Michael Hicks, 21 April 1987, transcript in possession of the author.

59. See Correspondence on Seminary Youth Concert, in CMD Correspondence 1967–77.

60. *Priesthood Bulletin* (First Quarter 1974), item 3.

61. Dayley Interview. A music blacklist was under consideration at least as early as spring of 1970: see Victor Cline to Alexander Schreiner, 13 April 1970, CMD Correspondence 1969–77.

62. Youth Music Task Committee Minutes, 4 November 1973.

63. See, for example, Tom Nolan, "The Family Plan of the Latter-Day Osmonds," *Rolling Stone,* 11 March 1976, pp. 46–52.

64. See Paul H. Dunn, *The Osmonds: The Official Story of the Osmond Family* (Salt Lake City: Bookcraft, 1975), p. 192. Much of the general information in this chapter about the Osmonds derives from this source.

65. See, for example, the reports in *Church News,* 15 July 1978, 10 February and 17 March 1979, and 26 January 1980.

66. C. N. Botting to "The General Authorities," 9 December 1973, CMD Correspondence 1969–77. On the intellectual response see, for instance, Wayne Booth, "Letters to Smoother," in Joy C. Ross and Steven C. Walker, eds., *Letters to Smoother, etc.: Proceedings of the 1980 Brigham Young University Symposium on the Humanities* (Provo: Brigham Young University Press, n.d.), pp. 15–16 (cf. pp. 103–4).

67. Michael F. Moody to Boyd K. Packer, 22 January 1974, CMD Correspondence 1969–77. See also Packer's antireligious rock comments in Sondrup, *Arts and Inspiration,* p. 8.

68. LeGrand Richards to Lloyd M. Gustavson, 19 October 1973, and Larry Bastian to Michael Moody, 9 November 1973, both in CMD Correspondence 1967–77.

69. Lex de Azevedo, *Pop Music and Morality* (North Hollywood: Embryo Books, 1982), p. 16.

70. On the relations and distinctions between "folk" and "popular" music see Arnold Hauser, *The Sociology of Art* (University of Chicago Press, 1982), pp. 580–610.

71. Fireside talks continue to be given in many Mormon communities, as in Christian churches at large, by itinerant "specialists" in rock music and lyrics. In north Utah, Mormon leaders recently issued a letter complaining that these talks "have gravely offended those in attendance [and] very often stimulate the imagination of the youth and often teach ideas, details or thoughts, that are highly questionable and totally out of place in a gathering of our members" (Utah North Area Presidency to Regional Representatives, 18 February 1986, photocopy in possession of the author). Religious attacks on rock music recently have been joined by secular critiques, from congressional hearings on the subject to best-selling books such as Allan Bloom, *The Closing of the American Mind* (New York: Simon and Schuster, 1987), pp. 68–81. For perhaps the most provocative study of the phenomenon of rock see Robert Pattison, *The Triumph of Vulgarity: Rock Music in the Mirror of Romanticism* (New York: Oxford, 1987).

12

Noble Savages

The desire to build Zion has energized Mormonism for a century and a half. Brigham Young was perhaps the most erudite in explaining what building Zion entailed, observing that it would be erected on the principle of gathering "truth from any source, wherever we can obtain it." Young taught that the citizens of Zion would acquire truth partly through revelation and prayer, and partly through the "arts and sciences," the latter being a catch-all phrase that for him included any social grace or refinement, from tempering copper to painting murals, from farming to music theory. And Young believed that some of those refinements might well lie outside of Western culture, that indeed the "arts and sciences in the so-called heathen nations in many respects excel the attainments of the Christian nations."[1]

In its isolated valleys and villages nineteenth-century Mormonism thrived under Young's leadership, evolving into what one sociologist has labeled a "near nation."[2] Their success in building a self-contained community spurred the Mormons to want to build a kingdom of colonies throughout the earth. As they did so, Mormonism's emphasis seemed to shift: rather than importing Zion, or building it for themselves alone, the Saints hoped to export the culture their faith had built. Brigham Young's calls for the Saints to educate themselves and gather to the Great Basin were quietly transformed into a Mormon desire to educate others in Zion's budding glories. This devout imperialism has been neither consistent nor free from ambivalence. One sees its fluctuations in the church's evolving responses to the indigenous musics of Native Americans, Polynesians, and West Africans.

Early American settlers regarded Indians through the eyes of both primitivism and puritanism. Native Americans were at once innocent citizens of the state of nature, devoid of civilization's discontents, and rude, or even diabolical heathen (except when they were consenting to the white man's occupation of the New World). Somewhere between these conflicting views lay the Book of Mormon's teachings, which described "native" Americans as descendants of Hebrew migrants, once noble but now degraded by apostasy from the true faith. For Mormons, Native Americans represented a sacred kindred to be reclaimed, literal descendants of Israel in need of civilizing.[3] And when they were converted, the Indians would not only be saved, they would become "white and delightsome," divinely readied to possess the continent.[4]

Indian dancing, like most any sort of dancing, troubled early denominational missionaries to the Indians. The music that accompanied it grieved them as well. Missionaries almost universally found its monophony, static melodies, and hypnotic drumming ugly, if not terrifying. They sought to replace it with revival hymns, or in the case of Catholic missionaries, with plainsong. None seems to have made any attempt to adapt Christian worship to the indigenous musics of the natives. This was chiefly because they considered these musics, as one scholar has expressed it, a "persistent phase of heathenism" and indeed not music at all.[5] A revivalist expressed this well when he recalled in 1846 the sound of converted Indians singing the hymns he had taught them, their strains "being made more strikingly sweet by the yelling and whooping of the wild Indians by whom they were surrounded. What a contrast!" he continued, "the woods made vocal on the one hand by Christian music, and startled on the other by the wild yells of the uncivilized! And yet both proceeding from the same race."[6]

Early Mormons expressed their unique empathy for Indians (or "Lamanites," as they called them) by frequently singing the American popular songs "The Indian Hunter" and "The Indian's Lament" as well as their own hymn "The Red Man." This last song spoke clearly of the Mormon's hope that Native Americans would "quit their savage customs," including, one presumes, their ritual music and dancing. Joseph Smith's responses to Native American music are unknown, but he did invite Sac, Fox, and other tribesmen around Nauvoo to dance for the Saints.[7] One LDS missionary to the Pottawatomies in this period referred to their singing without criticism and even spoke admiringly of their dancing, saying that he had never seen anyone keep such good time.[8] After the death of Joseph Smith, apostle Parley Pratt issued a proclamation on the Saints' duty to educate the Lamanites in all aspects of culture, including music and "all other things which are calculated in their nature to refine, purify, exalt and glorify them, as the sons and daughters of the royal house of Israel."[9]

During the Mormon trek to the Great Basin, a sympathetic non-Mormon observed the local tribes' curiosity toward the Saints' music on the plains, and wrote that the natives had a natural "inability to comprehend the wonderful performances."[10] In at least one instance, the Saints were equally awestruck by an Indian's music. In Nebraska the dark-skinned Indian William McCarey entered the pioneer camp claiming to be a Lamanite prophet and playing a variety of music on crude instruments. Wilford Woodruff, who had heard sophisticated European music during his British missions, wrote in his journal that McCarey was "the most perfect natural musician I ever saw on a flute fife, sauce pan, ratler, whistle, &c . . . . [he] made the most music on several instruments of any man I ever herd."[11]

In Utah, Brigham Young remained firm that white man's ways were superior to the Indians', and indeed that the Lamanites were looking to the Saints for both spiritual and cultural redemption. But little appears to have been said of Indian music in early Utah because the Saints were too concerned about the squalor in which the natives lived to pay much attention to the question of ceremonial culture. Not only did Mormons find Indians disease-ridden and poverty-stricken, they discerned serious vices among them: lying, stealing, gambling, idolatry, drunkenness, and bloodthirst, all vices they believed had been propagated among the Lamanites by white settlers. Young manifested the Saints' peculiar mixture of pity and cultural imperialism in this 1854 admonition: "Preach the Gospel to the natives in our midst, teach them the way to live, instruct them in the arts of civilization, and treat them as you would like to be treated, if you through the transgression of your fathers had fallen into the same state of ignorance, degradation, and misery."[12] While Young used the phrase "arts of civilization" primarily to denote technology and hygiene, he also may have intended the refinements of Western music and dancing, as Parley Pratt had written of earlier.

If native dancing was loathsome to some Mormons in this period, it was partly because they associated such dancing with aggression against whites.[13] Certain dances also struck some Saints as unchaste. In at least one instance, Young's solution to such dancing among converted Indians was severe. When bandleader Dimick Huntington, one of his chief ambassadors to the Indians, complained that some Mormon Indians were dancing what he called a "whore dance," Young is said to have advised him to whip them until they stopped.[14]

Mormon missionaries, like their denominational counterparts, probably agreed with the assessment of one elder, who found in Indian music "the most horrible noises I ever heard."[15] But the longer they lived among Native Americans, and the closer they drew to them, some Mormon missionaries became fascinated with Indian musical customs. One Mormon elder, Thomas D. Brown, described at length a Ute Indian "sing," a ritual during which the medicine man seemed to be healing a patient through his singing and gestures. Brown acknowledged the apparent medicinal powers of the strange singing, writing that it may have helped to induce faith in the sick person or even to cause a "magnetic stream" to pass through the sick person's body with "a mesmeric influence that heals.''[16] Perhaps because such approbation of Indian ritual, however cautious, was rare, Mormon successes among Native Americans were slight and short-lived.

Christian missionary societies had tried proselyting in Polynesia since the eighteenth century. Some denominational missionaries considered the Pacific natives' music and dance, like that of American Indians, symptomatic of their debasement. One wrote that Polynesian drum and flute music was ''loud and boisterous, and deficient in every quality that could render it agreeable to one accustomed to harmony.''[17] Nevertheless, Christian missionaries generally felt more comfortable with Polynesian music than with Indian music, for it at least had its own form of counterpoint and harmony. Indeed, its nasal melodies and thin harmonies seem to have borne a resemblance to ''old way'' singing and shape-note psalmody. And the dancing was often relaxed and graceful; some of it was performed sitting down.

During the late 1840s and early 1850s Mormon leaders began to view Pacific islanders as brothers to the Lamanites. In 1843 Joseph Smith directed Mormon missionaries to begin proselyting in the Pacific (although it is not clear that he personally considered Polynesians to be Lamanites). These missionaries used the natives' love of music to attract them to Mormon preaching. But like Christians generally, Mormon missionaries felt compelled to reset some of the islanders' songs with Western tunes.[18] As Mormon missions to the islands expanded in the 1850s under the belief that the natives were really Israelites, little was said of the islanders' musical habits, for the Saints regarded their poverty and squalor as the most pressing needs. But the Polynesians' love of religious dancing was something the elders hoped to suppress.

In the fall of 1851, Mormon elder James Brown visited a Putuhara feast and reported that amid the natives' semi-naked dancing ''the confusion was so great and turbulent that it looked more like an actual battle of savages than a dance.'' He went on to say that, in comparison to Native Americans' dancing, ''this excelled in confused savage deeds anything I ever beheld before.'' After making converts in this region, Brown and his colleagues held a massive Mormon conference among the Polynesians. During this conference the natives went into a religious ''frenzy'' of dancing in the new meetinghouse. Brown rebuked the crowd and ordered dancing be banned from the house, to which the congregation assented.[19]

By the late nineteenth century the Saints' intense interest in redeeming Native Americans led to rumors of a conspiracy between Mormons and Indians. Some observers believed that the Saints and the Indians might band together, war against the States, and set up a Mormon–Lamanite dynasty over the American continent. These rumors reached a summit during the intertribal Ghost Dance movement of the 1880s.

This movement took its name from the ecstatic dances of the Indians who proclaimed the advent of a new Messiah who would liberate them from white oppression. The Ghost Dance garment worn by these Native Americans was said to be impervious to the white settlers' bullets and some Americans linked its magic properties to the similar properties Mormons claimed their temple garments possessed. While evidence is weak that Mormons directly encouraged the Ghost Dance movement, some church leaders spoke approvingly of the Ghost Dance religion and said that they hoped that the Lamanites indeed would rise in power against their oppressors.[20] But their endorsement notwithstanding, many of these same Mormon leaders feared that the church might be linked to the "Messiah craze" and its wild dances. Their fear helped ward them away from Lamanite proselyting at the close of the century. The church would return actively to reclaiming Native Americans only after it had secured for itself a good reputation in the States—nearly halfway into the twentieth century.

As late as 1876 the standard view of Polynesian music and dance had been expressed in vivid tones in the *Juvenile Instructor:* "The acme of pleasurable excitement to them is a war dance, and if you could see, as I have, their violent exertions, demoniac grimaces and disgusting contortions while going through its performance, you would say it was one of the most laborious and horrid sights you ever beheld."[21] But as the church quietly closed most of its Indian missions and expanded its missionary efforts in the Pacific new attitudes emerged. Several of the most prominent Mormon elders sent to the islands during the 1890s were skilled musicians, and they seem to have found the natives' music enchanting, especially when the natives sang and danced for "joy at seeing the Lord's servants increased in number on the islands."[22] One missionary wrote of the natives' festive responsorial singing that the leader sang "in high treble, while the rest chimed in with a sort of chanting, which was neither alto, tenor nor bass, but withal harmonious and pleasing to the ear."[23] Another missionary described the Samoans' rowing songs similarly, adding that "the most accurate time is kept while they sing, and I must say at times sounds sweet and breaks the manotiny of the Ocean."[24] Only occasionally did a missionary write with deprecation about the native musical groups. One diary entry from Tahiti reads: "What they call the native band . . . consists of about a dozen women sitting around in a circle, one will start in a song and then all the others will join in the chorus, and what a noise they make. I don't see much of a band about it as there was only an accordian and a piccolo. They had a jug of rum which they passed to each other."[25]

Mormon missionaries to Samoa fell under the spell of casual island life and frequently exchanged songs and dances with the natives. The missionaries spent much of their time listening to indigenous hymns and teaching the Samoans the "songs of Zion"—primarily Sunday school songs.[26] The islanders craved Western music, even though they associated it with the colonial domination they had endured for decades. And while few natives spoke English, many had learned to read musical notation from Western sojourners.[27] The Hawaiian and Samoan Saints happily formed brass bands under the direction of Adelbert Beesley (a son of Ebenezer), modeling them upon the royal military bands they could hear at the docks and in the village squares. Several missionaries used hand-held instruments such as harmonicas, ocarinas, and guitars to accompany their Sabbath hymn singing. Elder Beesley ingeniously constructed a xylophone from timber salvaged from a shipwreck in Apia Bay. His frequent concertizing and hymn-accompanying on this instrument "surprised and pleased" the natives, and drew many to hear the elders' message.[28] Once converted, the Saints were summoned to church on Sabbath mornings by the drums that on weekdays were played in the native dances.[29]

Mormon missionaries thought most Polynesian dances hauntingly graceful. In turn, the Polynesians hoped to learn dances from their visitors. In one instance, a group of Samoans tried to execute a waltz for the missionaries, one of whom reported "they did not seem to understand much about it." The missionaries showed them how it should be done. But when the natives asked for lessons in the round dance, the elders demurred, no doubt conscience-stricken about corrupting the natives.[30]

To reject native cultures would have proven disastrous for the missionaries in Polynesia. Not only did the missionaries face a constant threat of expulsion, particularly as civil power struggles erupted in the islands from time to time, they also faced the constant harassment of well-entrenched Protestant groups. Coming to the Pacific in a position of relative weakness, the Mormon missionaries found that only making friends before making converts would ensure their continuance in the islands.

The Polynesian Saints also benefited from a new Mormon attitude toward the "gathering." Throughout most of the nineteenth century Mormon leaders had urged converts to leave their homelands and build up the culture in the Rocky Mountains. But after 1890 the leaders began to soften and even reverse their position. They now taught that Mormonism would not immediately triumph over the world, but would need to establish itself in all nations. This attitude encouraged the systematizing of LDS missionary work and Mormon schooling around the world in the early twentieth century. Although missionary forces dwindled during World War I, the 1920s saw the construction of Mormon schools in the Pacific and several apostolic tours of the missions. David O. McKay led one tour to the Pacific and found several Mormon brass bands there, especially at Sauniatu, the official gathering place of Samoan Saints. The genial apostle joined the natives in their dances and songs, so much so that they named a new band for him.[31] Missionary Matthew Cowley likewise endeared himself to the Maoris of New Zealand, singing and dancing in native style and encouraging the Mormon converts to amuse and recreate themselves freely.[32] Whatever "savagery" still seemed to cling to Polynesian music and dance, most Mormons seem to have regarded them as the quaint expressions of a friendly, open-hearted people.

By this time, pseudo-Indian tunes had become the source of much self-consciously "American" composition. Songs such as Thurlow Lieurance's "Waters of Minnetonka"—a Tabernacle Choir favorite—blanketed the United States. One church musician, William Hanson, emulated the Lieurance style by adapting Ute Indian songs and dances for his two operas, *The Sun Dance* and *The Bear Dance*.[33] But Mormon leaders remained virtually silent about Native American culture. One finds in the official writings and discourses of the early twentieth century only oblique remarks about the "degradation" of Lamanite culture, and, conversely, about its merits in comparison with white gentile culture.[34] However, a number of Mormon hymns perpetuated common ideas of Indian savagery. Hymn texts referred to the "barbarian" of the plains ("by darkness debased") seeking his "rude delights," and promised that, while the Indians' "arts of peace shall flourish ne'er to die," their "warwhoop . . . shall cease."[35]

In the meantime, writers and speakers throughout the church and the nation began to attack the new popular music styles, linking them with the primitive and barbaric in world culture. One Mormon author in 1926 pointedly complained that jazz had indeed been "copied from savage tribes."[36] As if to confirm the link between savagery and the new music, the *Salt Lake Tribune* carried an article in 1931 bearing the title "Indians Drop Tom-Tom for Modern Jazz." Implying a natural progression from the one style of music to the other, the article also mused on how powerfully white culture was eroding Indian life.

As denominational missionaries and sectarian schools began to fill the reservations, the Indian homelands became outposts of American mass culture. At the same time, native customs faded. Generations of Native Americans grew up with the belief that their own traditions were indeed debased and many of them gladly turned to the prevailing American customs of music and dance. Moreover, the radio brought popular music to the reservations. As it did, countless traditional Indian songs passed into oblivion.

Insofar as Mormon missionaries of the 1940s and 1950s tolerated what Native American traditions remained, they seem to have done so for one principal reason: "We feel this is a good way to get next to them & win at least some of them over.''[37] But the Mormon elders clearly were impressed by how well the Lamanites were able to adapt to the white man's music. As Indians gradually converted throughout the north- and southwest, they placed their talents at the service of the faith. Intertribal reservation choirs formed to sing Mormon hymns. One church leader requested that a southern Utah intertribal choir be brought to Salt Lake City to sing in the church's general conference. This would show, he said, how cultivated Lamanite music could be, although he conceded that the choir was "not the best."[38] A mission leader praised a Uintah children's singing group by saying that "their singing was probably better than the singing of white children."[39] As for traditional Indian music, the mission leaders occasionally allowed and even encouraged it in church socials and entertainments, where it could be kept separate from tribal rituals. But many of the Native Americans had already drifted far from their traditional ways. On at least one occasion a local Boy Scout troop had to provide the reservation dancers with some "genuine Indian costumes."[40]

By the early 1950s the church began trying to educate Indians through reservation seminaries, an "Indian Placement Program" (wherein Indian youths were sent to live with white families during school months), and a quota system for Lamanites at BYU. As early as 1950 a group led by white former missionaries to the Indians organized itself as a tribe on the BYU campus, calling itself the "Tribe of Many Feathers," complete with a chief and a tribal council. Among its aims was to "acquaint the student body of this University with some of the cultural contributions of the various Indian tribes."[41]

In Polynesia, wind bands continued to be organized in the 1950s, some of them at the behest of mission presidents. Tabernacle Choir broadcasts continued to be popular in the islands as well.[42] Between the bands and the choir, Polynesian Mormons developed a taste for the musical grandiosity that had filled Great Basin Mormondom in the late nineteenth century. According to one observer, by 1958 over half of the musicians in Samoa had joined the LDS church and many of these had begun to create a hybrid church-music style, a pseudo-oratorio tradition in which sacred words were set to band-tune medleys. The people called these medleys hymns, but they were really much more. One listener described them as four times the length of a typical choral anthem, "many Overtures merged in one . . . and it was one monotonous tempo and rhythm that blasted from the beginning to the end, with no consideration of dymanic whatsoever.'' The choirs and bands who performed these "hymns" in church services sometimes even marched into the meetinghouses in military fashion. For some years such exercises went on more or less unrestricted, with only an occasional critique from visiting church musicians.[43]

Meanwhile, plans were underway to create a church-sponsored cultural center in Hawaii that would preserve traditional native music and dancing. With the Church College of Hawaii drawing students from throughout the Pacific, local and general church leaders proposed building the center as a tourist attraction that could employ students to perform. Once it was established in 1963, the Polynesian Cultural Center offered entertainment that had its roots in tribal styles, yet was mingled with Mormon themes. There were, for example, the *Lakalaka* on the Joseph Smith story, and dances in praise of the beauty of the Mormon temple at Laie, recordings of the music of which appeared on a souvenir phonograph album produced by the center. During the 1960s through 1980s, the center drew huge crowds to hear traditional music mingled with Mormon messages. The cultural center became the core of church public relations in the Pacific.[44] Severed from their old pagan origins, the energetic music and dancing of Hawaiians, Samoans, Tongans, Fijians, Maoris, and Tahitians provided a healthy, wholesome image for Mormonism. But for mainland Lamanites the path to acceptance was not so clear.

As more and more American Indians enrolled at BYU in the late 1950s and early 1960s, the Tribe of Many Feathers helped keep native dances and medicine-man "sings" alive among them. Some campus advisers to the Indians counseled them to stop such practices because they violated the laws of the gospel and, indeed, were demonic. These advisers believed that the students were preserving Lamanite culture at the expense of their loyalty to Mormonism, that to perpetuate the singing and dancing was to perpetuate the legacy of the race's ancient decline. The paradoxes of Mormon attitudes during this period were great. At the same time that school advisers were decrying Native American customs they were presenting visiting Indian leaders with souvenir copies of the Polynesian Cultural Center phonograph album, a token of church-sponsored "Lamanite" culture.

Many Indian students bristled at the suggestion that their music and dance was satanic. George Lee, president of the Tribe of Many Feathers, insisted that the traditional social dances, at least, were as graceful as any European dances, while the ritual singing of medicine men was a gift from God to the Lamanite branch of Israel. Indian ways, Lee said, were probably more harmonious with the gospel than European ways because "many of our traditions held close ties to Israelite thought and expression."[45] After a number of private debates on the subject, the university's director of Indian affairs, Paul Felt, asked apostle Spencer Kimball to speak to the Lamanite students on the subject "Dangers in Placing Unique Emphasis in the Perpetuation of the Indian Culture."[46]

Kimball had sympathized with the American Indian peoples from his early childhood. His father, a former president of the Indian Territory

Mission, often sang tribal chants and recounted adventures from the reservation to young Spencer.[47] Called from his home state of Arizona to be a Mormon apostle (1945), Kimball was immediately assigned to Lamanite work. He treated Native Americans kindly and paternally. Throughout his life he spoke of the white Saints as the "nursing fathers and mothers" of the Indians, whom church members "must carry on their shoulders till they can walk straight and tall."

Kimball rarely discussed Indian music directly, although he was known to perform it from time to time in family gatherings. He wrote in 1963 that he hoped that music leaders in the church who were "possessed of much patience" would give free music lessons to the Lamanites until they could lead and accompany church music properly. He occasionally measured spiritual success among the Lamanites in musical terms and once remarked that it pleased him more to hear an Indian child playing a hymn on the piano with one finger than to hear Alexander Schreiner playing the Tabernacle organ. With proper schooling, Kimball hoped, American Indians would be able to compete with whites in the world of the arts.[48]

Felt's invitation to speak at BYU allowed Kimball at last to speak freely and in detail on Lamanite culture. In two addresses given on 5 January 1965, Kimball told the Indians at BYU that their culture was "distorted," and that it was wrong for them to try to maintain a cultural identity apart from that of historic Mormonism. To the surprise of many, he even attacked the fostering of traditional Polynesian culture: "Down in New Zealand I was the recipient of many, many courtesies while I was there. They sang and they danced. They sang their songs, and they rolled their eyes, and they stuck out their tongues. . . . And so we applaud them, you know; and they think that's wonderful to encourage the continuation of that culture. That *isn't* the Lord's culture. What they are doing . . . is perpetuating the paganism that they brought from the other islands." He urged that the islanders stop "digging up the cultures of yesterday that were paganistic. . . . Anything that is associated with paganism or sectarianism or devilism or anything, we eliminate." While he said that "any beautiful ideas not in conflict may be incorporated into the Program [of the church]," he insisted that all questionable practices be discarded by Latter-day Saints. Specifically, he said, Polynesians should give up their war chants, and Indians should stop having medicine-man sings.[49]

Over the next two years Paul Felt and other faculty members and students expanded on Kimball's remarks in memos to the university president and in editorials for the school's Lamanite newspaper, *Indian Crossroads*. Felt explained that, although he agreed that Polynesian dances were inherently as bad as Indian dances, they were more easily separated from their religious origins. (They thus could be performed acceptably by the school's folk-dancing groups.) But Indian dances, he argued, were too deeply rooted in paganism to continue on the campus. Some Indian students accepted the banning of the dances with little regret. Others fought the new policy vigorously. One of them even left the church and began to tour the reservations to urge Indians to reject Mormonism. When campus protests became too great, and the university's executive committee spoke its disapproval of Felt's tactics, Felt compromised, deciding that the students must be left to govern themselves in such matters.[50] But the precedent had been set for more cross-cultural regulation to come.

Denominational churches had wrestled for decades with the problems of internationalism.[51] Whatever debates lingered over how much primitive culture could be tolerated in Christian societies, there remained the separate question of what could be played *in church*. The Church Music Committee briefly discussed this question in 1967, admitting that it was becoming "increasingly acute."[52] They were well aware that the Catholic church had formally settled the matter during the Vatican councils of 1962–65, with the statement that missionaries should look toward "adapting worship to [the people's] native genius . . . [and] promoting the traditional music of these peoples, both in schools and in sacred services, as far as may be practicable."[53] One of the committee who endorsed the Catholic position was Alexander Schreiner, who observed that the Old Testament peoples had danced and clapped before the Lord with drums, timbrels, and cymbals: "In view of [this] I would recommend a very liberal and comprehensive allowance for approval of what is used in connection with worship. What I would be inclined to condemn would be for one person to dictate his own preferences in musical matters to others who have other feelings."[54]

As such topics began to be discussed in the mid-1960s, Native American Mormons persuaded the McKay administration to remove the remaining offensive treatments of their people in the hymnal.[55] But within a few years, as the church began proselyting in West Africa, deeply held views of culture, race, and religion resurfaced when black converts tried to drum and dance in Mormon meetings.

For much of the twentieth century the bush region of West Africa was filled with Anglican and Assemblies of God congregations, who tended to mingle freely their tribal and Western customs of worship. Pentecostalism found especially easy access into the hearts of West African blacks, in part because it allowed for intense physical worship. West African blacks generally considered a blend of New Testament grace theology with Old Testament worship styles the most congenial form of Christianity.

In the 1940s some Nigerians began writing Salt Lake City for Mormon tracts, hoping to found branches of the church in West Africa. Mormonism appealed to these inquirers for at least three reasons. First, it professed to be a restoration of Christ's original church and therefore might be more compatible with their non-Western ways. Second, it emphasized the importance of family and community, compelling virtues in tribal culture. Third, it was widely known once to have sanctioned polygamy, which was commonly practiced among the African blacks. While the church did send tracts to the African inquirers, it declined to send missionaries, chiefly because the church had not yet admitted blacks of African descent into the priesthood.[56]

At the close of the 1950s, David O. McKay considered the matter of opening a formal mission to Nigeria. When a group of missionaries arrived in Africa in 1961 to study the prospects, they found thousands of pseudo-Mormons, who had established their own congregations. These Africans conducted their own services in high Pentecostal style. The services lasted about five hours apiece and consisted mainly of public confession of sins, loud responsorial singing, and dancing to tribal drums. One of the missionaries showed his goodwill by dancing with the natives. But both he and his companion apparently were troubled by such worship and one wrote in his journal that the music was "very apentecostal" [*sic*], adding that "they have a lot to learn" about worship.[57]

The hoped-for mission to Nigeria fell through in 1963. Upon learning that the church proscribed blacks from its priesthood, the Nigerian government refused to issue the missionaries visas. Meanwhile, a charismatic Ghanaian had begun to found unofficial Mormon branches in his homeland after he saw a vision of "angels with trumpets singing songs of praise unto God," a vision in which he was told by Jesus to "take up my work."[58] Church leaders assigned various men to correspond with Africans interested in Mormonism, but abruptly stopped this in 1965. In the early 1970s several Mormons were assigned to inspect conditions among the pseudo-LDS groups in Nigeria and Ghana. One of them described the music in 1975: "Music is by the congregation, almost always in native languages, and introduced first by a song leader or minister, then echoed by the congregation. Hand drums are used to accompany the songs, and a song leader sometimes uses a megaphone. Members stand and add handclaps. Tunes are simple, very repetitive, and easy for young and old to sing. Part-singing consists usually of duets, with an occasional bass line added. It is a happy, lively service, similar in style, but more restrained as far as dancing goes, to the apostolic and pentecostal worship services we have visited."[59] The indigenous pseudo-Mormon groups who worshipped in this way received no support from the church until after it lifted its priesthood ban on blacks in 1978.

As soon as the priesthood was proffered to faithful Mormon blacks, the church sent missionaries to West Africa. These missionaries were married couples who could serve more or less as spiritual fathers and mothers to the natives. The missionaries quickly baptized hundreds of blacks and organized Salt Lake-approved congregations. Of the natives' boisterous worship style, one of the missionary couples reported that "as you become familiar with it, it was really not that objectionable, because they had nothing else." But this couple, like some others, were disturbed that the Africans "jazzed up" their hymns and sang indigenous sacred songs that, to the Americans, resembled rock music.[60] The missionaries were perplexed by the native worship, but at least one conceded that "they have such good harmony and unity and a sense of singing together that I stopped worrying about the accompaniment. . . . They have a very sophisticated sense of musical composition and keeping together. . . . They're much better than we are."[61]

The mission president responded perhaps the most negatively to the music and dancing in Mormon services, flatly declaring that it was satanic and that it had descended from the culture of Cain himself. He ordered all drumming and dancing in church stopped and the native percussion instruments replaced by cassette tapes of organ music. The missionaries were to teach their converts that God was pleased by quiet reverence, especially during the sacrament. But many natives feared that God would think them timid for keeping their peace in worship. Hence, the congregations complied outwardly, but with evident sadness. "It was like asking them to give up their right arm to give up those drums," one missionary explained. "Their countenances would fall. . . . Some even cried. They asked, 'But why? Why do we have to give up our drums?' "[62] Some members, unable to cope with the loss, held services in their old style each Sunday when the missionaries left their areas.

Spencer Kimball, now president of the church, was partially incapacitated in his old age and could not directly deal with the questions raised by the musical worship in West Africa. He did inquire if the blacks were "singing the songs of Zion," to which the mission president replied, "yes, and with gusto"—a reply which was said to have pleased the infirm leader. Feeling assured that Kimball would have encouraged his attempts to "civilize" the Africans, the mission president worked to eradicate indigenous styles from church.[63] In time, hundreds left the church over the restrictions placed on their worship. As the church shrank in the bush areas, it flourished in port cities, urban centers where European- and American-trained blacks could lead the services.

The church's early experiences in West Africa suggest that further conflicts over style will come. So far, Mormon leaders have avoided public discussions of such issues. Some scholars in the church have challenged the continuing cultural imperialism, while others have resigned themselves to it, feeling that the westernization of alien cultures is inevitable.[64]

In the absence of official debate, a quiet synthesis continues. West African blacks have added subtle syncopations into their performance of Sunday school songs. Polynesian choirs have rearranged by ear the standard hymns into their traditional seven- and eight-part harmonies. On some reservations, and among Lamanite performing groups at BYU, Native Americans have synthesized their traditional music and gospel hymnody, bringing sacred chants and ritual percussion instruments into the service of Mormon song.

Perhaps more important than questions of style are the questions that cross-cultural encounters pose about the place of music in human life. Many societies regard music as a magic that invokes the divine in virtually every act that accompanies it. Indeed, in some societies music is so much a part of other activities—marriage, medicine, cooking—that their languages lack a separate word for "music." To them, the meaning of tonal art lies precisely in its use, its power to complete some human action, without which, in turn, the "music" could not fully exist. But for most of the Christian world music has entered churches only through a tradition that tolerates it for its power to indoctrinate and unify. And Christianity remains an anomaly among world religions: a faith with no sacred dance.

Mormons now aspire to penetrate further into the Third World and Communist Asia. As they encounter some of the world's most ancient musical traditions, they will grapple with a longstanding dilemma: whether to pry their converts away from those traditions or to preserve the traditions from cultural erosion. And as Zion implants itself in nations whose identities are inseparable from their music, it will find fresh dilemmas about its own music, its own identity.

NOTES

1. For the Young quotations see *JD* 14:197, 8:171. For a further study of this see Michael Hicks, "Notes on Brigham Young's Aesthetics," *Dialogue* 16 (Winter 1983): 124–30.

2. Thomas O'Dea, "Mormonism and the Avoidance of Sectarian Stagnation," pp. 285–93.

3. For a general study of American attitudes toward Native Americans, see Robert F. Berkhofer, Jr., *The White Man's Indian: Images of the American Indian from Columbus to the Present* (New York: Knopf, 1978), pp. 71–104. On Mormon attitudes see Arrington, *Brigham Young: American Moses*, pp. 210–22, and that work's bibliography on the subject, pp. 467–68; Leonard J. Arrington and Davis Bitton, *The Mormon Experience* (New York: Knopf, 1983), pp. 145–60; and David J. Whittaker, "Mormons and Native Americans: A Historical and Bibliographical Introduction," *Dialogue* 18 (Winter 1985): 33–64. For a history of Christian missions to Indians, as well as to Polynesians and West Africans,

to Polynesians and West Africans, see J. Herbert Kane, *A Global View of Christian Missions from Pentecost to the Present* (Grand Rapids: Baker Book House, 1971).

4. See especially Grant Underwood, "Book of Mormon Usage in Early LDS Theology," *Dialogue* 17 (Autumn 1984): 42–45.

5. Frances Densmore, *The American Indians and Their Music* (New York: The Womans Press, 1926), p. 59.

6. Thomas L. M'Kenney, *Memoirs, Official and Personal, with Sketches of Travels among the Northern and Southern Indians* (New York: Paine and Burgess, 1846), pp. 83–84, cited in Hamm, *Music in the New World,* p. 20. See also Stevenson, *Protestant Church Music in America,* pp. 3–11, and Leonard Ellinwood, "Religious Music in America," in James Ward Smith and A. Leland Jamison, eds., *Religious Perspectives in American Culture* (Princeton University Press, 1961), pp. 289–95.

7. See *HC* 4:401 and 6:402; also Joseph Smith Diary, 22 and 23 May 1844.

8. Jonathan Dunham in *HC* 5:545–46.

9. *Proclamation of the Twelve Apostles of the Church of Jesus Christ of Latter-day Saints* (Liverpool: Wilford Woodruff, 1845). For more on the evolution of official attitudes toward Indian music see P. Jane Hafen, " 'Great Spirit Listen': The American Indian in Mormon Music," *Dialogue* 18 (Winter 1985): 133–42.

10. Kane, *The Mormons,* p. 31.

11. *WWJ* 3:139. For more on McCarey see Newell G. Bringhurst, *Saints, Slaves, and Blacks: The Changing Place of Black People within Mormonism* (Westport, Conn.: Greenwood Press, 1981), pp. 84–85.

12. Clark, *Messages of the First Presidency,* 2:143.

13. See Daniel W. Jones, *Forty Years among the Indians* (Salt Lake City: Juvenile Instructor Office, 1890), p. 397, and James S. Brown, *Giant of the Lord: Life of a Pioneer* (Salt Lake City: Bookcraft, 1960), pp. 340–42.

14. Manuscript History of Brigham Young, 8 September 1856, cited in Arrington, *Brigham Young,* pp. 220–21.

15. Elijah Nicholas Wilson, *Among the Shoshones* (Salt Lake City: Bookcraft, 1969), pp. 26–27.

16. Juanita Brooks, ed., *Journal of the Southern Indian Mission: Diary of Thomas D. Brown* (Logan: Utah State University Press, 1972), p. 23.

17. *History of the Establishment and Progress of the Christian Religion in the Islands of the South Sea* (Boston: Tappan and Dennet, 1841), p. 53.

18. Brown, *Giant of the Lord,* p. 506. Despite such attempts to civilize the Polynesian natives, some Christians attributed Mormon successes in the islands to the natives' attraction to anything degraded. See Rufus Anderson, *History of the Mission of the American Board of Commissioners for Foreign Missions to the Sandwich Islands,* 3rd ed. (Boston: Congregational Publishing Board, 1872), pp. 257–58. Much of the general information concerning the Mormon Pacific islands missions may be found in R. Lanier Britsch, *Unto the Islands of the Sea: A History of the Latter-day Saints in the Pacific* (Salt Lake City: Deseret Book, 1986). On Mormon views of the genealogy of Polynesian races, see Russell T. Clement, "Polynesian Origins: More Word on the Mormon Perspective," *Dialogue* 13 (Winter 1980): 88–98.

19. Brown, *Giant of the Lord,* pp. 232, 237–38.

20. The best treatment so far is Lawrence G. Coates, "The Mormons and the Ghost Dance," *Dialogue* 18 (Winter 1985): 89–111.

21. Hugh Knough, "Fun," *JI* 11 (1 November 1876): 250.

22. "Ejay" [Edward J.] Wood, "My Samoan Experience," *JI* 28 (15 May 1893): 328.

23. Henry L. Bassett, *Adventures in Samoa* (Los Angeles: Wetzel, 1940), p. 57.

24. Joseph Quinney Diary, 3 December 1895, holograph in HBLL.

25. Eugene M. Cannon Journal, 21 March 1893, holograph in HBLL.

26. On this period in Samoa see Britsch, *Unto the Islands of the Sea,* pp. 358–74. On singing exchanges see Eugene Cannon Journal, 1893, passim. This source, 17 December 1893, also describes one of the Tahitian Protestants' "himene" meetings, a hymn-singing session after Sabbath services.

27. William Alfred Moody, *Years in the Sheaf* (Salt Lake City: Granite, 1959), p. 153.

28. On these musical developments see Bassett, *Adventures in Samoa,* pp. 52, 55–56, 75; Joseph Dean Diary, microfilm of holograph in HDC, 11 June 1887, 12 October 1888. The Dean diary entry for 27 October 1888 contains an apparently typical program of a missionary feast. It includes three Sunday school songs sung in English, one song each in Hawaiian and Samoan, three xylophone solos by Beesley, and a duet for violin and guitar by Beesley and Dean. In another episode, a Samoan chief called the elders to come and play harmonicas for him (Quinney Diary, 8 November 1895).

29. Moody, *Years in the Sheaf,* p. 62.

30. See Quinney Diary, 9 and 21 October 1895, and Moody, *Years in the Sheaf,* pp. 69, 77.

31. See Britsch, *Unto the Islands of the Sea,* pp. 389–90, and Clare Middlemiss, comp., *Cherished Experiences from the Writings of President David O. McKay* (Salt Lake City: Deseret Book, 1970), pp. 66–67, 75. On the expansion of missions during this period see Alexander, *Mormonism in Transition,* pp. 212–38.

32. See Henry A. Smith, *Matthew Cowley: Man of Faith* (Salt Lake City: Bookcraft, 1954), pp. 45, 58, 262.

33. See "Preserving the Music and Legends of the Utes for Future Generations," *DN,* 7 March 1925, and William F. Hanson, *Sun Dance Land* (Salt Lake City: J. Grant Stevenson, 1967), passim.

34. See Joseph Fielding Smith, *The Progress of Man* (Salt Lake City: Deseret News Press, 1936), pp. 263–65.

35. See Hafen, " 'Great Spirit, Listen,' " pp. 134–38.

36. Bennett, "Why Not Abolish Jazz?," p. 273.

37. Evan Gardner to Golden Buchanan, 19 October 1950, Indian Relations Committee Correspondence, microfilm in HDC.

38. S. Dilworth Young to Spencer W. Kimball, undated report of July 1951 visit to Kanab Stake, Indian Relations Committee Correspondence.

39. Milton R. Hunter to Indian Relations Committee, 15 August 1951, Indian Relations Committee Correspondence.

40. Unsigned report on meeting of Piute Indians of Cedar Stake, 22 November 1950, Indian Relations Committee Correspondence.

41. "The Constitution of the Tribe of Many Feathers," dittoed copy of typescript, and Melvin D. Thom to Will Rogers, Jr., 31 January 1961, both in Institute of American Indian Studies Papers, HBLL. For a survey of Indian education in the church see Wilkinson, *Brigham Young University: The First Hundred Years*, 3:503-35. For a different perspective and critique of Mormon Indian programs see Robert Gottlieb and Peter Wiley, *America's Saints: The Rise of Mormon Power* (New York: Putnam, 1984), pp. 157-77.

42. See Britsch, *Unto the Islands of the Sea*, pp. 67, 313.

43. On this "hymn" practice see Kipeni Suapaia to Harry Dean, 14 March and 23 May 1958, "History of the Revised Edition of the Samoan Hymn Book," manuscript letter collection in Harry Dean Papers.

44. For the history of the center see Britsch, *Unto the Islands of the Sea*, pp. 186-89.

45. George P. Lee, *Silent Courage* (Salt Lake City: Bookcraft, 1987), pp. 273-74, and Lacee Harris, "To Be Native American—and Mormon," *Dialogue* 18 (Winter 1985): 148-49. Indeed, some Indians were troubled by the close dancing of males and females at school dances, which violated certain tribal customs. See *Me and Mine: The Life Story of Helen Sekaquaptewa*, as told to Louise Udall (Tucson: University of Arizona Press, 1969), pp. 117-18.

46. Paul E. Felt to Spencer W. Kimball, 30 December 1964, Institute of American Indian Studies Papers.

47. Edward L. Kimball and Andrew E. Kimball, Jr., *Spencer W. Kimball* (Salt Lake City: Bookcraft, 1977), pp. 236-48.

48. For the quotations and information in this and the preceding paragraph see Spencer Kimball, "The Lamanite," address given at Regional Representatives Seminar, 1 April 1977, reprinted in Jeffrey L. Simons and John R. Maestas, comp., *The Lamanite*, rev. ed. (Provo, Utah: privately distributed, 1981), copy in HBLL; Indian Committee to James Mathews, 15 October 1963, and Spencer Kimball to James Mathews, 19 May 1963, both reprinted in James D. Mathews, "A Study of the Cultural and Religious Behavior of the Navaho Indians Which Caused Animosity, Resistance, or Indifference to the Religious Teachings of the Latter-day Saints" (Master's thesis, Brigham Young University, 1968); Edward L. Kimball to Michael Hicks, 29 September 1987; Bryan Espinscheide, telephone interview with Michael Hicks, 19 August 1987.

49. The typescripts of these two addresses are in the Institute of American Indian Studies Papers. Compare the edited version of these remarks in Edward L. Kimball, *The Teachings of Spencer W. Kimball*, p. 394.

50. See Paul Felt to Hal Taylor, 26 April 1965, Paul Felt to Ernest Wilkinson, 21 April 1966, Ernest Wilkinson to Paul Felt, 13 May 1966, and Paul Felt to Ernest Wilkinson, 10 August 1966, all in Institute of American Indian Studies Papers; also the editorials in *Indian Crossroads*, 28 February 1966 and 18 April 1966. For the varied views of some students see Mathews, "A Study of the Cultural and Religious Behavior," pp. 47-48.

51. See, for example, the discussions of the legitimizing of the American Indian Sun Dance by Christians in the 1940s, Åke Hultkranz, *Belief and Worship in Native North America,* ed. Christopher Vecsey (Syracuse: Syracuse University Press, 1981), p. 229; of Christian adaptations of Krishna worship, W. K. Lowther Clarke, ed., *Liturgy and Worship: A Companion to the Prayer Books of the Anglican Communion* (London: Society for Promoting Christian Knowledge, 1932), p. 822; and of syncretism in East Java, Philp van Akkeren, *Sri and Christ: A Study of the Indigenous Church in East Java* (London: Longworth, 1970), pp. 82–87. See also the various articles in William Smalley, ed., *Readings in Missionary Anthropology* (Tarrytown, N.Y.: Practical Anthropology, 1967).

52. CMC Minutes, 25 October 1967.

53. Walter M. Abbott, ed., *The Documents of Vatican II* (New York: Herder and Herder, 1966), pp. 172–73.

54. Schreiner to Joe L. Spears, reprinted in Alexander Schreiner, Oral History, p. 25 of typescript.

55. See Joe E. Weight to David O. McKay, 5 January 1965, and Leroy J. Robertson to Alva R. Parry, 16 April 1965, both in CMC Subject and Correspondence Files.

56. Many sources have treated this subject. Among the best is Lester Bush, "Mormonism's Negro Doctrine: An Historical Overview," *Dialogue* 8, no. 1 (1973): 11–68.

57. See Lamar S. Williams Diary, quoted in Davis Bitton, *Guide to Mormon Diaries and Autobiographies* (Provo: Brigham Young University Press, 1977), p. 385, and Marvin Reese Jones Diary, microfilm of holograph in HDC, 22 October 1961. On the general history of the mission and experiences of Mormon missionaries to West Africa, I have relied upon Emanuel Abu Kissi, address to conference on African religions, 22 October 1986, BYU (notes in my possession); Bryan Espinscheide, personal conversation with the author, 22 October 1986, and telephone interview with the author, 19 August 1987; E. Q. Cannon to Michael Hicks, 2 October 1987; Murray Boren, telephone interview with the author, 19 August 1987; Murray Boren, "Worship through Music Nigerian Style," *Sunstone* 10 (May 1985): 64–65; M. Neff Smart, "The Challenge of Africa," *Dialogue* 12 (Summer 1979): 54–57; Janet Bingham, "Nigeria and Ghana: A Miracle Precedes the Messengers," *Ensign* 10 (February 1980): 73–76; and Rendell N. Maybey and Gordon T. Allred, *Brother to Brother: The Story of the Latter-day Saint Missionaries Who Took the Gospel to Black Africa* (Salt Lake City: Bookcraft, 1984), especially pp. 70–72 (on native worship meetings).

58. See J. W. B. Johnson to First Presidency, 9 September 1978, in Edwin Q. Cannon, Papers, holographs and photocopies of holographs in HDC.

59. "Summary [of] Mormon Church of Nigeria," a report apparently written by Lorry Rytting, photocopy of typescript in Edwin Cannon Papers.

60. LaMar S. Williams and Nyal B. Williams, Oral History, interviewed by Gordon Irving (May 1981), pp. 101–3 of typescript, Moyle Program.

61. Edwin Q. Cannon, Jr., and Janath R. Cannon, Oral History, interviewed by Gordon Irving (1980), Moyle Program, p. 21.

62. Williams, Oral History, p. 117.

63. Espinscheide Interview. Generally, local cultural expressions among West African blacks appear to have been tolerated in social settings apart from worship services.

64. See Soren F. Cox in Spencer J. Palmer, *The Expanding Church* (Salt Lake City: Deseret Book, 1978), pp. 159–60, and, conversely, Moody Interview. The most erudite exploration of Mormonism and world cultures is F. LaMond Tullis, ed., *Mormonism: A Faith for All Cultures* (Provo, Utah: Brigham Young University Press, 1978). See also Don Hicken, "The Church in Asia," *Dialogue* 3 (Spring 1968): 134–42; Wesley Craig, Jr., "The Church in Latin America: Progress and Challenge," *Dialogue* 5 (Autumn 1970): 66–74; John Sorenson, "Mormon World View and American Culture," *Dialogue* 8, no. 2 (1973): 17–29; and *Dialogue* 13 (Spring 1980), passim.

Epilogue

Many Mormon diaries contain accounts of musical dreams and visions. One of the most detailed of these was left by David Patten Kimball following a siege of pneumonia in 1882. Consuming only Jamaica ginger and pepper tea for relief, Kimball fell into a trance and saw hundreds of dead relatives standing around his bed and in the valley outside his window. As these relatives spoke with him he could hear in the distance "the most beautiful singing I ever listened to in all my life."[1] He wrapped himself in two blankets and went out into the autumn night looking for the choir. He could not find it, and the singing vanished at dawn. But he never forgot the words of the first refrain the heavenly choir had sung: "God bless Brother David Kimball."

Music has played a like part in the dreams of the Mormon people. In their direst hours it has joined them to legions of unseen forebears who sing the hope for a heaven on earth. Kimball's heavenly choir expressed his fervent yearnings to live. Twenty years earlier the yearnings of a generation of Saints had been rolled into one "national anthem"—"God Bless Brigham Young." And all of the music of over a century and a half of Mormonism has had one implicit refrain: "God bless Zion."

The church's dreams for itself have been to gather Israel and build Zion with the confidence that God and all of history have ordained it to such a task. The realities it has faced, like the bleak dawn Kimball found when the heavenly singing stopped, have been played out in a sometimes tortuous drama of wits and wills that shows few signs of abatement. (Even the last decade has witnessed a revival of anti-Mormonism that at times echoes national anti-Masonic, anti-Catholic, and anti-Semitic movements.) But as it dreams of Zion in a strange land, Mormondom has declined to hang its harps in the willows. Rather, it has made music a preserver of its vision of a better kingdom.

The shape of that vision necessarily has changed. The church's membership has increased a millionfold from its founding group of six members. In the process, the ferocity of Mormon rhetoric has dissipated considerably. The solitary gathering place in the mountains has dissolved into a network of gathering places around the world. And the overseership of the prophet increasingly filters out through a bureaucracy of departments and committees. As it has grown, the church has been transformed, yet still clings to its origins. Just so, Mormon musical habits have changed, yet still recall their first impulses.

The impulses have not always been harmonious. In 1957 Mormon sociologist E. E. Ericksen discussed two distinct traits of Joseph Smith's personality. One of these, he said, was Smith's ability to look forward toward new possibilities, an ability that nurtured "the dynamic and creative spirit of the prophet." The other trait was Smith's ability to look into the remote past for models and patterns, an ability that fostered "the conservative and authoritative qualities of the priest." Ericksen observed: "These two facets of his personality and thinking have become deeply embedded in the institutions of the church and in the mind of his people. The tension between these two principles (the prophetic and the priestly), the dynamic and the conservative, the inspiration toward the new and the stabilizing and the authoritative power of the old, constitutes the problem of twentieth century Mormonism. Herewith lies its strengths as also its limitations and its frustrations."[2]

The history of Mormon musical life manifests the tensions Ericksen described. The "prophetic" spirit has led the Saints to elevate their aesthetic standards, to gather in the best music from many sources, to appoint schooled performers and composers to govern sacred musical practice, and to educate the unschooled. The "priestly" spirit has led the Saints to reject sectarian musical practice, to warn against aestheticism, and to resist the influences of foreign cultures. Much of the time, to be sure, the prophetic and the priestly interpenetrate, as in the pursuit of "homemade music"—to improve upon the old by creating fresh works, yet somehow to preserve the distinctly Mormon character of the Saints' established musical canon. Moreover, powerful events and personalities have joined with the revelations pronounced by Mormon leaders to dictate the dominant spirit of this or that moment in the church's musical history. Yet certain trends are apparent. Insofar as the Saints enjoy independence, acceptance, and security, they tend to express their essentially "dynamic and creative" musical impulses. And insofar as they feel threatened, maligned, or rejected, their "conservative and authoritative" musical traits emerge.

This then may be the essential conundrum for the Saints and their music as they push forward toward the Millennium: how to reconcile their thirst for progress with their fear of contamination. While the Saints once wondered how they could sing the Lord's song in a strange land, they now wonder if they can sing a strange song in Zion. The musical cultures of many nations have had similar fears of contamination, yet have managed to survive those fears and to prosper, often with a richer and more varied means of expression in the end. American music in particular has flourished amid the constant transformation of its forms by new ideas, whether their source be from within or from without the nation's borders.[3] Mormondom, like its native land, has demonstrated a persistent power to attract fresh minds and ideas to its cause, a fact which suggests that the dream of the heavenly city will not collapse under the burden of its fears. The harps of the Mormon Zion will continue to be played, if at times only by the winds of change.

NOTES

1. *Helpful Visions: Designed for the Instruction and Encouragement of Young Latter-day Saints* (Salt Lake City: Juvenile Instructor Office, 1887), pp. 10–11.

2. Ephraim E. Ericksen, "Priesthood and Philosophy," *Utah Academy of Sciences, Arts, and Letters: Proceedings* 34 (1957): 14–15. Compare Ericksen's terms and definitions with those of Max Weber, *The Sociology of Religion,* trans. Ephraim Fischoff (Boston: Beacon, 1963).

3. In this I agree with and echo the sentiments of Hamm, *Music in the New World,* pp. 655–56.

General Index

Index of First Lines and Titles
of Hymns and Songs

Titles are listed in italics. Many hymns and songs were published without separate titles. In those cases where an enduring hymn or song has taken on its first line as a title, it is listed here as a title only.

A Note on the Author

Michael Hicks is Assistant Professor of Music at Brigham Young University. He has published articles about music theory and aesthetics in *Perspectives of New Music* and the *Journal of Aesthetic Education* and essays on Mormon culture in *Sunstone, Dialogue,* and *Brigham Young University Studies.* He was a contributor to *Wagner in Retrospect: A Centennial Reappraisal* (Amsterdam, 1986). Professor Hicks also has composed numerous works for chamber ensembles and instrumental soloists and is director of the university's Group for New Music.